49.95

The German Public and the
Persecution of the Jews, 1933–1945

The German Public and the Persecution of the Jews, 1933–1945

"No One Participated, No One Knew"

Edited by
Jörg Wollenberg

English edition translated and edited by
Rado Pribic

 HUMANITIES PRESS
NEW JERSEY

3 28. 2995

Originally published in German as "Niemand war dabei und keiner hat's
gewußt." Die deutsche Öffentlichkeit und die Judenverfolgung © 1989
by R. Piper GmbH & Co. KG, München, Germany

English translation first published in 1996 by
Humanities Press International, Inc.
165 First Avenue, Atlantic Highlands, New Jersey 07716

This English translation © 1996 by Humanities Press International, Inc.

Library of Congress Cataloging-in-Publication Data
"Niemand war dabei und keiner hat's gewusst". English.
   The German public and the persecution of the Jews, 1933–1945 : "no one
participated, no one knew" / edited by Jörg Wollenberg : English
edition translated and edited by Rado Pribic.
      p.   cm.
   Includes bibliographical references and index.
   ISBN 0–391–03913-X (cloth).—ISBN 0–391–03914–8 (paper)
   1. Jews—Germany—History—1933–1945—Congresses. 2. Holocaust,
Jewish (1939–1945)—Germany—Congresses. 3. Jews—Persecutions—
Germany—Public opinion—Congresses. 4. Public opinion—Germany—
Congresses. 5. Germany—Ethnic relations—Congresses.
   I. Wollenberg, Jörg. II. Pribic, Rado. III. Title.
DS135.G3315N5313   1995
940.53'18—dc20   95–17600
                                  CIP

Printed in the United States of America

10 9 8 7 6 5 4 3 2 1

Contents

II. INTERPRETATIONS 57

APPENDIX 177

A Note on the Translation

Every attempt has been made to retain the original narrative and analytical style of each contributor, although some of the authors do not use the most literary language in accordance with German grammatical and stylistic rules. However, compromises were also made in order to keep the English translation relatively clear and fluent.

R. P.

Fifty-Five Years after
Reichskristallnacht

Seven thousand Nazis, mostly young people, march and demonstrate with flags, songs, and slogans in the Hessian city of Fulda. The police smile and watch the parade, and the mayor only shakes his head. Is this Germany in the 1930s? No, this happened on August 14, 1993. Private citizens are outraged. One demands that the bishop of Fulda take some action against the neo-Nazi mobs parading in front of his church on Fulda's downtown square. But the bishop refuses. This square is public property, and it is the business of the city authorities to restore order. Another citizen confronts the police officers who tolerate the display of outlawed insignias and songs, songs which call for the purification of the Aryan race and the expulsion of unwanted foreigners. The same citizen screams: "Have you not learned anything in your history classes? Were you asleep?" But the police only stand by, keeping order by preventing "left-wing radicals" from charging into the crowd of neo-Nazis "thereby creating riots."

Have we learned any lessons from history? Why is there such an alarming rise of right-wing activities not only in Germany but all over the world? The Fulda demonstration was attended by British, French, and Dutch neo-Nazis, in addition to the German ones, who tried to commemorate the death of Rudolf Hess, who they claim was killed by the Allies in his Spandau jail cell in 1988. In Germany foreign workers are accosted, and homes of asylum seekers are being torched on a regular basis. Most recently, neo-Nazi skinheads attacked the U.S. national luge team members who were training in eastern Germany. Several bomber-jacket-clad youths taunted the group's only black member, beat him up, and yelled pro-Nazi slogans.

In France right-wing parties propagating "cultural purity" are gaining in popularity at every election. In the Netherlands the cemeteries for World War II veterans are desecrated by Nazi swastikas. In the Baltic states history is again being rewritten, and the local fascist henchmen from the Second World War are now presented as great patriots. Croatian television gives interviews to children of former fascist leaders and members of "elite" units. These units also include foreign right-wing mercenaries and fight in the civil war under old fascist emblems and insignias. In Italy thousands of neo-fascists stage demonstrations in the streets of major cities, and the granddaughter of Benito Mussolini is seeking election to a major political office. Finally, nowadays one does not even take notice of the numerous reunions of Nazi veterans of the Second World War, the most recent being the gathering of the SS Galizien Division, which was attended by close to eight thousand people in the summer of 1993 in the Ukrainian city of Lvov.

It is now November 1993, exactly fifty-five years after the infamous Reichskristallnacht (Reich's Crystal Night), and it should be obvious, noting the events mentioned above, why there is a need once more to look into our collective history. The public needs to be reminded of where simple acts of intolerance can lead. A frequently quoted Jewish adage states in part: "The secret of redemption lies in remembrance." The contributors to this very important volume illustrate vividly how *all* segments of German society were drawn directly or indirectly into participation in discriminatory actions against their fellow citizens. This discrimination, of course, did not stop there but eventually led to a genocide unparalleled in history.

The German president Richard von Weizsäcker, in his remarkable speech during a commemorative ceremony in the plenary room of the German Bundestag (the lower chamber of the parliament), on May 8, 1985, the fortieth anniversary of the end of the Second World War, perceptively characterized the genocide of Jews:

> This crime was perpetrated by a few people. It was concealed from the eyes of the public, but every German was able to experience the range of emotions that his Jewish compatriots had to endure—from plain apathy and hidden intolerance to outright hatred. Who could remain unsuspecting after the burning of the synagogues, the plundering, the stigmatization with the Star of David, the deprivation of rights, the ceaseless violation of human dignity? Whoever opened his eyes and ears and sought information could not fail to notice that Jews were being deported. The nature and scope of the destruction may have exceeded human imagination but, apart from the crime itself, there was an attempt by too many people, including those of my generation who were young and uninvolved in the planning and execution of these events, to ignore what was happening. There were many ways to avoid burdening one's conscience, to shun responsibility, to look the other way to keep mum. When the unspeakable truth of the Holocaust became known at the end of the war, all too many of us claimed that we had not known anything about it or even suspected anything.
>
> There is no such thing as the guilt or innocence of an entire nation.

Guilt is, like innocence, not collective, but personal and individual guilt is either discovered or concealed. There is guilt which people acknowledge or deny. Everyone who directly experienced that era should today quietly ask himself about his involvement then.

Unfortunately, not all Germans, or even non-Germans, are willing to confront their collective history. Even the present-day chancellor of the Federal Republic of Germany, Helmut Kohl, plainly states that he is blessed "by the grace of late birth" (Gnade der späten Geburt).

On Tuesday, November 9, 1993, the German Bundestag president Rita Süßmuth warned at a special session against drawing a "final line" (Schlußstrich) under German history. "November 9, 1938, was the day from which one unstoppable process led to the deportation and mass annihilation in Auschwitz, Majdanek, Treblinka, and other places." She proceeded to evoke the lessons from history in warning against the present-day violence against foreigners in Germany. Since 1991, 4,500 shameful right-wing extremist acts of violence have occurred in the Federal Republic of Germany. As a result of these disturbing acts, twenty-six people have been killed and 1,800 have been injured. Unfortunately, the xenophobic violence and the hatred of foreigners has also manifested itself in the desecration of Jewish and Allied soldiers' memorials and cemeteries.

November 9 is a fateful date in the history of Germany. Four significant years are 1918, 1923, 1938, and 1989. On November 9, 1918, the Social Democrat Gustav Scheidemann proclaimed the First German Republic, the so-called Weimar Republic. This action, of course, meant the conclusion of the reign of the authoritarian Prussian Hohenzollern dynasty as well as the end of the Second Reich (which was a monarchy). November 9, 1923, marked Adolf Hitler's putsch in Munich when the fledgling National Socialist party made a violent and unsuccessful grab for political power in southern Germany. This resulted in Hitler's incarceration and his writing of *Mein Kampf*. The night of November 9 to November 10, 1938, marked the infamous Reichskristallnacht, organized by the Nazis. Ironically, the Berlin Wall fell on the same date in 1989, opening the way for democracy, self-determination, and German (re)unification. Obviously, this fateful date is to be celebrated, on one hand, and commemorated, on the other.

One should also recall some important dates in the history of the Third Reich as background to the discussions presented in this volume. On January 30, 1933, Adolf Hitler became the Reich's chancellor, and less than two months later, on March 23, 1933, he was empowered by the Enabling Act (Ermächtigungsgesetz), which was accepted by the Reichstag, to decree laws. Still in the same year, Germany signed the Concordat with the Vatican (July 7) and left the League of Nations (October 14). After the death of the Reich's president Paul von Hindenburg, on August 2, 1934, the German military (Reichswehrmacht) swore the Oath of Allegiance to "Führer and Reich's Chancellor" Adolf Hitler. On March 7, 1936, German troops marched into the demilitarized Rheinland, after military conscription was reintroduced on March 16, 1935. Also in 1936 Germany signed alliance treaties with Italy (October 25) and Japan (November 25). On March 12, 1938, German troops marched into Austria (Anschluß), and, after having invaded Czechoslovakia on March 15, 1939, they attacked Poland on September 1, 1939, and thus started the Second World War. The Sixth German Army surrendered on February 2, 1943, at Stalingrad, Russia, and on June 6, 1944, the Allies landed on the beaches of Normandy, France. Germany twice signed an unconditional surrender in Reims, France, and Berlin-Karlshorst between May 7 and 9, 1945. The important conferences in which the victorious Allies determined the fate of Germany took place in Casablanca (January 14–25, 1943), Teheran (November 28–December 1, 1943), Yalta (February 4–11, 1945), and finally in Potsdam (July 17–August 8, 1945). On October 1, 1946, the Nuremberg war-crime trials came to an end with the passing of sentences.

To understand fully the extent of one of the greatest, if not *the* greatest, tragedies in human history, one should be familiar with the gradually escalating, step-by-step process, in the destruction of German Jewry which eventually led to the "final solution." The following table describes the significant legislation and events:

April 1, 1933	One-day boycott of Jewish stores, physicians, and lawyers
April 7, 1933	With the exception of war veterans, Jewish civil servants are forced into retirement
April 21, 1933	Ban on kosher rituals
July 14, 1933	German citizenship can be taken away from "undesirables"
September 6, 1935	Sale of Jewish newspapers in the streets is prohibited
September 15, 1935	Laws for the Protection of German Blood and German Honor (Nuremberg Laws): only Germans or people of "related blood" can become citizens of the Reich; Jews are not allowed to marry "Aryan" citizens

September 30, 1935	All Jewish civil servants are placed on leave
March 7, 1936	Jews lose their right to vote in elections for the Reichstag
July 2, 1937	Severe limitations on the numbers of Jewish pupils (already partially restricted in 1933)
November 16, 1937	Only in rare cases can Jews obtain passports for foreign travel
April 26, 1938	Jews are required to turn over their property
July 6, 1938	Certain professions are placed off limits for Jews (e.g., tour guide)
July 23, 1938	A new law decrees that as of January 1, 1939, Jews are required to carry special identification cards
July 25, 1938	A new law decrees that as of September 30, 1938, all Jewish physicians can call themselves only *Krankenbehandler* (caretakers of sick)
July 27, 1938	All Jewish street names are changed
August 17, 1938	By decree, Jews as of January 1, 1939, may have only Jewish first names; if they keep an "Aryan" name, they have to add Jewish middle names such as "Israel" or "Sara"
October 5, 1938	Jewish passports are designated by a *J*.
October 28, 1938	Approximately fifteen thousand "stateless" Jews are deported to Poland
November 7, 1938	Assassination of the German embassy consul vom Rath in Paris by Herschel Grynszpan
November 9, 1938	Anti-Jewish pogrom takes place as vom Rath dies: Reichskristallnacht
November 11, 1938	Jews may neither carry nor possess arms
November 12, 1938	German Jewry as a whole has to pay an "atonement fee" (Sühneleistung) of one billion Reichsmarks for the damages incurred during the pogrom, and they have to clean up all the mess in the streets; Jews are prohibited from attending theaters, movies, concerts, and exhibits; Jews are no longer allowed to own stores and artisan businesses
November 15, 1938	All Jewish children are expelled from German schools

November 23, 1938	All Jewish-owned plants are dissolved
November 28, 1938	Introduction of curfews and off-limit places for Jews
December 3, 1938	Jews may no longer keep their driver's licenses and vehicle registration papers
December 3, 1938	Jews are forced to sell their securities, their jewelry, and their businesses
December 8, 1938	Jewish students can no longer attend German universities
April 30, 1939	Jews lose their right to rent protection
July 4, 1939	All German Jews have to become members of the Reich's Association of Jews (Reichsvereinigung der Juden)
September 23, 1939	All Jews have to turn in their radios to the police
October 12, 1939	Beginning of deportation of Austrian Jews to Poland
October 19, 1939	The "atonement fee" for Jews is increased to 1.25 billion RM and has to be paid by November 15, 1939
November 23, 1939	The Star of David is introduced in Poland
February 6, 1940	Jews lose their eligibility for clothing coupons
February 12, 1940	First deportations of German Jews
July 29, 1940	Jews are not allowed to have telephones in their homes
June 12, 1941	Jews have to designate themselves only as "without faith" (glaubenslos)
September 1, 1941	Jews in Germany now also have to wear a Star of David; they may not leave their home district without a police permit
October 14, 1941	Beginning of general deportations of German Jewry to the concentration camps
December 26, 1941	Jews are no longer allowed to use public phones
January 10, 1942	Jews have to turn in all their wool and fur clothing
January 20, 1942	Wannsee Conference announcement of the "final solution for the Jewish question"

February 17, 1942	Jews may no longer subscribe to newspapers and magazines
March 26, 1942	Jewish dwellings have to be marked by a Star of David
April 24, 1942	Jews are no longer allowed to use public transportation
May 9, 1942	Jews are not allowed to enter beauty parlors and barber shops
May 15, 1942	Jews are not allowed to keep pets
June 9, 1942	Jews are required to turn in all their "excess" clothing
June 11, 1942	Jews cannot receive cigarette ration cards
June 19, 1942	Jews have to turn in all their electrical and optical appliances, as well as typewriters and bicycles
June 20, 1942	All Jewish schools are closed
July 17, 1942	Blind and handicapped Jews may no longer display special armbands for the disabled
September 18, 1942	Jews are not entitled to buy meat, eggs, and milk products
October 4, 1942	Beginning of deportation of all Jews from concentration camps in Germany to Auschwitz

This listing speaks for itself. At the time of Hitler's "power grab" in 1933, approximately half a million Jews lived in Germany. According to the Nazis' statistics, there were 215,000 left in 1939 and only 130,000 at the conclusion of 1941. By the end of 1944 only ten to fifteen thousand Jews survived in the German Reich. Of the twelve to thirteen million victims murdered in Nazi concentration camps, primarily in Eastern Europe, at least six million were Jews, most of them from Poland and the Soviet Union.

In conclusion, I can give an update on the Nazis' files. The files are kept by the United States government at the Berlin Document Center. They contain thirty million documents, including the membership files of some 10.7 million members of the National Socialist German Workers party (NSDAP), as well as personnel files for six hundred thousand SA men, 230,000 members of the SS, and sixty thousand SS officers. Additionally, there are files for 490,000 members of the National Socialist Federation of Teachers, numerous members of the Reich's medical personnel, members of the Cultural Chambers, the judicial system, and papers from the Race and Resettlement Department (Rasse- und Siedlungshauptamt).

At the end of the war all these documents were ordered to be destroyed. But the orders were not followed, and most of the files were discovered at a Munich paper mill by U.S. soldiers in April of 1945. With the Cold War, the de-Nazification of Germany was reduced to a low priority, and, as some of the contributors in this volume correctly indicate, many perpetrators escaped with very mild punishment or none at all. In 1985 the Bundestag passed a resolution requesting that the files be transferred to the German government. The German–U.S. negotiations were concluded in June of 1993, and an agreement was signed on October 18, 1993, declaring that the administration of the Berlin Document Center would be transferred to Germany effective July 1, 1994, and would be managed by the Federal Archive in Koblenz. However, before the transfer U.S. authorities were to be able to microfilm the files, and after July 1994 the microfilms and the original files in Berlin were to be available to the public in accordance with the regulations of each country's archive.

Rado Pribic
Easton, PA

JÖRG WOLLENBERG

No One Participated,
No One Knew

The Public Persecution and Destruction
of the Jews in Germany

After the many events commemorating the Jewish pogrom of 1938 in the Federal Republic of Germany—from reports of contemporaries, lectures and seminars in the evening schools, exhibits in the museums, memorial celebrations in the cities, radio and television programs, to the speech by the president of the parliament, Jenninger, to the Bundestag—Michal Bodemann, a sociologist at the University of Toronto, articulated his uneasiness about Germans' dealings with the darkest chapter of their history in a speech to Berlin's Jewish groups:

> One cannot speak anymore in the Federal Republic today about an attempt to demonstrate that the Nazis' crimes were insignificant. The culture of commemoration which has suddenly sprung up does not question the extent of the crimes. The question is, however, how should Germans today deal with their feelings of guilt in order to assure a positive national identity? According to Jenninger's speech, there should be a nationwide ecologically conscious message in order to help the world heal again through this newly enlightened German character. Therefore, Jenninger's speech, which was often attacked but which was still honest and certainly popular, was the highlight of this year's exculpation rituals.[1]

Indeed, the remembrance of the Reich's Pogrom Night of fifty years ago had, in many cases, little to do with the history and the culture of the Jews in Germany. Concrete events of the persecution and destruction of the Jews retreated more and more into the background. On the other hand, questions about broken national identity and the problems of coping with feelings of guilt stood and continue to stand in the center of many events. Therefore the level of knowledge about the forms of suffering and the injustices inflicted upon the Jews by their

1

fellow German citizens is still low. The flood of publications in most recent times did not change this situation much.[2] Even the term "Reich's Crystal Night" (Reichskristallnacht) is today still being interpreted in different ways. For many, this term derived from Goebbels's Propaganda Ministry and is therefore being interpreted as a cynical expression of the Nazis with which they tried to reduce the pogrom to a few destroyed glass windows. For others, the term is an expression of Berlin's local dialect, an ironic word creation which uncovered the deeds of the Nazis. The damage which the Nazis caused with their persecution and destruction of the Jews deprived Germany of a large segment of its artistic, scientific, economic, and technical know-how. Even on the eve of the fortieth anniversary of the foundation of two German republics, the consequences of this deprivation have still not been fully digested and analyzed.[3]

Nuremberg is an especially suitable place to lose this particular and contemporary heavy baggage of German history, because Nuremberg is the city where the old Reich's celebrations took place [for many years the German emperors were selected and crowned in Nuremberg; Am. ed.]. It was also the center of the Third Reich's Party Days which were organized by the Nazis. Nuremberg is a modern industrial city as well as the city of the *Stürmer* [the official newspaper of the Nazi party; Am. ed.]. It is also the city of the Nuremberg Laws of 1935 and of the Nuremberg trials from 1945 to 1949. This is a list of immanent contradictions which continues with the mention of debts which were more or less pushed aside and the availability of educational opportunities. At the same time, these contradictions indicate that during the Weimar Republic one of the most republican cities was involved with National Socialism in a special manner and had already developed early terrible forms of anti-Semitism.

Hitler's intimate friend Julius Streicher was especially responsible for this. In August of 1923, he founded the weekly which soon became the symbol of the National Socialists' anti-Semitism. Every week, the former Nürnberg elementary school teacher spread among "the people's community" the constantly repeated and (by Streicher) consciously adopted motto "The Jews are our misfortune!" in the almost five hundred thousand issues of the hate publication, *Der Stürmer*, the "German weekly in struggle for truth." This motto was coined by the Berlin historian and demagogue Heinrich von Treitschke in 1879. Nuremberg became the center of anti-Semitism in Germany only through the *Stürmer*. Shortly after November 9, 1938, the Stürmer Publishing House published a voluminous "provocative publication" about "the Jewish question throughout five centuries" which was dedicated "with gratitude and adoration" to "the leader of the Franks, Julius Streicher." The publication states, among other things:

> And just as Nuremberg's solution to the Jewish question served at the beginning of modern times as a model for the whole nation, so also may Nuremberg today pride itself to have carried the storm banner in the final struggle of the German nation against the Jews, according to the old motto: Franks foreward.
>
> Therefore, the Führer's laws for the Protection and the Purity of the German Blood justifiably carry the name "Nuremberg Laws."[4]

Indeed, the Franks acted in an "exemplary manner." *Der Stürmer* and Julius Streicher were "the powerful sword" which prepared and aided in the achievement of "the final victory" (Stock). One can also accuse the fanatic self-proclaimed "leader" of the Franks of beginning the intensive agitation against the Jews in Nuremberg even before 1933. Furthermore, Streicher had instigated the destruction of the main synagogue of the Israelite cultural community on Hans Sachs Square in August of 1938, three months before the organized November pogrom.

The Jewish pogrom of 1938 is an act unparalleled in its level of expropriation and expulsion of Jewish enterprises. This was true not only in Nuremberg, but throughout the entire Reich. The demolition and Aryanization of Jewish shops, banks, and department stores followed the destruction of the synagogues and the ransacking of Jewish cemeteries. Thirty thousand Jews, most of whom were wealthy, were arrested and deported to concentration camps. The repression process, which began in 1933 with the exclusion of Jews from specific professions, continued through the 1938 boycott actions and the subsequent enrichment of private interests at the expense of the deprived Jews. The events ended in physical destruction and plunder.

The Nazis used the assassination of the mission secretary Ernst vom Rath in the German embassy in Paris by the German-Polish Jew Herschel Grynszpan on November 7, 1938 as the inducement for sounding the last alarm signal before the Final Solution Pogrom. However, while the National Socialist rulers pretended that the brutal transgressions were a spontaneous reaction by the "raging people's soul" to the murder of vom Rath, they were in reality organized and inflamed by the highest authorities.

Hans Jürgen Döscher has convincingly proven in a recently presented study that the pogroms of 1938 appeared to be "a new radical approach on the path toward the existential destruction of the Jews in the German Reich, which was welcomed and tolerated by large circles of the population." This theory stands in contrast to the previous interpretations of the pogrom as a "fatal year" (Barkai), a "turning point," or as "a stage of a new policy."[5]

The National Socialist leadership used the "unfolding of the Jewish question from below" through the mobilization of the "people's anger" as the means for the removal of Jews from all areas of culture, the sciences, and the economy.

After restricting the public and legal position of the Jews through the Law for the Restoration of Professional Civil Servants of 1933 and the Nuremberg Laws of 1935, the National Socialist rulers used the pogrom of 1938 as a method of exerting anti-Semitic pressure through anti-Jewish activities. They primarily used the assassination in Paris as the pretense to prepare the "final solution of the Jewish question" through a multitude of laws. However, everything that occurred throughout Germany during the night of November 9, 1938, by order of SA chief of staff Lutze and the Nazi supreme leadership, immediately after Goebbels's inciting speech in remembrance of the "old fighters" of the Hitler coup of November 9, 1923, took place before a broad public. Many participated, and the majority of the population knew about it. Some German citizens distanced themselves from the brutal excesses, riots, and murders during the Jewish pogroms of 1938. But hardly anyone objected, first, to the legislation that followed excluding Jews from economic life, then, to the deportation, and finally, to the extermination that also followed, because "the Jew was the most important person in Hitler's state" (Victor Klemperer). The Jewry created the plagues of capitalism and communism in the world, it especially sought to bring about Germany's misery and destruction, it decomposed the purity of the race, the ability to resist, and it stirred up discord among fellow citizens. However, the German citizens of the Reich supposedly did not grasp the plan for the "final solution of the Jewish question"—the "extermination anti-Semitism" (Silbermann)—which Hitler created with unparalleled energy. For more than forty years the generation of perpetrators has refused to answer the question of what it actually thought during the greatest crime known to history.

Against this background of a continuing claim of ignorance, the fiftieth anniversary of the Jewish pogrom of November 1938 gives us the opportunity to compare the completely public persecution of the Jews which took place on the streets, as well as in published laws and decrees, with the mystery of the places of extermination. Can one fundamentally differentiate between the known and the so-called unknown in millions of cases? Or is there a difference between a death sentence and an execution? Should one place the Reich's bank officials who used melted down gold teeth to make Prussian state coins on a differ-

ent level of humanity than those police officers who shot at the Jews
during the raids? Are the employees of the welfare organization who
redistributed the laundry and the dishes of the deported Jews after
the Reich's Crystal Night of a different quality than those physicians
who did their duty at the peepholes of the gas chamber? Did the public and secret segments of the prosecution of the Jews join so simply
and normally as was common during administrative procedures? The
deed was unique, but the methods were customary. Even the gassing
of enemy civilians circulated in the world of imagination. All of Germany trained with gas masks. One did not hear of any of the Reich's
citizens experiencing a shock when they were sent into the gas plants
after 1942. However, they perceived, just as Himmler and Eichmann
did, that the physical extermination was, for the most part, more vigorous
than the reports which circulated in official documents led one to believe.

The fact that the European Jews were being destroyed was not horrible, but the notion of it was.

Today it is exactly the opposite. In the meantime, every schoolchild
grew accustomed to the idea of Auschwitz and Treblinka. In contrast,
the truth of the Aryanization documents is now as it was before, the
iron secret of the company archives. The winners of the Aryanization
process—who include the "later fathers" of the post-War German economic miracle, such as Horten, Neckermann, Ries (Pegulan); or the
large banks before and after 1933, such as the Deutsche Bank and the
Dresdner Bank—are suppressing this chapter of their enrichment.
The memory of the extermination of the Jews came to us in a muddled
and disconnected form. The fires of the so-called Reich's Crystal Night
and the Star of David are registered in the German national memory,
but the deportation history of the cities and districts has hardly been
processed. Who, for example, knows of the Gestapo's deportation list
which contains the names of 1,631 Nuremberg citizens who were deported to the Theresienstadt and Auschwitz concentration camps between 1941 and 1944, of whom only seventy-two survived? The SS
brigadier Dr. Benno Martin, who was the Gestapo administrator responsible, was acquitted by the state court in Nuremberg on July 1,
1953, after a trial which lasted four years.[6]

It is time to work through this dark chapter of German history and
make it the focal point of educational work at institutions for continuing education. Consequently, one should not restrict the memory of
the so-called Reich's Crystal Night of fifty years ago only to the realm
of SA clubs. One should discuss the whole system of robbery, persecution, and destruction of the Jews which was accepted by the majority of the population. The cultural and educational institutions of

Nuremberg, Fürth, Erlangen, and Schwabach are making efforts toward such a differentiated approach. The exhibit on Jewish history and culture in Bavaria which took place in the Germanic National Museum and the House of Bavarian History under the theme "Nothing Was Known and No One Participated" was accompanied by a program of more than four hundred various activities (lectures, eyewitness reports, seminars, film series, open readings of publications, cultural activities, and exhibitions). These activities were very well received and served as an introduction to the continuous journey of discovery into a repressed chapter of the German history. One of the high points is being documented in this volume: a symposium with the theme "Nothing Was Known and No One Participated: The Public and the Persecution and Extermination of the Jews in Germany from 1933 to 1945" was organized on November 15 and 16, 1988, by the Educational Center of Nuremberg. One could investigate the various vestiges of violations and deeds with the aid of fourteen contributions by eyewitnesses, scholars, and writers.

As the organizer of the symposium and the editor of its proceedings I would like to thank the contributors for commenting on, and answering questions, which are still debatable, in front of several hundred highly attentive listeners.[7]

I am especially indebted to Jörg Friedrich. As he had done during the "Nuremberg Dialogue 1987" which dealt with the removal of the taboos of the war-criminal trials,[8] Mr. Friedrich again helped me with the preparation and presentation also of this symposium. I would also like to thank Mrs. Ingrid Weiß-Albert, Mrs. Doris Baptistella, Mrs. Kunigunde Hamouda, Mr. Friedrich J. Bröder, and Mr. Manfred Schwab for helping with the preparation of the symposium and for the printing of its records.

I offer continued warm regards to Nuremberg's scholastic and cultural advisors for their commitment. Without the generous support of Hermann Glaser, the larger projects within the educational center's historical workshop would have failed in their initial phase. Furthermore, since today's climate seems to be suitable for a new historical debate, as well as for the formation of visions of the future based upon past experience, we are making a conscientious effort to continue the "Nuremberg Dialogues," which Mr. Glaser initiated, with new themes and symposia.

The so-called historians' debate is one last attempt to fortify old legends with the use of thought which is contrary to the times. Theses by Ernst Nolte, which are trying to present the past as harmless, fail to notice, among other things, that the Federal Republic of Germany is no longer without a history and that, rather than hide in the shadow of the past, many would like to shed more light on the past's shadow. Also, the president of the Federal Republic, Richard von Weizsäcker, who is committed to this sad historical work, spoke out against the strategy of closing the discussion at the Bamberg Historians' Day in October of 1988. Only one who can remember and is willing to work through the past can gain the future. Of course, such an approach includes not only the publicizing of the history of 1933 to 1945 and the intensifying of political education, but it should also include post-world-war history with its repression of the brown past [Nazi era; Am. ed.] and the mistaken developments in the history of the foundation of the Federal Republic of Germany as the consequence of the "second guilt" (Ralph Giordano).

At the same time, November 9, 1938, alludes to the history of the foundation of the First German Republic. This is because it was always Hitler's declared goal to reverse the November Revolution of November 9, 1918. Hitler believed that the activity of the "November criminals, who stabbed the German army in the back in 1918," was a Jewish tool. When the first Hitler coup failed on November 9, 1923, it was imperative for the Nazis to persecute the Jews as the "scapegoats" following their takeover. After the April 1, 1933 appeal to the population to boycott Jewish stores, physicians, and lawyers, the burning of the books in the "struggle against the non-German spirit" of May 1933, and the Nuremberg Laws of September 15, 1935, for the "protection of the German blood and the German honor," there followed, after a phase of relative calm, an escalation which manifested itself in the form of the Pogrom Night of 1938. This must be interpreted as the consciously planned first step toward Auschwitz. Whoever would like to explain this apparently inconceivable phenomenon must not only remember historical events during memorial days. One must certainly also look at present radical social changes and their consequences. Furthermore, the significance that remembering holds for the future not only involves dealing with historical details but investigating how the National Socialist period and the Jewish pogrom are perceived and interpreted today in the public's conscience. How, for example, do the politicians in the community, state, and federal governments treat ethnic and political minorities and applicants for asylum?

I. EYEWITNESS REPORTS

Arno Hamburger

The Night of the Pogrom of November 9–10, 1938 in Nuremberg

It was cold on November 9, 1938. I was fifteen years old at that time. I was born in Nuremberg, like my father, but we were not allowed to feel at home in this city, which was always my hometown. Certainly I had a longer nose than my Aryan colleagues in school. As a joke someone called it "the key to the synagogue," and some people laughed themselves silly over this expression. I was a "Jewish pig," a subhuman. My family, the Hamburger family, had lived in Franconia for four hundred years. My father was born in Schweinau.

On November 9, 1938, I rode on my bicycle, as I did every day, to Erle, a Jewish electronics store in Johannis. I had been an apprentice there for a year, since I was not allowed to attend high school at Egidienberg. I was expelled from school when I beat up a fellow student who called me a "Jewish pig." Before I rode to the store that morning of November 9, we knew that things would become worse and that it would be more than just a matter of someone calling us "Jewish pigs." It was written clearly in the newspaper on November 9: "The German people are not taking this anymore." The reference concerned the assassination of vom Rath, the German diplomat, in Paris two days earlier by seventeen-year-old Herschel Grynszpan. The day passed by normally. In the evening at nine o'clock my father sent me to bed. "Something will happen," he said. "We have to remain quiet." Shortly afterward there was a knock on the door. There were eight SA men. "We have to search everything," they said. Nothing was broken, and none of us were touched. They searched the apartment and left. In my grandparents' house on Schweinauer Street the same thing happened—exactly the same thing: they searched and left again.

My uncle Justin Hamburger lived on Landgraben Street. He was part owner of the Luma brush factory. I called him there, but he did

11

not answer the phone. So my father sent me on my bicycle to his home. An SA sentry stood in front of the house and the lights were on inside. "Where are you going?" the SA man asked me. I said that I wanted to see my uncle. He responded, "You little Jewish pig, get going." Recently I had gotten used to this—the Jewish pig and the obedience. I returned home again, and on the way I saw that the SA had done a thorough job in the neighborhood. On Essenwein Street the synagogue was burning, Jewish stores were ransacked, the furniture was thrown onto the street, and the SA was watching so that no one would disturb the fire. The next day I rode again to the Jewish electronics store, Erle, in Johannis. It was no longer an electronics store— only a pile of broken furniture and equipment with a swastika on the wall. "It is the end," Mr. Erle said. "I do not have any work for you anymore." After this I returned to my uncle's apartment to find everything destroyed—glass was broken, books were torn apart, chairs and beds were cut into pieces, and the closets were broken into. Later, I read in the paper who had done these things on the night of November 9th. It was not Mr. Hitler, nor Mr. Streicher, and not the SA but supposedly a spontaneous uprising of the people.

On this night, hordes of SA men took their anger out, especially in the city of Nuremberg. First, they attacked the large stores, breaking the windows with the bars which they had brought with them, and then, they ransacked the stores with a mob which had already been informed that these events would take place. After this they proceeded to the dwellings where Jews lived. The non-Jewish tenants were instructed earlier to open the apartment house doors and, if the door was not opened, it would be broken down. Many of the "spontaneous" avengers were equipped with pistols and knives, while each group brought along axes, large hammers, and iron bars to force entry into Jewish homes. Several SS men had bags for collecting money, jewelry, paintings, and other valuables which they hauled off. The apartments were supposedly being searched for weapons because of a new law enacted the day before that forbade Jews to possess such items. Glass doors, mirrors, and pictures were broken. Paintings were cut with knives, and beds, shoes, and clothes were cut apart. Everything was broken into small pieces, and so, on the morning of November 10th, the victimized families had nothing left. Most had no coffee cups, no spoons, no knives, nothing at all. Any money that was found was confiscated along with valuable papers and savings books. The worst violence was aimed against Jewish apartment owners; both men and women were badly mistreated. The SA men drove a number of men to the jail. On the way there, the prisoners endured constant beatings and jeers from the crowd. The women who were also brought to the jail were usually released by the authorities after several hours. The men, among them boys under fourteen, were squeezed tightly into cells in great numbers. After more than a hundred males were turned-in in such a fashion, they were driven off in police trucks to the court jail and placed in its gymnasium. Toward the evening an additional number of Jews from the city of Fürth were brought in. The next morning around four o'clock all Jews under sixty years of age were deported to Dachau. The Gestapo officers arrested the secretary of the Jewish community, Bernhard Kolb. During the night SA men violently entered his apartment and struck him on the head. He was driven by car to the office of the Jewish Cultural Society, where he was imprisoned with other male prisoners. More and more Jews were brought in. Kolb reported that many Jews had been beaten severely.

On the night of November 9 to 10 nine people were killed in this violence in Nuremberg. On the same day the city coroner certified the suicides of ten Jewish citizens in Nuremberg. The Nazi lord mayor Liebel reported to the city council that twenty-six Jews did not survive the night of the pogrom. That number was certified in the city registers; the number of Jews who died shortly after the so-called Kristallnacht [Night of the Broken Crystal; Am. ed.] is significantly higher. Since the cause of death was not indicated, however, it is difficult to say precisely how many of them were direct victims of that night.

Of the ninety-one murders which occurred during that night within the entire German Reich, nine were in Nuremberg. This shows the brutality with which the campaign was carried out in that city, even though the uncertified numbers which I have mentioned earlier are not included. During that night more than a hundred million marks worth of material damage resulted in Germany. At least 7,500 stores were destroyed; the damage to the glass windows alone surpassed six million marks. At least 267 synagogues were destroyed, and around thirty thousand Jews were arrested. They were sent to Buchenwald, Dachau, and Sachsenhausen concentration camps. The damage to the German economy was tremendous. However, the organizers of that night found a solution for this problem. On November 14, 1938, the Jews were ordered to pay a collective punitive fine of one billion Reichsmarks for the damages incurred to "the property of the people's community," as the perpetrators called it.

The last phase of the "solution to the Jewish question" had begun. That night was not only about broken glass and crystal; no, it was a night of murder in which more was broken:

The dams of hate and prejudice were broken.

The concepts of friendship and humanity were broken.

Human hearts were broken; the confidence in a nation and in German people were broken.

No, it was not only a night of broken crystal.

A community broke here without recourse, a community of a nation. And everyone knew it and watched it, and no one could or wanted to help. One must have been deaf and blind during that night not to have known what was happening. If someone was able to say up until that point, "What business is that of mine?" or "I do not know anything," then everyone should have known after this night. It was one of the most shameful nights in German history. The last chance for a collective scream against further escalating injustice was lost. The crime which occurred in front of everyone's eyes was relegated to an everyday event because of the lack of action. This ordeal preprogrammed the beginning of the end of Jewish life in Germany and in Europe!

I immigrated on August 22, 1939. Alone. To Palestine. On May 27, 1945, I returned to my hometown as a soldier in an English uniform. I stood at the Plärrer [a main square in downtown Nuremberg; Am. ed.] and saw no houses, no streets, no trees, and almost no people. I had to think back to the night of November 9, 1938. I remembered the swastikas on the walls of the houses, the broken glass in the home of my uncle Justin, the ransacked stores, the burning synagogue, and the flames in the whole city. These memories will probably never die.

HERMANN GLASER

The Majority Could Have Stayed Away without the Risk of Repression

I cannot quite claim to be an eyewitness of the time in the fullest sense of the word; I was only ten years old in 1938. Wouldn't this therefore be beyond me? Wouldn't it? Didn't I know anything? After all, the National Socialists demonstrated and practiced their inhumanity in front of everyone. Everyone who lived at that time can testify to this. There was no secret in the explosion of the violence which the state organized in November 1938, nor in the systematic, inhumane, defaming, and depriving policy toward the Jewish population. Everyone, young, middle-aged, or old, could witness the destruction of public morality. However, one still had to be able to make ethical judgments.

The day after the night of the pogrom in Nuremberg a large demonstration took place on Adolf Hitler Square (which is called the Main Market today): A "huge moving sea of human beings"; Julius Streicher, the "Führer of the Franconians," "summoned" the population of Nuremberg and it came: "Although it became known only in the late hours of the afternoon that the Führer of the Franconians would speak to his fellow Nurembergers, almost a hundred thousand fellow citizens came to the historic meeting place. It was impossible to look over the huge mass of humanity. . . . Could the voice of a nation ever speak clearer than it did in this case?" Unfortunately, one must agree with the reporter from the *Fränkische Tageszeitung* (of November 11, 1938) who observed that it is appropriate to be collectively ashamed due to the fact that this infamous triumphant event ("the seed which he [Streicher] spread has blossomed") found such a large voluntary participation. One does not see many "assigned" uniformed participants in pictures of the event. "Eternal jubilation met the Führer of the Franconians when he appeared on Adolf Hitler Square. There was a storm of enthusiasm which subsided only after quite a while." The

15

overwhelming majority of the women and men of Nuremberg could have avoided this event without any danger of retaliation. Instead, they applauded these national criminals. "Words and pictures are not able to approximate what we saw with our eyes. Furthermore, one cannot begin to describe the atmosphere which enveloped the large square; that atmosphere which united the fanatic hate against the nation of Jewish criminals with the joyful belief in a great future for Germany."

The data have been researched; the facts are in front of us. I'm blessed by the mercy of late birth [a term used by Chancellor Helmut Kohl to exonerate his generation of Germans; Am. ed.] when confronted by this oppressing meanness; I must not feel like I am a "criminal of the time." However, whoever does not remember, supports either directly or indirectly the "second guilt"—the suppression, the reckoning, and the glossing over of the facts.

There is not much that I can report, but it still seems like a lot to me: I will never forget that night; I have to thank my parents for sensitizing me to the "violation of civilization," in other words, the loss of culture which the Third Reich presented. During the night of November 9–10 my spiritual biography was coined; my youthful "educational experience" (the experience which has shaped me and has remained with me) is recorded in an artistic and compact manner as "A Page in an Album" for a neighbor. (The three memoirs are taken from Hermann Glaser, *Spurensuche. Deutsche Familienprosa* [Frankfurt am Main and Berlin, 1987].)

> Solidarity was slowly but steadily growing in the Schulze family without Jewish haste because of a multistoried building from the foundation era which the family owned for a long time. Initially, the wholesale dairy products business was not much larger than a small retail business. First there was a three-wheel Hanomag vehicle, then a four-wheel electric cart with a high loading platform. The sales volume grew. The courtyard was always clean. Laundry was hung every Monday on the terrace above the storage area. The little garden in front of the building and the flower beds next to the driveway were always raked and watered, and the empty egg crates and butter boxes were neatly piled up in the back to the right. The fallen fruit underneath the pear tree was regularly collected. The ivy around the window was cleanly cut. And the son grew into the business; the daughters married hearty men; later one of them got divorced. Early in the morning, old Schulze was already at work. Milk for vespers and thick yellow butter spread on black kernel bread. And on Sundays, the family went on an excursion; later it would be

by car. When the door of the storage area was open one could smell the cool, appetizing milk products. Everything was as fresh as the people in the brochures from the dairy which for many months told the entire Nibelungen tale [the German medieval heroic epic tale which was also widely popularized through Wagnerian operas; Am. ed.] in pictures. One could see that Siegfried and Kriemhild [the heroes of the epic tale; Am. ed.] surely ate a lot of butter and drank buttermilk; in contrast, Hagen [the antagonist of the tale; Am. ed.] looked rancid. The brochures were made of pure flint-laced paper, and in the backs of the booklets one read the praises for unbottled and bottled fresh milk. Low-fat milk, which appeared slightly bluish when it was taken out of the large containers, came later. One night there was a loud and long ringing next door. Since our living room was across from the entrance of the neighboring house, we turned off the light and listened. Schulze, the SA member, was supposed to go into action with his comrades within an hour, and everything was supposed to be secret. After half an hour he was ready to march: boots, shoulder straps, brown shirt with the swastika sling, a cap on his white hair, and a walrus mustache. He was so happy. During that night, they ransacked Jewish apartments and stores. The next morning the neighbor's brown shirt was already washed and hung on the terrace above the storage building; lonely, it flew in the morning breeze; because the laundry was just washed. Schulze, dressed in his white coat, piled the egg crates neatly one on top of each other in the back of the courtyard to the right next to the pear tree.

A day later, another page from the "Album"—again from the daily, bourgeois routine.

The apartment of Knöchlein, the secondary school teacher, was located on the top floor; several of the rooms had slanted walls; this was the reason why it was so comfortable in that apartment. There were several photographs on his writing desk; two sons in uniform; five sharpened pencils, precisely aligned; a stack of notebooks piled exactly one on top of the other; two small cactus flowers. Books and coffee cups were on the bookshelf. A banged-up steel helmet hung on the wall; from Verdun. I knew the apartment quite well because whenever we had vacations we would always carry the flowerpots from the classroom into the teacher's apartment, where they would be cared for. The teacher wore a smoking jacket at home but he did not smoke. In the school, he wore a brown worker's coat on which one could see traces of white and colored chalk. He immediately hung his suit jacket in a closet where there was also a towel and soap; the little stick with which he occasionally disciplined the students was also in there on a shelf. Oftentimes, in sessions called "paws," the teacher would hold a delinquent's thumbs or the child had to hold his hand freely; if the student pulled his hand away, Knöchlein would laugh heartily; He would then hit the upper side of the fingers, which was more painful. Therefore, very few pulled their hands away.—We painted pictures of the place where the Führer was born; It was the town of Braunau with its many house decorations and its two towers; I received a "very good"; how the Führer founded the National Socialist party of Germany and became the savior of Germany; I had to erase the swastika since I drew it the wrong way. After the instruction in local history we would sing; the teacher had a strong voice—"with whom God was merciful . . ." Knöchlein was a German nationalist; from an old family of teachers; I also came from an old family of teachers; he got together with my grandfather in the teachers' association.—In November 1938 when the shops and the apartments of the Jews were being destroyed, when we fearfully squeezed by the furniture which was thrown out of windows—the doors were broken down and the windows were smashed to pieces in many homes—when we went to school that morning we met our teacher on the way; we felt safe again. He cheered us up and laughed; he stroked his mustache. A pile of feathers, which flew in the air when we walked by laid in front of a home; the feathers came from cut-up bedding. They have played a little trick-or-treat today he said; and he adjusted the rag with which he cleaned the blackboard, but it got stuck when he closed his folder, and hung now like a little flag and he laughed once again; During the local history class he told us how the Führer recognized the power of the Jews for the first time in Vienna.

I didn't carry flowerpots into his apartment anymore. Next year, however, I went to the secondary school anyway.

The National Socialist crimes were possible only because the perpetrators found incredible support for their ideology and propaganda, their actions and plans; because the enthusiasm for the Führer and the National Socialist regime could not be shaken, not even by undisguised barbarism. The aura of mass murder was hardly scratched until the end of the war; the violation of civilization was not a mere collapse, it was total devastation. What Philip Jenninger, the unfortunate Bundestag president, presented in a partly linguistic role identification with the low point of political culture at that time is unfortunately correct. He was incapable of putting his level of objection to what the people thought and felt at that time into perspective from today's point of view: It is unfortunately true that Hitler's policies were celebrated fanatically. The facade of "German values" from behind which disaster lurked was praised. Morality could only be found in remnants in a few enclaves far away from the mainstream of events. One must always recall painfully that National Socialism was not the product of a few shrewd, demonic seducers who secretly carried out their crimes with the aid of a handful of primitive and brutal executioners; the overwhelming portion of the population knew of the crimes, frequently participated in them, and did not even offer inner resistance. The "fellow citizen" is especially characterized by the lack of any feeling for humanity and morality.

I would like to report a third recollection—the story may have taken place at the end of 1938—the year of the November riots. Christmastime. "The gingerbread peacefulness" of Nuremberg.

The Seltsam family had everything, a five-room apartment with a bathroom; a weekend home in the countryside; they went skiing after the New Year; this was especially impressive, because who was able to leave around that time? The father had an upper management position with the postal or railroad service; they had a lot of toys and always the newest ones; a three-speed bicycle; ice-skate boots. He was able to play the hit parade on the piano; in the gym he always had the highest grades. He was a leader in the youth organization and was soon to become a "flag leader"; athletic, blond, well tanned; he was a joy to his parents, the Führer, and his teacher; one could be sure that he would soon be admitted into a Napola [abbreviation for "Nationalpolitische Erziehungsanstalt," an elitist political educational institution for young Nazis; Am. ed.]. The Hitler Youth leadership's benevolent eye rested upon my schoolmate who was almost my friend. I was always invited to his birthday celebration: a major afternoon cake-eating.—Once, close to the village of Boxdorf, we followed mysterious tracks in the fields and a cable which of course was only a severed wire, not a secret phone line for agents. Close to Buchenbühl we discovered a puddle which also appeared curious to us; however, we never uncovered the secret. Of course our bicycle tours and meetings became less and less frequent since the Hitler Youth Organization claimed more and more of his time; Gerd had to fulfill his leadership duties; therefore, he had little time. However, next Christmas another large gathering took place; it was already beautiful at his house; they had a large Christmas tree with many stars made out of straw as well as Winter Relief Fund figurines [figurines given annually to donors of money, food, and/or clothing; Am. ed.]; his father put a down payment on a Volkswagen (the certificate was placed on the table with Christmas gifts); many gift-wrapped books, the bows with their attached Christmas cards appeared untouched; the new picture was already on the wall; it showed the end of a work day; a peasant with a scythe in the sunset glow, a woman behind him with an open blouse, a locket around her naked neck; around her skirt several blond children looked up at their parents. The naked breast made us uncomfortable, but we secretly looked at the picture. But then came the great surprise: he received a book which appeared to be the most precious gift of this Christmas; he was already laughing when he unwrapped it; colorful with many verses, a youth book prepared by Streicher— *Don't Trust a Fox on a Green Meadow or a Jew in His Oath*. The fat meaty figures were pictured in all their infamy and were described in verses. Outside snowflakes were falling. It was a white Christmas, which was rare and gave us special joy. The mother read aloud and laughingly—the mother who had a breast almost as large as the one in the picture and who already looked so athletic, fashionable, and healthy before the ski trip. And now subconsciously, she made a mistake by saying: "Don't trust a Jew on a green meadow or a fox in his oath"—it was wrong but also funny; we laughed and then we received hot chocolate. A blessed Christmas. Gerd was supposed to go to leadership school soon; he had more specific information sent to him. Of course, later, he never went to leadership school. Whenever it was possible during class time he would paint— he sat next to me—he painted meatly Jewish noses on scratch pads and blotting paper; one only had to draw a number six and you already had a caricature.

In this context I would like to remember the very few women and men of Nuremberg who did not allow the inhumanity to become a state and societal principle, and who—if they did not actively resist— at least tried to lessen this cruelty and thereby retained a shred of decency. So, for example, we have the teachers of Nuremberg—although, as mentioned, only a few—made it very clear to Jewish children and youth that not all Germans had replaced poets and thinkers with judges and executioners.

And without any consideration, I would like to discuss those who fortified the official sadism with their own private variety and who made sure that the psychological and physical torture of the victims would know no limits. For example, one of the worst "writing desk executioners" was the Nuremberg city school counselor, Friedrich F. By spreading hatred against the Jewish population, through the distribution of the unmentionable Stürmer-books within the school system, he proved to be a man of the basest character, a pedagogical governor in an empire of the lowest demons.

We must lose the habit of ignoring and forgetting the guilt of the pioneers and perpetrators of the mass murder simply because they eventually became old and "jolly" and because their time has passed. The victims' pain makes it imperative that the culprits are named.

One should not allow the meanness to pass into the underworld without a sound—especially while the pretension of well-calculated reconciliation is spreading. The abyss of the crime cannot be covered with a verbal foam. By the way, the city school counselor of Nuremberg, Friedrich F., died recently—"went home in God's peace," "equipped with the comforting of the church." So it was written in the obituary, which began with a quotation from Pope Pius XII: "There is no farewell for those who are united with God." In such fashion, individuals and groups constantly deceive themselves about the terror of historical truth.

"'I remember Auschwitz' must accompany all of my ideas," Theodore W. Adorno has thus formulated the categorical imperative of contemporary history. In the text, *Far Away from the Shot*, written in the fall of 1944, it says in the "Minima moralia": "It is idiotic to assume that after this war life can continue 'normally' or that the culture can be 'reconstructed'—as if the reconstruction of culture alone is not already its negation. Millions of Jews were murdered and this is supposed to be an interlude and not the catastrophe itself. What is this culture still waiting for?"

Soon, however, everything was moving again; the culture was waiting to be only culture and nothing else. The elimination of critical consciousness allowed the dead to rest. It let Auschwitz pass. Adorno noted ten years later: "The relationship to the spiritual past is poisoned in improperly resurrected culture." Is this statement also valid for our immediate present? Does one have to repeat it for the imminent fin de siècle? "Life" hovers over the mass graves; the unfortunate unconsciousness dissolves in a vacuum. Senseless happiness is threatening. So that Auschwitz does not happen again, there is a desperate wake-up call for political morality and an ethical culture. This culture seeks to carry on the concept of enlightenment, with great exertion. There is also a place for memory.

ERNST WALTEMATHE

The Race between Life and Death: The Mixed-Breeds

It is very difficult for me to describe objectively the special problem of the "mixed-breeds"; first of all, I cannot be objective, since I was affected subjectively. And second, I was a child who directly experienced what children usually go through without being able to digest the events at the time. My comments will therefore begin with my personal experiences which will be supplemented at the end with what I later researched and read.

Both of my parents come from workers' families, and my father was a blue-collar worker. They met during an event sponsored by the Workers' Youth International; my father belonged to the German section of the Workers' Youth International, and my mother, an Amsterdam Jewess, belonged to the counterpart organization there. They married on December 29, 1929. Therefore, my mother became German and from then on lived with my father in the city of Bremen. My brother was born in 1930, and I, in February of 1935.

I was three years old at the time of the Reich's Pogrom Night. I did not consciously experience that night, and I have no memory of it. However, my life was later affected by this event, and my personal history could not be explained without an awareness of it.

A month later, in December of 1938, my mother, my brother, and I moved to my (Jewish) grandparents' home in Amsterdam. Of course, that was supposed to be only temporarily. My parents, who were politically committed people, thought that the Hitler empire would be too dangerous for the family, and therefore my mother and we children had to flee the Nazis.

My parents were divorced in 1939 for this reason. This was necessary for both parties: my father, who was a locksmith working for a railroad repair company in Bremen, had difficulties because he was married to a Jewess; my mother had to try to regain her Dutch citizenship in order to be eligible for social benefits in Amsterdam or to find job opportunities there.

22

My mother was named as the guilty one in the divorce decree because she "willfully" left the family. This decree was tactically well calculated so that the children were given to the "Aryan" father, who, however, relinquished their education to the Jewish mother in the Netherlands. My parents' decision later proved to be crucial, since it saved the lives of us children and my mother.

In fact it would be another ten years until our family "reunion." From then on I grew up with German citizenship as a Netherlander and lived with my mother and my brother together at my Dutch-Jewish grandparents' place.

Up to this point, this has been a sober narration of a single human destiny in the year 1938.

The pogrom against the Jewish population in the Nazi Reich forced my parents to give up their togetherness for the time being, in favor of an uncertain future. The family was separated; I grew up without a father.

The reasons for the separation, however, were already firmly stated in a political sense in the National Socialists' "racial politics." In spite of, or because of, this ideology which was based on a scientific racial theory, the Nazis came to power and did not hesitate to put this theory into practice after the "power grab." The superiority of the Aryan race, which was supported by the scientific methods of the anti-Semites and the racial purists, became the foundation for the legislation which was immediately enacted in 1933.

According to the racial purists' theories, the "contamination" of the "national Aryan body" came about through the progress of civilization, since modern medicine and social reforms were increasing the lifespans of the "inferiors," as well as their reproduction rate. Therefore, the purists demanded a direct action by the state. After 1933 the state, which inscribed its racism on its banner, took action:

The adoption of the Law for Prevention of Descendants with Hereditary Diseases on July 14, 1933, led to forced sterilization and euthanasia. Soon the Jews were disfranchised by special legislation. The Reich's Citizen Law of September 15, 1935, distinguished between those who were only state's citizens and thereby had no legal rights, and those who would receive the distinction of being citizens of the Reich. We mixed-breeds, for the time being, received the same rights as state's citizens with German or related blood. The Law for Protection of German Blood and German Honor prohibited marriages between Jewish and non-Jewish citizens.

With these laws, the state legalized racism, discrimination, and later persecution. Additionally, Jews were excluded from all public life with the help of professional bans, school dismissals, and cancellations of state assistance. No one could claim to be unaware of all of this. In fact, many people advocated such clear legislation and disfranchisement, and several profited very well from it.

By 1938 the gradual disfranchisement of the Jewish population had progressed quite far. The Reich's Pogrom Night was a well-calculated public event which was supposed to provoke fear and terror among the victims and demonstrate that the disfranchisement of the Jews included even their right to life. That evening, however, was more than a night of terror. It was supposed to set the tone, and viewed historically, November 9, 1938, was the high-point on the road toward the "final solution."

Up until 1938, a broad segment of the Jewish population caved in to public discrimination and made great sacrifices. By now, the Jews knew that the Nazis were serious, that their lives were threatened. The systematically executed disfranchisement of the Jews took an alarming turn toward physical terror on this day. Arson, destruction, and murder were the predecessors of the Holocaust.

From my own experience, I can report on what was happening in Holland. From this, one can surmise what would have happened to me in Germany if our family had remained there. According to the Nuremberg Laws, it was clear that "mixed-breeds of the first degree" from then on had to be considered Jews. This was based not on membership in the Jewish religious community (to which I never belonged) but on the "Jewish blood" principle (whatever that meant). The entire paradox of National Socialist race theory (i.e., to connect religion with racial traits) was demonstrated in the borderline situation of the mixed-breeds, in their position between Jews and Aryans. Religion was used as a biological criterion in order to define mixed-breeds. On one hand, this may have led to their special place between Aryans and Jews while, at the same time, it held the sword of Damocles over their heads. On the other hand, "legal desk executioners," such as Hans Globke [a high-level justice department official who became an advisor to West German Chancellor Konrad Adenauer after the war; Am. ed.] were cold-blooded enought to include this association, without any rational thought, in their interpretations of the first decree of the Reich's Citizen Law: "What is important for judging whether someone is a Jew or not is fundamentally *not* membership in the Jewish religious community but Jewish blood. In order to preclude dissension during argumentation it is, however, definitely determined that a grandparent who belonged to the Jewish religious community is without a doubt a Jew, thus a being of Jewish blood; a counterargument is not valid." Therefore, any contradiction was not allowed.

The movement to place mixed-breeds outside of the jurisdiction began in 1940; the persecution of the mixed-breeds started after 1942. At the Wannsee Conference of January 1942 [when the Nazi Hierarchy decided on the "final solution" for the Jewish population; Am. ed.] the debate ensued as to whether the mixed-breeds shoud face forced sterilization or whether they should be deported and/or completely eliminated. The deportation began in 1943. Heydrich, the chief of the Reich's Main Security Office, suggested the following at the Wannsee Conference: "Mixed-breeds of the first degree are, in view of the final solution to the Jewish question, classified as being equal to the Jews." Therefore, in Germany I would have surely become a victim of the Holocaust.

In the Netherlands, which Hitler's Germany attacked on May 10, 1940, and which was eventually occupied by the Germans, the policies of the "final solution" began as well in 1942. In May of 1942, the Star of David was introduced, which my mother had to wear.

The first crackdown on our street occurred in September 1942. My grandfather was taken away and sent via Theresienstadt to Auschwitz and the gas chamber. Many relatives of my grandparents' and my mother's generations faced the same or a similar fate. My mother was not taken away. She had two advantages: she was able to speak German and therefore was able to make herself understood; however, she was especially able to point to the fact that she had two children (at that time eleven and seven years old) who belonged to an Aryan husband.

In contrast to many completely Jewish families who lived on our street with children of the same age and who were all taken away together, we remained in Amsterdam. My grandmother, who at the time of the crackdown was seriously diabetic and was therefore not able to be transported, was not taken away. She died six weeks later in a hospital in Amsterdam.

A second crackdown took place in June 1943. I remember it as being lengthy and spooky. My mother contributed to this by wearing black because a message arrived through the underground a week earlier that her sister, a well-known artist who had been hiding since 1942, had been betrayed and had been picked up by the Gestapo. However, she succeeded in swallowing the poison which she always carried with her and died later in the hospital in Hengelo. My mother apparently also had trouble explaining again (I did not understand a word of the conversation in German) that no one could arrest her because her children were in fact Aryan and "belonged" to a father, who could not take care of them due to his shift duty with the railroad. I do not know how long the two state security agents remained in our apartment, but it seemed to me like an eternity. In any case, my mother was not taken away.

The bureaucracy was also thorough in Germany. Soon after our departure, with my father remaining in Bremen, the child support which the railroad district of Altona had been giving to my father was cut. The explanation that was given was that the children who were adjudged to him were growing up in a non-Aryan household. Therefore child support—the war would be a reason later—was nonexistent.

From this account, one could conclude that the mixed-breeds of the first degree, according to the Nuremberg Laws—which Globke supposedly singled out in order to protect the Jews—were really a generation between life and death. They were victims of the Holocaust, when they lived as a *complete* family because only the Aryan part was spared from the crackdowns. Thus, the mixed-breeds of the first degree shared the same fate as their Jewish parent.

The placement of mixed-breeds outside of the civil laws can be documented as can the measures intended for their persecution. The facts demonstrate that while the persecution of mixed-breeds took place later than that of the Jews, they were eventually threatened by the same fate.

1940   Placing of personal data into the Jewish index card record, discharges from the army (also for the Aryan husbands)

1942   Memorandum by the Interior Ministry, that requests by Jewish mixed-breeds for marriage will not be accepted for the duration of the war—marriage ban

1942   Exclusion from school instruction (a memorandum of the People's Education Ministry)

1943   "Extermination through work": Göring ordered that all mixed-breeds and Aryan men who were married to Jewesses were to be picked up for the work campaign of the "Death" Organization (Organisation Tod). The labor camps of the "Death" Organization were not much different from the concentration camps.

1943   Beginning of the deportation to Hadamar for the purpose of "euthanasia" murders. A registered nurse from Hadamar reported:

> In May of 1943 mixed-breeds—all children—were brought to the Hadamar institution. I cannot name the number of

children exactly, but to the best of my knowledge there were fifteen to twenty girls in the group. Almost all of these children were healthy. A few had skin rashes. The children were all killed by injections. When I returned to Hadamar in October of 1943 from a twenty-four-day-long vacation, someone told me that all of these children had been eliminated.[1]

1943   Beginning of the deportation to Theresienstadt. Known systematic arrests of mixed-breeds in the cities of Cologne, Berlin, Augsburg, Oldenburg, Dresden. On February 18, 1945, transports arrived with 169 people from Leipzig, 195 from Frankfurt, 146 from Halle, and from other cities. Supposedly, in 1945 an additional 1,954 mixed-breeds arrived in Theresienstadt.

This data devulges a lot about the initial operation of the state murdering apparatus, about the institutionalizing of mass murder, but nothing about the lives spent in fear and powerlessness.

At the beginning, I said that as a victim I cannot be objective. By the way, one can use objectivity as a convenient excuse to distance oneself subjectively from the historical events and their implications for today. It is probably better not to refer to the clemency of birthdates [a reference to Chancellor Helmut Kohl's well-known claim that he was blessed by the grace of "late birth," i.e., his generation was too young to have any influence on the Nazi regime; Am. ed.] but to empathize with the feelings of others. One should try to understand them in every sense when one deals with overcoming the past. Furthermore, the creation of an anti-fascist future should not be pursued with abstract columns of numbers and lifeless statistics. It would be much too easy to recognize only digits, which one can easily overlook, instead of human beings in need.

I would like to complete my treatment of my personal experiences with a passage from my speech in front of the Bundestag on March 29, 1979. At that time, this was my contribution to the debate concerning the question of whether the murders committed during the Nazi regime should become null and void under the statute of limitations and whether the statement "Murder is murder" made by Wehner [a leading left-wing politician in the Social Democratic party; Am. ed.] is appropriate:

Perhaps one must have to have experienced firsthand the terror of being a victim of governmentally-organized measures which the majority of the population accepted quietly and cowardly. One cannot forget the meaning of the fundamental, existential fear when recalling the rattle of the SS boots on the stairways, the grandfather who was picked up at the apartment, the wish that mother would not also be taken, the uncertainty, the mixture of hope and terror. One clung to the prospect that surely no harm would befall simple people who after all were not guilty of anything, and small innocent children, but one knew precisely—one knew already by that time—that the shipment which was assembled was destined for an extermination camp. "Picking up": that was a completely simple and innocent name for that which was hiding behind it, the so-called final solution. In the term "final solution," moreover, the deaths of millions of human beings were hidden. It must be acknowledged again and again that one is not dealing with a number here but with countless individuals, good ones and bad ones, likeable ones and dislikeable ones, rich ones and poor ones, industrious ones and lazy ones, young ones and old ones, children and adults, Germans and foreigners, sick people and healthy people, but in each case a human being, an individual who had the right to his own life.

In this context, however, I would like to say that as a child in Holland, I experienced the concrete meaning of human solidarity and resistance. In any case, there were human beings—in Germany as well—who did not look away, who did not ask what career opportunity they would lose if they put themselves against the movement, who did not ask about the danger into which they put themselves. They just asked a simple question—and answered it by their actions: in what kind of trouble are my fellow men, and how can I help them?

For me, heroism often manifested itself as human responsibility, as unarmed action against injustice, as resistance in the face of temptation to participate and accept. Personally, I especially connect the term "resistance" with those friends and neighbors who, as simple people, were not looking for some sort of public glory when they helped the persecuted. They did not ask whether the people in need were Christians or conservatives or Communists or Socialists or trade unionists or something else.

On the other hand, in judging the bravery of this resistance today it should be immaterial what those who resisted fascism were themselves.[2]

In conclusion, I have formulated the following theses from all of the above:

- The fascism of the German Reich sought, as does that of today's fascist regimes, to construct a system in which the aim justifies the means and in which individual humans are degraded into recipients

of orders or, if they are on the other side, become victims.
- In regard to governmental actions, indifference, unwillingness to understand, and looking away pave the way for the growth of fascism.
- Resistance and an unconditional adherence to human rights must be organized against injustice and inhuman actions, regardless of the reputation of the oppressive regime and irrespective of world opinion and religious attitudes toward those who are being oppressed.
- Xenophobia is yet another symptoms like anti-Semitism. By spiritualizing the superiority of one's own nationality and therefore the inferiority of another, one also implies a justifiable inferiority of one's fellow human beings.
- Whoever wants to have democracy must practice tolerance.

Walter Grab

"The Jews Are Vermin, Except for Grab, My Jewish Schoolmate"

I am the son of a Jewish middle-class Viennese family, born in 1919. If one had asked me who I was, when I finished high school in 1937, I would have identified myself as an Austrian, not a Jew. Although I was a Jew, I was not a believer, and I did not follow any of the religious conventions. Therefore my confession seems irrelevant to me. Nowadays one defines oneself by nationality and not by religion. When I was a pupil, it seemed to me that my identity as an Austrian was obvious. In high school I was taught the essence of enlightenment, humanism, international friendship, and world citizenship.

I was in the second semester of my studies at the University of Vienna when Austria was annexed by Nazi Germany in March of 1938. My life appeared to be at an end. I was lucky that my mother had relatives in Jerusalem. I did not know them, and I never would have emigrated if the Nazis had not seized power in Austria. These relatives saved me and they saved my parents later. I obtained a student certificate to study at the University of Jerusalem, and I emigrated in July of 1938, after four months of Nazi rule in Austria.

I have lived in Tel Aviv for the last fifty years, though intermittently for the last quarter of a century. Since 1965, I have been a professor at the University of Tel Aviv, where I taught contemporary history up until my retirement in 1986. In 1971, I founded the Tel Aviv University Institute for German History, and I often traveled to the Federal Republic of Germany and to other European and non-European countries for workshops, lectures, and to conduct research. However, Tel Aviv is still my home, as before.

As a historian, I view personal experiences within a historical context. I believe that a new chapter of the Nazi period had already begun by March of 1938, and not first of all because of the pogrom of November 1938. The annexation of Austria had demonstrated to the Nazis in the German Reich that one could very easily ignite and mo-

30

bilize the so-called people's anger in order to use it for one own's enrichment and in order to rob the Jews. This had happened on a large scale from below for the first time in Austria in March of 1938. Up until then, much was organized in Germany from above, i.e., by the Nazi government. What happened in Austria in March of 1938 was, to a great extent, an eruption of the masses, who wanted to enrich themselves with Jewish property. Thousands of Jewish apartments, stores, shops, enterprises were "Aryanized" in a powerful raid which lasted from March to November of 1938. Many people had only waited for the moment to deprive the Jews and make themselves rich. Therefore a new chapter began, and I believe that the robberies and pogroms in November of 1938 throughout the Reich, including Austria and the Sudetenland, were a consequence of what the Nazis had learned from March 1938 in Austria.

Immediately following the annexation of Austria in March of 1938, Vienna, which was home for 175,000 Jews, experienced tremendous anti-Semitic excesses which, up until that time, had not even been seen to such an extent in Nazi Germany. I would like to mention only one fact in this context: in the first weeks after the German army crossed the Austrian border, three thousand Jews were arrested and imprisoned in Vienna; many ended up in concentration camps. These Jews were registered in lists which were compiled by the Austrian Nazis (an illegal party from 1933–38) who had already targeted the well-known and wealthy Jews as victims and objects of their greed long before the annexation. Among the names were those of my two uncles—brothers of my mother—who were well-to-do lawyers. The Nazis locked them up in a prison where they were forced to donate their estates to the German Reich. One of them contracted blood poisoning in jail, and died a few weeks after his release from prison; his servants, who turned out to be Nazis, stole most of his valuable furniture in the meantime.

I was on my way home on the afternoon of April 25, 1938, six weeks after the Nazi takeover in Austria. There was a Jewish gymnasium close to our apartment, in the cellar of the house at 20 Liechtenstein Street. I sometimes went there to do gymnastics when I was a child of seven or eight years old. When I came close to this house, I was stopped by a chain of Nazis who wore armbands with swastikas. One of them yelled at me: "Are you a Jew?" When I said yes, he pushed me towards the house where the gymnasium was and ordered me to climb down the cellar stairway. Jewish children used to exercise in this large cellar, which was approximately thirty meters long. There was a lot of exercise equipment, and there were also rooms where Jewish boys and girls could change clothes. In the gym's lobby, I saw about twenty to thirty Jews who the Nazis had caught before me. They were crowded into a corner. A Nazi pushed me in there, too. The large gym as well as the lobby were—if you'll pardon the expression—completely full of shit. The floor and the walls were entirely covered with excrement. It stank savagely. By my estimation, a whole regiment of the SA or the SS or some other Nazis relieved themselves shortly before they began to round up the Jews; the excrement was still fresh and moist. Fifteen to twenty Nazis stood in the changing rooms in addition to the Jews. Behind me more Jews were pushed down the cellar stairways so that there were finally thirty-five or forty of us—only men. The Nazis had great fun; they amused themselves tremendously because they could now show off their courage with these helpless and confused Jews whom they chased into this gymnasium filled with excrement. They laughed and yelled for ten or fifteen minutes and made fun of us because we were afraid. Finally, one of them stepped in front and said: "You Jews have left your gymnasium to us in such a filthy state. Jewish gymnasia are so dirty. Again, one can see how filthy Jews are. And now you have to lick everything clean." What can one say when at the mercy of these barbarians who appear as if they have a human face? Nothing. We stood there silently. We were at their mercy, and anything seemed possible to us. However, they only wanted to have a little fun. They came up with this idea in order to insult and demean the Jews. This was not an ordered campaign like the pogrom of November 9, when Jews' stores were plundered and their apartments were destroyed. No, this fun was genuinely mob-inspired. I am not sure whether jokes like this took place in other cities, but they took place in Vienna. We were completely at the mercy of these Nazis. And they had tremendous fun while we squeezed together in fear. How could one lick this Nazi excrement?

Then one of them yelled: "Let's go to work!" And several Jews really tried to collect the excrement with their hands and throw it into the toilet bowls. That, however, was impossible. At best, one could only smear the excrement. It was impossible to clean the entry room and the gymnasium in this way. The Nazis laughed at and ridiculed us, but they finally brought a shovel, a broom, a bucket, and a few rags. We turned on the water faucet. However, one would have needed a fire hose for this job. I took one of the rags, in terrible fear of being killed by one of these Nazis in this cellar, and threw the excrement into the toilet bowl while trying to hide behind other Jews. The whole thing lasted a quarter of an hour to twenty minutes, during which time we were trying to obey the Nazi's orders. We were not very successful. And while I squatted and bent over in order to make myself, in my fear, as little as possible, I lifted my eyes up, just in time to meet precisely the gaze of one of the laughing Nazis who were standing there with their swastika bands on their brown shirts. I recognized him right away; he was a classmate of mine from the elementary school. Although I had left that elementary school in 1929, and nine years had passed in the meantime, I knew right away that this Nazi was a boy with whom I had gone to class for the first four years. Once we even sat next to each other and played in the courtyard together. His name was Lichtenegger. I will never forget that.

And this former schoolmate Lichtenegger looked at me—and recognized me just as I had recognized him. This recognition was uncomfortable and embarrassing for him. I noticed this in a split second; I felt that he did not want to lower me, the Jew who he knew, but the anonymous Jew, the Jewish stereotype of Nazi racial madness. "The Jew" is vermin which needs to be squashed, destroyed, but the classmate Grab who he knew as a fellow human being was excluded from this rule. These were his thoughts; I understood this within a second when our eyes met. I then got up to throw away the rag and walked up to Lichtenegger while the other Jews were trying to clean up the excrement. In my best Viennese accent I said to him: "Listen, Lichtenegger, you know me, let me out of here." He lowered his eyes, tore off a piece of newspaper which was lying around for cleaning the excrement, and wrote on it: "The Jew can walk out of here." Apparently, he had some kind of small authority; he was some kind of a subleader of these Nazis. After he gave me the piece of paper without saying a word, I went to the cellar stairway and told the Nazi who guarded it: "Lichtenegger said I can get out of here," and I showed him the piece of paper. Then I ran upstairs, showed the piece of paper to the Nazi at the door, and ran home as fast as I could. No more than an hour had passed from the moment that I was stopped on the street until my flight from the gymnasium.

I believe that this small episode illustrates the contradiction between the anti-Semitic racial madness and the personal encounters between Nazis and real Jews.

Maria Countess von Maltzan

Hiding at the Home of Strangers

At Easter time in 1930, I moved from Breslau to Munich in order to continue my studies, and I felt very much at that time that I was in the "Capital of the Movement." One could already see very distinct masses of people who believed in National Socialism there. As we all know, the "Brown House" [Nazi Party Headquarters in Munich; Am. ed.]" was there. The Nazis also made tremendous propaganda. I remember being in a movie theater at the end of 1932 where a film by Henri Bauer was being shown when a detachment of Nazis suddenly attacked the movie house. They cut off the projection of the film, and started beating up on people who still wanted to see the film. I was not able to get too involved but I was able to trip a few of the "storm troopers" who were running back and forth. Several of them fell to the ground. It was clear to me, at that time, what was going on. I realized that the hatred for the Jews, which appeared to me to be completely unjustified, was fanatical.

Then came the day of the "power grab," which was celebrated in Munich with overwhelming enthusiasm. SA and SS men marched everywhere all of a sudden. Then the wave of incarcerations started: at first, the Communists and the Social Democrats filled up the concentration camps, but well-known Jewish intellectuals were also already under attack at that time.

At the universities, students suddenly began to mutiny against their Jewish professors. In this context, I remember a wonderful example of helpfulness and civil courage: Borsig, who was a young student at that time, confronted his National Socialist classmates. He yelled at them and called them cowardly swines for attacking an old man with a large group. He then protected his professor until he found safety in the dean's office. I admired him very much for that!

In Munich, I had as friends many couples where one or both partners were Jews. They were refined, cultivated people whose intellects attracted me and whom I liked and appreciated. It was most terrible to witness the fact that human beings suddenly started to be "careful"

34

with whom they associated and avoided all their old friends after Hitler came to power. I belonged to a circle in Schwabing [city district of Munich; Am. ed.] which did not like what was happening. Everything was becoming coordinated very slowly. When it was announced over the radio on February 27 that the Reichstag was burning, we of course hurried immediately to all of our friends who held dangerous opinions and made sure that they did not return to their homes for a few days. Several were already incarcerated, but we were still able to hide quite a few so that they at least did not become victims of this highly-incited rage.

Then April 1 arrived, when all Jewish-owned stores were smeared with swastikas and Stars of David, and the SA and the SS forbade customers to enter. Thank God, I was still rebellious enough at that time to push the SS men aside and say: "You should have no objection if I, as a good German, pay my bill to a Jew." Some of the brown shirts stood there with cameras and recorded who entered—but I did not care. Even then, I remained a customer in many Jewish stores. But at the same time many people started to become afraid. It was pretty bad, especially in Bavaria, because the Nazi movement was stronger there than it was, for example, in Berlin. And everything was already moving toward the inevitable next step: the book burning of May 10.

This was one of the most horrifying things I could imagine. I had known, for example, Thomas Mann and his wife personally, and I enjoyed their hospitality. It was terrible to hear how they were denounced. It must have also been horrible in front of the university in Berlin. It was completely incomprehensible to me that even students and academicians could be persuaded into participating in such barbaric events.

At that time, I occasionally wrote articles for a south German newspaper in order to improve my meager monthly income. The editor and chief of that newspaper was in quite a hurry to become a member of the Reich's Archives Chamber (Reichsschrifttumskammer) in order to avoid jeopardizing his career. Fortunately, there were those with different attitudes. After all, I met Father Friedrich Muckermann through the editor's office. At this point, he already needed people who could actively help. We reported by mail the terrible things that were happening in Munich to a newspaper in Innsbruck. I also managed to deliver quite a large amount of mail across the border. Once the SS people in Munich dared to take my suitcases away and tried to check my mail. I simply refused to open the suitcases. They were stunned because SS men were no longer used having their orders disobeyed. I told them that every lock would be worth a shot of schnapps, and thereby put my trust in my Silesian stamina. I triumphed because, in the end, the same SS people personally took care of forwarding my mail.

Money-making became progressively more important because more and more Jews lost their jobs and were now in need. I often went to the embassies and consulates in Berlin, and I negotiated for the Jews and asked that they be given the chance to emigrate—especially those who were not wealthy, because, at that time, emigration was still relatively easy for those who had money.

After the semester break, I returned to Munich and noticed that the city was already devoid of my good friends. In part, some wealthy Jews were able to emigrate right away, at least to Paris or Holland and from there, they could try to emigrate further. Fortunately, many of them succeeded in not falling victim to the Holocaust. Of course, I and many others who thought like me helped them as much as we could. I was also never "embarrassed" to greet my friends openly on the streets and to walk with them. It was simply incredible how a city and its people changed under a regime. People, whom one assumed were respectible colleagues, suddenly became loyal party followers who professed "Aryan" and "German" interests. They, of course, angrily cursed the Austrians because they could not cross the border—in short it was an ugly atmosphere. One had to always be prepared to help someone spontaneously because terrible things were constantly happening.

At the institute in Munich, I often visited my mentor, Professor Frisch, whom I admired very much because he uncompromisingly and successfully objected to the dismissal of his Jewish assistants until they found positions abroad. They were all highly qualified scholars, so it was not too difficult. Indeed, this honest man succeeded in standing up to the regime; he was, however, an Austrian and had to be careful that nothing happened to him. In hospitals, however, Jewish doctors were kicked out in large numbers—which was also very bad for the patients.

Officially, a ban on practicing one's profession had not yet been pronounced. Thanks to my connection to Father Muckermann, I often received important information early; it was amazing how well the intelligence service of the Catholic Church worked! So we found out about the planned incarcerations, and we were able to bring the victims to safety in time.

I lived in Berlin again in the summer of 1935. Berlin was much more pleasant compared to Munich. Since there were foreign embassies and consulates, there was a somewhat international atmosphere. Besides, there were friends who lived in these extraterritorial areas who helped tremendously. I know that people were hidden in some embassies until they were finally taken out of the country.

In Berlin, I knew mostly well-to-do or wealthy, cultured Jews. It was upsetting that we had to use all of our powers of persuasion to convince them that they were in danger and that they should leave the country as fast as possible. There were still several among them who believed that the pogroms which eventually could happen would be aimed primarily against the Eastern Jews who immigrated after 1918! It was almost as important to succeed in convincing them of the danger as it was to help them.

Through Father Muckermann, I received an inquiry from Munich as to whether I could house people who were released from concentration camps. My first guest was as shy as a beaten dog—unfortunately, the comparison was fitting: his back, from the neck to his rear, was black and blue from beatings. I kept him as long as he needed to recover not only physically but also psychologically, and humanly— to get back on his feet again.

In the meantime, our efforts continued to pave the way for Jewish emigration. It was almost insurmountably difficult, however, for those who had no money. Unfortunately there were many who wanted to be paid for their help. The question of trust was the greatest risk with the paid help. Could the "helpers" be trusted?" Regrettably, the denunciations business was also flourishing. Refugees had to be channeled to one of the borders—for example, Holland or Denmark. For leading the Jews some helpers took away half of the cash and valuables from them. Then they were led around for a while until the Gestapo finally caught them with the rest of the valuables. Therefore, one was not allowed to trust anyone they did not really know. Furthermore, constant caution and distrust were additional handicaps for the victims as well as for the helpers.

When the Nuremberg Laws were passed in 1935, a new wave of arrests began which not only threatened the Jews who had "Aryan" girlfriends or male friends but their Aryan partners as well. The new term was called "disgrace by blood" (Blutschande). This again started a new wave of denunciations: one denounced and denounced and denounced; in this handy fashion a person could also settle many a personal score of jealousy, envy, and dislike.

The ban on Aryan women working in Jewish households soon followed. This was carefully prepared by wrongful accusations of rape.

Things became more and more difficult. The so-called privileged marriages were still protected, i.e., the marriages in which one of the partners was not Jewish. But then suddenly one day we found out that during the following night the husbands from such marriages had been "picked up." My friend Zivier spent the night in my place with his wife and child. Many others who we were able to warn in time were also brought to safety in friends' houses. However, many were still surprised and arrested. In Berlin, for the time being, all of the enemies of the state who were arrested were brought to Große Hamburger Street. At this point, I have to praise the Berlin wives who appeared there the next morning in force and made so much noise that their husbands were freed within twenty-four hours! That was a great achievement at that time. They also could have kept fearfully quiet, and could have gone into hiding to at least protect their children. But they preferred confrontation—and this was the only time that I experienced when the Nazis gave in, probably because the number of people involved was too large.

That was in 1935. I had just been divorced from my first husband, and I returned to Munich. I became seriously ill and a Jewish physician operated on me. The Gestapo was stupid enough to interrogate me in the hospital and denounce me because I allowed a Jew to treat me—this, however, impressed me very little, because the doctor did his job well, and that is the only thing that was important to me. At that time there was no ban which prohibited Jewish doctors from treating Aryans—but everyone who dared to consult a Jew was put under significant pressure. In this fashion one was probably trying to create the "healthy (Aryan) people's perception"! I, of course, kept my doctor as long as I could without endangering him.

In the hospital I was visited by the wife of the hairstylist Ernst Moritz Engert and my good friend Eva von Carlberg, the sister of the famous dancer. Both of them were also in my room when another fine female acquaintance brought in a new friend and colleague, a Tyrolian. At that time I did not know that she worked on Prince Albrecht Street. This young man was very unpleasant, and he bothered us with his Nazi slogans. I can remember that he told us about how he suffered when the Italians marched in, to which I remarked that he must have probably been two years old at that time and was still sitting on a training pot. He did not forgive me for this, and while I was making dinner, he "found" my passport on my desk, which contained several stamps from my African trip. This man reported me to the Gestapo and claimed that anyone who traveled so much must be politically suspect and was surely an agent. At that time we all ridiculed him— therefore, he also reported my girlfriends and they were also summoned by the Gestapo before I was released. Fortunately, they were both able to get out of this trouble by dismissing the situation as trifling in the same way. As soon as I left the hospital I had to go to the Gestapo and find out why I was suspect: how could I have traveled around so much, when it was unlawful to have foreign currency? My arrogant answer, that I belonged to international nobility and therefore all the castles were open to me, surely contributed to my registration in the blacklist. However, I was not arrested. Now I knew I had to be especially careful.

In 1936 I still had a number of Jewish friends in Berlin, among whom were the Hahn family. They were the parents of a girlfriend from school and I often frequented their beautiful house on the Wannsee. The father told me that his daughter would enjoy seeing the military riding competition at the Olympics tremendously, and I promised to do whatever I could. Thus in the early morning we drove out to Döberitz. Since I had no tickets, I decided to bluff myself in, and when I was asked politely about my tickets at the entrance, I replied, "Tell me, you don't recognize me?" The ticket checker became unsure of himself right away and did not dare protest when we simply walked past him. Encouraged by this success, we aimed straight for the best seats, and we eventually enjoyed the competition from General Blomberg's personal seats. This daring act proved to me once again that it was not only better but it was also more successful if one did not hide from the Nazis but on the contrary, appeared decisive and self-assured.

In the course of time, I hid many Jews and helped them to flee. This became progressively more difficult. In 1939 I befriended a Jewish writer, Hans Hirschel, and by visiting his house regularly I found out from the closest proximity everything that happened to this man. First, the lease to his large apartment was canceled, and he and his family were moved to a smaller apartment; however, they were still allowed to remain (in Berlin). Then the day came when they were not given substitute living quarters. At that moment, we knew that the deportations were just around the corner.

It was already known that Jews were being transported toward the East from the Grunewald railroad station. These were terrible transports which did not always even reach Auschwitz but ended somewhere in forests where the passengers were simply shot to death. Gradually, more and more news also reached us which reported that the Jews who reached the camp had no chance of survival there. Thus we had to contemplate how to help them.

At the beginning of the war, the situation changed somewhat for the time being; the German soldier in the field was much more endangered than the Jew who was "unfit to serve," as my friend Zivier— himself a Jew—noticed. However, everyone felt that the development of anti-Semitism continued. In 1938 we experienced the Reich's Crystal Night. Throughout that entire evening, I helped a businessman bring his goods to a safe neighboring apartment. After that we saw so many terrible things that we were preoccupied with only one question: "How can we protect human lives?" And whenever someone came and said that he was afraid to remain in his apartment, we, of course, took him in. Persecuted people often spent the night in my small apartment on Detmold Street, not only Jews but also Communists and other people of different persuasions who lived in deadly fear of the Gestapo and had to be protected.

The fruits of the terror regime were ripening: denunciations were daily events, because the general pressure did not spare anybody and most people lived in constant fear as they tried to save themselves by denouncing their fellow citizens to the Gestapo. However, of course, there were still people of integrity who remained true to their friends and supported them, hid them, and covered for them. There was a relatively large circle in Berlin—more numerous than I have experienced anywhere else. The Berliners said, "They are not to blame," and they risked their hearts and souls in order to help the persecuted.

In the meantime the deportation trains were constantly moving, and if people claim today that they did not know about them, they are lying: we saw those trains, and the people who lived along the tracks saw them rolling by—after all, the circumstances under which human beings who were squeezed into cattle wagons were transported could not have remained hidden. Should people have thought nothing at all?

I was drafted at the beginning of the war, and was assigned to the mail censorship office because of my knowledge of foreign languages. This was a terrible job. However, I was also able to help—especially there. Not only I, but many of my coworkers made the opened letters of harmless contemporaries disappear, so that neither the writer nor the recipient of the mail would be endangered. That was also not very pleasant. One had to swallow letters daily because one could not risk that treacherous little pieces of paper would reappear in a toilet.

Moreover, I know that there were also some officers in charge at my office who closed their eyes. Unfortunately, they were the minority; most of them spied on their fellow human beings in order to "blow up" at them at the slightest opportunity.

When I was denounced and therefore terminated from the military service without recourse, I reported to the Red Cross, since the National Socialist state made it everyone's duty to belong to some kind of organization. At that time, I thought of the Red Cross as the least harmful of the organizations in the Nazi state. I now was assigned to an awful office at the Möckern Bridge which was mainly responsible for Poland. At the beginning of the war, there was already a smear campaign against Poland which denounced all Poles. Thus the people who asked the Berlin Red Cross for help or information were treated accordingly. However, here too it was important that a few people with normal attitudes could help those poor people who, for example, searched for family members who, as a rule, were deported or assigned to forced labor. Naturally, it was strictly forbidden to give out such information, and the spying system was effective. Nevertheless, there were small successes. So, for example, we succeeded in not only telling a young woman the location of her husband but also in making a visit with him possible. The man was a gynecologist, and she wanted him to check her out because she was pregnant. Later the woman asked for my first name and said she wanted to give it to her child in case it was a girl. Was that child ever born?

The bombing started, and in a sense the chaos brought us little relief. However, the persecuted and hidden people could not protect themselves from the bombs, and many of them lost their lives. A good number of the air raid wardens were strictly loyal to the regime, and one preferred quick death by a bomb to torture by the Nazi executioners.

The Swedish as well as other Nordic churches did some incredible deeds in those terrible times. Fearlessly and without much bureaucracy they built aid organizations that collected money, clothing, and food; they hid people and brought them out of the country by using all of their extraterritorial resources and contacts. The effort was well-organized and effectively carried out. Therefore, many refugees have them to thank for their lives. I collaborated with the Swedish church located on Landhaus Street in Wilmersdorf on a number of assignments. I felt that we Germans owed them help in these risky undertakings which they conducted for our compatriots who our state was persecuting, even though that state was not ours by choice.

Prisoners of war, deported people, and forced laborers were another group of people who needed help; they had it a little better than the Jews. I was able to take two Russian children into my household, even legitimately, because the older girl was assigned to me as my household helper. Her little sister was supposed to be a worker too but I succeeded in having her "work booklet" closed. These children lived through such difficult times that they thereby became independent and introverted, but yet still helpful. From the beginning I trusted them so much that I could let them live together with my hidden husband without worrying that they would, even by coincidence, betray us. They helped me tremendously as interpreters during the capture of Berlin, and they passionately supported me.

Moreover, I must say that among the people the willingness to help was quite strong—perhaps not so much quantitatively, if one would compare the number of helpers with the total number of the population, but qualitatively, because even the smallest gesture of help demanded much civil courage and great sacrifice. This began with the problem of feeding the people without food cards; often the last crumb was shared. Every helper also knew that he was exactly in the same danger as his protectee, or even in greater danger, because he was after all registered and watched. He exposed his whole family to the danger of blackmail or imprisonment. It would be nice if this attitude, these actions, and this civil courage could become more of a gauge and a model than career, success, and everything else that is propagated today.

AXEL EGGEBRECHT

In Berlin There Were People Who Were Willing to Help

(From an Interview)

I was thirty-nine years old on November 9, 1938; I lived once again in Berlin and survived the concentration camp, a prison, and various other things. My friends, among whom many were Jews, told me after my first stormy experiences under the National Socialist incarceration: "You have it good now, it is behind you. You must remain here. Later you have to tell us what happened."

There were, for example, the bad experiences in 1936: the Olympic games had been the worst for everyone who was against the regime. I spoke to Englishmen and Frenchmen in Berlin who said: "What do you really want, why are you so against the regime? We were treated wonderfully here." They fell for the Nazi propaganda. They overlooked a lot of things, they also could not see many things, e.g., the inscriptions on the benches in the parks: "Not for Jews." That inscription was removed, but it returned in the winter of 1937. The Nazis hid everything very skillfully. One has to consider this, if one tries to imagine how suddenly the event of November 1938 befell the large number of Jews who were still living in Berlin. They were truly robbed, physically and materially, from one day to the other.

I have to say it over and over again; it is terrible when one has experienced life among people where the majority at that time actually affirmed this regime. On the other hand, the Berliners were shocked by the so-called Reich's Crystal Night! Only very few people were enthusiastic about it. Even later, many behaved with expressed solidarity and decency toward the Jews who had to wear the Star of David. I believe that a significant number of Berliners recognized too late that something inhumane was happening here. And many a Berliner was glad when he was able to contribute by helping them with small gestures and favors. Nobody knew of the plan for the extermination of the Jews yet.

43

I was looking, for example, for somebody who could transcribe film manuscripts, and I found a lady who eventually emmigrated to New York. It was a little bit risky to permit a Jewess to work. "A criminal act against the state, nation, and the Führer." Think about it . . .

In about 1937 an old friend of mine who, thank God, survived the Third Reich, arrived in Berlin from Königsberg and called me. I said: "Should we meet?" "That's impossible." "Why not?" "Yes, can you do that?" That meant that in Königsberg it was not possible to simply meet a Jewess in a restaurant. She thought that she would cause me trouble if she met me. However, I was constantly meeting Jewish friends. The wife of my best friend even returned from exile (from Paris) to Berlin in order to visit her mother, who lived there. Her husband did not come. He was a well-known physicist. He was right to be afraid of being arrested.

Then, however, November 9, 1938 arrived. From that moment on, nobody was able to deceive himself into thinking that nothing would happen. Of course nobody believed that a total extermination would eventually occur (Wannsee Conference 1942). After all, Jewish stores, law offices, and medical practices were destroyed during this one day in Berlin; it was obvious that life would never again be even halfway normal in Nazi Germany.

On the morning of November 10, I found out about the events from a former editor of the *Red Flag*—one of my Communist friends, who had also already survived the concentration camp. This gentleman, Otto Steinicke, who was not a Jew and who subsequently lost his life during the bombing of Berlin, called me and asked: "Did you read the newspaper already?" "No." "Well, then take a look at what is happening around here. Is everything calm at your place?" Thereupon, I went down Sächsische Street to the Kurfürstendamm, and I then saw the whole story. All the windows were broken in the stores which belonged to Jews or were suspected of belonging to them. Then I returned home again and did something crazy: I called up a man who successfully survived the Third Reich although his life was in danger many times. His name was Ernst von Salomon.

He was the one who took care of me in Berlin when I got out of the concentration camp, because he opposed the Nazis for a number of reasons. Salomon was a supernationalist and an eternal cadet. He was the type of man who "never got over the fact that he did not die at the battle of Langemarck," during the attack at the end of 1914. This man was a militarist who became completely converted in his old age; he was also a friend of Richard Scheringer. I called him and said, "Do you know what is going on?" He said: "Yes, it's crazy." "What can we do now?" I said. "How about calling the police and telling them that the mob is plundering." "That would be a good idea." This plan of course, failed completely. "Keep calm," the police said. They assumed, therefore, that we were excited citizens who did not understand that the events were the result of political initiative.

I would like to make a short comment now which is essential to one's ability to understand the mentality of that time. There were no computers in the Third Reich, and the telephone surveillance was ridiculous. We were genuinely sure that Ernst von Salomon, who participated in the Free Corps in 1918 and 1919, was not under surveillance. Thus I spoke with him openly. Perhaps I was under surveillance. After all, I spent some time in a concentration camp. A few people knew that even without a computer! When I was arrested under the Third Reich for the second time (winter 1934), the Nazis on Prinz Albrecht Street in Berlin did not know that I had already spent some time in a concentration camp in 1933. Furthermore, I was lucky enough to have a former Prussian police inspector help me with the SS after endless interrogations: my friend Paul Baudisch, the famous translator of American literature, who was the cause of my second imprisonment emigrated via Switzerland to Sweden (just like Tucholsky [well-known German writer; Am. ed.] had done), and he never returned. This police inspector advised me indirectly, so to say, to inform Baudisch. "Are you going to see his wife now?" I said: "Oh, his wife is still here?" "You are entirely aware of this." I said: "The hell I will. She is probably under surveillance day and night." "Oh, we would have too much to do, if we kept every relative of a suspect under surveillance day and night." Thanks to this man's help, the moment I left Prinz Albrecht Street, I went straight to Mrs. Baudisch.

I relate this only as an example: Today, of course, life in a dictatorship has become much more dangerous due to technology and electronics. Naturally, there were people who were forced to leave Germany. For example, people who had come from Poland in the last twenty years. They were regarded as particularly bad Jews. And I must say, unfortunately, that the Jews were partly responsible for this classification. The Eastern Jews were treated as something inferior by Jews who had been living in Germany for a long time. One has to admit this today with the hindsight of many decades.

Later during the war I hid a Jewish girl in our apartment, probably for about half a year. Her only official paper was a Czech postal service ID. She was considered a forced laborer in 1940–41. And when, for example, the landlord came, she identified herself as a Czech guest worker. There were thousands of them. And one tried to help these people everywhere. I have never understood the difference between the Germans and the German Jews. But now Germany was without Jews. Of course, it was not completely without Jews. In Leipzig there was a Nazi official who was a full-blooded Jew. He was accepted. And there was Field Marshal Milch, who was also a full-blooded Jew. Furthermore, how can it be explained that Helene Meyer won a gold medal in fencing during the Olympic games in 1936? Because she received special permission. She emigrated before 1936 but returned again. Everyone was not aware of it, but in Berlin, many people knew that she was a Jewess. The Nazis, of course, wanted to have medals.

A Germany without Jews—I could not imagine this. Everything connected with culture in Germany had received positive influences from Judaism. My beloved *Weltbühne* (World Stage), which is my intellectual home, was made possible only because the small circulation was supported in part by a group of interested Jewish citizens. They also supported art journals, art galleries, academies, every aspect of intellectual life. We only have to look into the world of newspapers, where supposedly or factually, the Jews played an extraordinarily important role in Berlin. I can only say that my career as a writer began in 1925–26. And as a non-Jew I was given almost preferential treatment by the editorial boards of newspapers such as the *Voßische Zeitung* or the *Berliner Tageblatt* where I wrote much of the time. I was recommended to others, and I was supported. Thus when the Nazis claimed that poor German Aryan writers could not make a living because the Jews were in power everywhere, I did not notice any of that. The opposite was true: Siegfried Jacobsohn, the head of the *Weltbühne*, taught me what writing was. Contemplating and writing. He also taught this to Tucholsky just as much as he did to Ossietzky [German Nobel Prize–winner who later died in a concentration camp; Am. ed.]. He recognized the tremendous journalistic talent of this magnificent editorialist who proved to be a brilliant writer even there, where he formed false opinions. After all, we all made errors in judgment. Although we perceived the great danger of Hitler, we did not take the man seriously. For aesthetic reasons, we found him inferior. After all, such a character could not rule over Germany, nothing could come of this. One can also consider the strange events in Munich in 1923. However, we believed, Ossietzky included, that the danger was over, especially after the election in November 1932, when the percentage of votes for the Nazi party decreased significantly. We also underestimated the racist anti-Semitism of the Nazis and its effect.

However, many friendships fell apart between 1933 and 1938, even though this was a time when it was quite harmless to associate with Jews. These cautious and cowardly German masses had a premonition which moved them in the following direction even by that time: we would rather be careful in regard to relationships with Jews; we would rather avoid them. And still there were people in Berlin who were willing to help. However, that was difficult during the bombardment, when Berlin was destroyed. When the city became a pile of ashes and rubble, when one was only able to save oneself in cellars and bunkers for the time being, when many people streamed into these hiding places and the Jews themselves did not dare go there, it became more and more difficult to hide someone. At that time, I experienced the most adventurous events as well as examples of great daring.

There was, for example, a man by the name of Behrisch. I believe he had something to do with publishing. As a joke he always introduced himself: "Behrisch wie arisch" [Behrisch, as in Aryan; Am. ed.]. He was married to a woman who was not Jewish. (For a while that was a certain kind of protection but not later.) He and his wife decided to be on the safe side. That would only be possible if others would help them. They discovered people who they could trust completely, in the rural area not far from Berlin. One could always find people like that. (It is interesting to note that the island of Föhr became a place of choice for Jews who were hiding. This had something to do with the fact that very many Friesians traveled all over the world, knew America, and spoke English.)

But for now let us return to Berlin, to the Behrischs. They proceeded in the following manner: they took clothes, a little money, food, etc., and found a refuge about twenty kilometers from Berlin. After they did this (by this time, the last of the Jews had been picked up from their homes), the wife went to the police (she must have been a great amateur actress), and made a major scene: "Where is my husband?" "Why, who is your husband?" "Behrisch is my husband. You know that." "We do not know him." "Of course you know him." "Well, you know . . ." "No, I do not know anything. Where is my husband? I want to know where my husband is." And so she bothered these people for four or five days. She did it, until they said: "Well, he may have committed suicide. We do not know him." "Then help me." As a result of this, they drove the wife to a morgue on Oranienburg Street, took her to the ice-cold storage rooms, and asked: "Could he be that one? Perhaps he drowned himself, or he shot himself, or he took poison?" To this she replied: "It could perhaps be that one, but he is so disfigured." And she acted on and convinced them that she had apparently calmed down with the discovery that her poor husband had committed suicide. However, they met secretly every eight or fourteen days. And he survived the war that way. That was only possible because certain people hid him.

Another example:

When I returned to Berlin in 1934, I rented a small apartment in a house which was divided into several small apartments. A Mr. Königsberger and his non-Jewish wife lived next to me. Everything went well for a while. But at the beginning of 1942 trucks with SS people in them roamed the streets and picked up the last Jews. Suddenly my doorbell rang: "Come next door, come next door," yelled Mrs. Königsberger. The tubes were still lying there on the floor. He swallowed Veronal, part of which he puked out again. He turned blue. It was some kind of death by strangulation which the person doesn't feel because he is completely anesthetized. She screamed: "Get him a doctor." I said: "It is no use, it's all over for him." And sure enough, half an hour later, after the man apparently died, the bell rang and there was a knock. The SS came and said: "Where's the Jew Königsberger? Damn it, there's another one who got away." Just like that. The next day the wife came by (a truly sentimental story), and thanked me for having prevented her from reviving her husband. A true story.

Of course, there were places where one was able to hide quite successfully. The daily life and work of people in the film industry, for example, was almost like life insurance because one could tell exactly who was a supporter and who was a dissenter. There was a much smaller percentage of National Socialists or even fellow travelers among the artists, especially the performing artists, producers, actors, makeup artists, in comparison to officials, medical doctors, military officers, and lawyers. There never was, after all, much settling of scores. This happened relatively rarely among the actors. It is possible that there was more of that among the writers. But a case like Höfer's is still eye-opening after forty years. It is a story of someone who apparently wrote too much . . . But one must not forget that in the age of mass communication, which began at the same time as National Socialism, it was no longer possible to write between the lines as it had been during the times of Heine or Börne. One had to do something harmless like writing scripts for entertainment films. I was not allowed to do anything else.

By the way, I was protected by a man in an SS uniform, an officer by the name of Lienhard. This man was executed in connection with the twentieth of July [1944—assassination attempt against Hitler; Am. ed.]. I received help twice. First, from the police inspector who helped me during my second arrest. And second, from the SS man in some type of cultural office who arranged for me to receive a limited work permit. I believe it was the Reich's Archives Office. And that man told me: "One day, we must draft a letter in which you will state that you only want to write movies for entertainment and that you are not interested in politics at all. And I do not know whether you can do it, but you have to sign with Heil Hitler." This statement, "... I do not know whether you can do it." convinced me that he wanted to help me. And all my Jewish friends who I consulted told me: "Of course you will sign the letter. It doesn't matter at all, everything is merely nonsense."

Therefore, I made movies like *Bel ami, The Comedians, Vienna Blood* with Willy Forst, and many others. Of course none of them were political movies. Today, one can say: "Well, even in this manner, you had supported the Third Reich." That's correct! The physician who treated the sick had done the same, as well as the baker who baked rolls. Is that so simple?

Let us consider, for example, the case of Emmrich. After the war, Dr. Kurt Emmrich, who later became well-known as Peter Bamm, hosted topical shows such as "Echo of the Day" on German Radio's First Program here in Hamburg. He was a physician by profession. In his book *The Invisible Flag*, he described precisely how he defended soldiers who, for example, shot themselves in the hand and were later indicted for it. As a physician he did not resist, but he helped those who did not want to support Hitler anymore. Another reason for his involvement was that self-mutilation carried a death sentence. He never had even a trace of anti-Semitism in him throughout his entire life. He was conservative but not reactionary: a very important difference. Conservatives were often willing to help where one was able to. And of course one could not help without the assistance of others.

One of the people who I helped to hide in Berlin was Hans Brodnitz, the director of several large first-run movie theaters up until 1933. We had hidden him with people who lived on Uhland Street in Berlin. And now the man needed something to eat. Everything was rationed because of the war. And we were not rich enough to be able to buy everything on the black market. But I knew an enterprising movie producer from whom I would pick up a number of food coupons which he received every month. And therefore Brodnitz did not starve. In spite of this, he was caught and eventually killed in the last year of the war. That was the type of help which one was able to give. In the inferno of terror which was eventually joined by the storm of destruction under which cities were destroyed, with alarms, sirens, and announcements about bombing squadrons which approached Berlin, one was preoccupied at the same time with saving individual human beings, the last Jews, and others who were persecuted by the Nazis.

ROBERT M. W. KEMPNER

The Truth about the Reich's Pogrom Night

The Reich's Crystal Night, which, more appropriately, should be called the Reich's Pogrom Night, made its worldwide impact on November 9, 1938. The actual start of the abuses against the Jews did not fall on this date, however. The real beginning was on January 30, 1933, when Adolf Hitler was appointed as German Reich's chancellor by Paul von Hindenburg, who was the Reich's president at that time. A new era began then in the German empire. Clearly stated, it was an era where the Jews were murdered and robbed. Murder and robbery started to become "legal." Whoever does not believe this need only read the register of German laws, decrees, and other ordinances in the official bulletins. One of the last decrees of the National Socialist regime of February 16, 1945, says: Anti-Jewish material should be destroyed, "so that it is not captured by the enemy."

I observed the persecution of the Jews not only since the so-called power grab of January 30, 1933, but before, when the persecution of the Jews in the Reich had not yet been legalized. It grew stronger and stronger in the final years of the twenties. At that time, the persecutions manifested themselves in store robberies and denunciations of businessmen, lawyers, physicians, university professors, and journalists. Mostly, National Socialist organizations were the instigators. They denounced colleagues for certain "deeds," and this was published in the Nazi press. It was difficult for the authorities to persecute people on the basis of false statements. This changed after Hitler's power grab. Whatever was used against the Jews became valid and punishable.

Up until the time when Hitler took power, I worked as a justice administrator in the Prussian Ministry of the Interior. I was responsible for almost one hundred thousand police officers. Nazi crimes became more and more frequent in the years before 1933—during the time of the Weimar Republic—so we, therefore, faced a growing number of serious problems. The struggle against these crimes was often successful via legal channels, under the leadership of Otto Braun and Carl Severing. But the drive for a legislative ban against the Nazi party never received the proper support under the leadership of Chancellor Heinrich Brüning and Franz von Papen. Many highly-placed officials within the Reich had the crazy notion that they could make a deal with Adolf Hitler and his cohorts during the elections. The most important official conceptions on how to combat the outbreak of barbarism, which were signed by Prussia's president Otto Braun, were, for example, labeled "Remains unanswered!" in the Reich's Chancellory.

Interestingly enough, I was sitting in my office at 74 Unter den Linden in Berlin, in the early days of February of 1933 when the newly named Prussian president Hermann Göring called me to a conference. At that time, he explained to the few high ministry officials that everything in the ministry was in order and that everyone would remain in office as long as one did not declare oneself explicitly against the Hitler regime.

When I returned to my office a message was already waiting for me which said that I should report to the personnel officer. This gentleman, who had just joined the National Socialist German Workers party, explained to me that I was suspended immediately from my service in the ministry. I would receive further notice. With this, my career as a Prussian state official came to an end. Later, I received a questionnaire asking me about my "race." I responded in brief fashion: I will begin an investigation on that question. Furthermore, I had already become a soldier in the World War at the age of seventeen, just like the Führer.

I still remembered this event, twelve years later in October 1945, when, as a member of the American Indictment Staff in Nuremberg, I had to interrogate my former boss Hermann Göring about his crimes. At first he tried to skirt the issue by remarking that, in the meantime, I had become an American and that I was surely opposed to him. "But Mr. Reich's Marshal, I'm grateful that you had dismissed me from the civil service in such a timely manner. Otherwise, shortly thereafter, I would have ended up in one of the chimneys which you stoked up!" After this, he calmly allowed us to interrogate him for a long time about the numerous deeds which we considered to be his war crimes and crimes against humanity. After he was sentenced to death, he committed suicide in the Nuremberg prison.

The following fact should demonstrate, by the way, the seriousness with which Göring considered the terms "race" and "Aryan." He himself was raised and supported by a doctor at Veldenstein castle, who was his mother's lover for years but who, however, did not exactly belong to the racial Aryans! Göring himself made sure that one of his closest collaborators, Field Marshal Erhard Milch, a non-Aryan, became "Aryanized" through skillful maneuvering with the aid of the Interior Ministry. After the occupation of Paris, Göring ensured that Jewish possessions and artifacts worth millions were confiscated. He gave this task to Alfred Rosenberg, the head of the enforcement staff, who was later sentenced to death in Nuremberg because of his numerous crimes. After the confiscation of Jewish property in Paris, for example, that of the Rothschilds, Göring personally wrote to Rosenberg in a letter, which I found in the Rosenberg file: "Since I ordered you to supervise the confiscation of Jewish property in Paris, I expect you to pass on 10 percent of the profits to me." The close connection between personal acceptance of Jewish money and the general plundering measures which occurred immediately after the Reich's Crystal Night becomes quite obvious from the minutes of the meetings with Hermann Göring, who was empowered by the Reich. These minutes are printed to a large extent in the protocols of the Nuremberg trials.

I emphasized at the beginning of my statement that the robbery of Jewish property and the personal extermination of Jews had already begun in January of 1933, and not during the Reich's Crystal Night. All of these occurrences were patterned after the methods of the mafia.

Hitler plundered one region after another. It was the largest raid in history. Those officials who were viewed in the National Socialist perspective as unreliable were fired. At first the veterans of the World War remained unaffected. Some physicians, lawyers, university professors, and others were able to remain in their positions up to 1938, but promotions became more and more difficult to obtain. The results were detrimental for society. We know from medical statistics that the exclusion of Jewish doctors caused harm to hundreds of patients. Studies concerning the Berlin-Moabit municipal hospital indicate a decline in the quality of treatment for patients. I personally was able to determine, based on official health statistics from the years 1933 to 1938, that the number of communicable diseases had increased during the Nazi period.

Although the income of professionals increased significantly after the dismissal of Jewish colleagues, the public losses could not be recouped. The survivors themselves were partly to blame, because they had personally denounced their former Jewish colleagues at the Gestapo office. There are hundreds of examples of this behavior. The National Socialist professional organizations of physicians, lawyers, teachers, engineers, etc., some of which already existed in 1933, believed it was their duty to cleanse the Jews from the entire state system. They also enlisted the Gestapo for this purpose. Confiscated "Jewish" apartments were distributed among the ministries; the new owners pretended not to know who these apartments came from. On September 30, 1938, the 3,152 Jewish physicians who still remained lost their licenses. A small group of them was later allowed to care for Jewish patients as Krankenbehandler (caretakers of sick). The Jews had already lost their civil rights by September 1935.

Nationalist Socialist literature hardly ever mentioned the tremendously damaging effects that these rapacious acts of violence—against academicians, and particularly those in many of the technical professions—inflicted upon the German Reich. The loss proved to be especially heavy in light of the German rearmament which began in 1933. American universities and institutions of higher learning had accepted many exiled Jews from Germany. Many of them later found relevant work in the U.S. Army.

All of this had already taken place prior to November 7, 1938, when the desperate seventeen-year-old stateless German-Polish Jew Herschel Grynszpan assassinated the German consul Ernst vom Rath in Paris. Vom Rath died on the afternoon of November 9. The day before he delivered his bullets, Grynszpan received a desperate postcard from his sister in Germany complaining about the deportation of family members to Poland. Joseph Goebbels's Propaganda Ministry used the shooting as a pretense for an unprecedented anti-Jewish propaganda campaign. It sought to prove that Grynszpan acted under the orders of the "international Jewry." This National Socialist propaganda could not be substantiated throughout the course of the numerous investigations which the French legal authorities had undertaken in Paris, which was still unoccupied at this point. The following is a better depiction of the actual events: After his immigration from Germany, young Grynszpan lived in Paris for several years without ever having a regular job. He associated with homosexual circles. As I have discovered from interrogations, several members of the German secret police, which was well represented in Paris, also belonged to those circles. They had ties to the members of the German embassy in Paris. All this happened before the beginning of the German-French war, which took place about ten months later. There was a relationship between Grynszpan and vom Rath, who was twelve years older, because Grynszpan tried to obtain a travel permit to Germany through vom Rath. He must have also had some other relationship with vom Rath, because he was able to visit him at the embassy without a formal announcement. In the meantime, however, it became known through investigation that vom Rath himself belonged to homosexual circles. He had only recently returned to Paris, after having been treated for venereal disease in Germany several months earlier. The statements of the Jewish doctor who treated him are available.

Therefore, there is no justification whatsoever for the attempts to play up the excitable young Grynszpan's act against vom Rath as an assassination by the "world Jewry" against the Third Reich. Another question is whether Grynszpan was manipulated by Nazi agents. After all, it was the National Socialist agents' business to perpetrate crimes in Europe and then blame them on foreign countries. We know from manuscripts that an official from the Foreign Office sent a telegram to Berlin in 1939 before the occupation of the city of Danzig. The location of the (Polish) weapons depot had already been secured. The attack on the German radio station in Gliwice (Gleiwitz) was carried out by German agents in 1939. And German agents set fire to German cars in Slovakia in order to point toward Slovak misdeeds.

Thus the assassination in Paris on November 7, 1938, had nothing to do with worldwide action by the Jewry. Nevertheless, the Foreign Office, with the help of Friedrich Grimm, the law professor who was on its payroll, tried to stage a show trial in front of the Reich's court in Leipzig. They had already been in touch with officials in Leipzig and other places in an attempt to find witnesses, etc. I had thoroughly interrogated Grimm in Nuremberg in 1947. Several Foreign Office officials were involved in this endeavor. However, the trial never took place because Leopold Gutterer, the state secretary of the Propaganda Ministry, with Goebbels' support, persuaded his colleagues to stop this project with an energetic statement: "We would be terribly embarrassed if the truth were to come out during this trial."

Nevertheless, Ernst vom Rath was promoted to the rank of an embassy consul on his deathbed as a victim of Jewish vengeance. Grynszpan was transferred to Germany after the beginning of the war. He remained in the Sachsenhausen concentration camp for several years, where he died. The date and cause of his death were never announced. His parents later testified in the Eichmann trial in Jerusalem.

The political consequences of the Parisian assassination became well known by November of 1938. Outwardly, it was the so-called Crystal Night; in clear language: the almost complete robbery of the property which the Jews still held. The principle participants were the Reich's Central Security Office, the state Finance Ministry under Lutz Schwerin von Krosigk, as well as Hermann Göring, the administrator of the four-year plan. Other offices were busy in their spheres of responsibility. Many of the plans for robbery, which had been in the works for years, were realized. Jews could barely bring along essential belongings to deportation camps. I found what "remained" in the boxes and cases of the Reich's district bank in Frankfurt am Main after the war—broken gold teeth and other personal valuables. Jews were not allowed to travel abroad since October 23, 1941. These were the external consequences of Crystal Night which had been planned for years. The last step was the "final solution to the Jewish question." My associates and I discovered the protocol of January 20, 1942, which was the basis of the murder plan, in the files of the Foreign Ministry which was run by Ribbentrop. Today, it is located again in the secret archives of the Foreign Office. It is one of the most terrible documents of the Second World War.

II. INTERPRETATIONS

ULRICH KLUG

Permission for Murder

The Justice System and the Persecution of the Jews

If someone asks today whether murder was allowed during the Nazi period, one could actually reply relatively quickly: yes, that's the way it was. However, this is perhaps not quite the correct way of looking at it, because such a thesis states, after all, that something as inhumane as murder was allowed, according to the existing legal system.

And what is happening to the concept of justice in our century which is now slowly coming to an end? What was happening to the concept of justice in the century before? Of course, one cannot and should not deal with this historical development in detail now. One should simply try to present a legal association by remembering important jurists.

It is strange that one does not always remember that there are important personalities in our culture who were lawyers. The jurists have sometimes forgotten that, but, at times, they do refer to it with pleasure. In order to characterize a certain historical period only four men may be named here, namely, Goethe, E. T. A. Hoffman, Eichendorff [important German poets and writers; Am. ed.], and Kant, who was a legal philosopher. They were either actively working around 1800 or they had just been born at that time. In any case, they are associated with the end of the eighteenth and the beginning of the nineteenth century.

The basis for this association is the following: without having to be familiar with all the legal details, what kind of legal culture existed at that time, when honest personalities served as jurists? Could it have been a legal culture in which murder was allowed? Of course not! And if the National Socialists allowed murders based upon "law," then this is a tremendous break with the legal culture. The thesis that the National Socialists allowed murders from the beginning needs a somewhat more concrete justification than the fact that later one was able to observe millions of murders which were obviously permitted. According to the perverse National Socialist concept of justice, political and racial murder was allowed from the beginning. This began with a decree of Reich's President Hindenburg released on March 21, 1933, which I shall quote here. First of all, one should mention its provocative title: *Decree of the Reich's President on the Exemption from Punishment*. This decree, which, in the history of modern law, is quite sensational and which was enacted a few weeks after the beginning of the Hitler dictatorship, states in Paragraph 1 (RGBI I 134):

¶1

In regard to punishable deeds which were committed in the struggle for the national uplifting of the German people, toward their preparation for this, or in the struggle for German soil, punishment will be omitted according to the following provisions.

It goes on to say, in an unconstitutional manner:

¶2

Sentences which are recognized as legal on the effective date of this decree and which were not yet served will be suspended.

Such exemptions also apply to overdue fines and expenses which have not yet been collected by the treasury of the Reich or the Länder [Gm. states; Am Ed.] and which were imposed to compensate for secondary infractions or safety violations.

If an appeal or annulment is recognized, then the matter can rest.

¶3

If the deed was perpetrated before March 21, 1933, then the current proceedings shall be terminated; new proceedings will not be initiated.

The decree ends with Paragraphs 6 and 7, after several procedural rules for sentencing whose details are not of importance here.

¶6

The decree should be used in matters for which the courts of the Reich and the Länder are responsible.

¶7

The decree becomes valid on the day following its announcement. Berlin, March 21, 1933.

THE PRESIDENT OF THE REICH
von Hindenburg
THE CHANCELLOR OF THE REICH
Adolf Hitler
THE REICH'S MINISTER OF THE INTERIOR
Frick
For the Justice Minister of the Reich
THE DEPUTY OF THE REICH'S CHANCELLOR
von Papen

That was a decree which referred to very concrete and contemporary crimes, considering the conscience of the country at that time. It dealt especially with murders, in which sentences were handed down before 1933 in jury trials that took place in a constitutional state. Thus, in retrospect, murders were declared legal. In this context, one must consider that a Reich's president acted and thereby broke his oath as a Reich's president, simply through this decree. This was obvious to everyone who followed the events conscientiously. One can also prove that the Reich's president had broken his oath several times. However, it is probably appropriate that one should point out, especially in this context, the criminal behavior that the decree for the exemption from punishment represents. In light of this, one should always reflect when encountering one of the many Hindenburg streets in our country.

Everyone who signed this document knew that such a decree stood opposed to the Weimar state, which was truly a constitutional state. Through this rectification which, in truth, standardized injustice, the terrible gate was opened which led to the road on which thousands and finally millions of murders were committed—murders for which the National Socialists are responsible.

The decree for exemption from punishment, which was enacted so quickly after the "power grab," was a break in the dam. It was quickly followed by other events which can be characterized by their growing degree of lawlessness. First, there was the *Law Concerning the Reconstruction of the Reich* of January 30, 1934 (RGBI I 75) with its hypocritical preamble and dramatic Article 4. It was brief and drastic:

> The plebiscite and the elections of November 12, 1933, have proven that the German nation has fused together into an insoluble domestic unit despite all internal borders and contrasts.
>
> The Reichstag therefore unanimously agreed to the following law which will be announced hereby with a unanimous agreement of the Reichstag, after it is determined that all conditions for a change of constitution are met.

Article 1
The people's representatives of the Länder are dismissed.

Article 2
(1) The Reich is assuming control over the jurisdiction of the Länder.
(2) The governments of the Länder are subservient to the government of the Reich.

Article 3
The "governors" are subordinate to the Reich's Minister of the Interior.

Article 4
The government of the Reich can pass a new constitution.

Article 5
The Reich's Minister of the Interior decrees the necessary constitution and governmental regulations required for enactment of the law.

Article 6
This law becomes official on the day of its announcement.
Berlin, January 30, 1934.

THE REICH'S PRESIDENT
von Hindenburg

THE REICH'S CHANCELLOR
Adolf Hitler

THE REICH'S MINISTER OF THE INTERIOR
Frick

Hindenburg also signed this law together with Hitler. It is unique to modern German legal history that such an obvious change from a previously constitutional state took place, especially with Article 4 and its blanket empowerment for constitutional change. This change prepared the way for historical laws which are perhaps also known to nonlegal experts. They were the result of those murders which were perpetrated by National Socialist units as a result of an inner party conflict on June 30, 1934, and where one could also find democratic politicians among the victims. On July 3, 1934 (RGBI I 329), the decree was issued and read in a "single article":

THE LAW CONCERNING MEASURES FOR THE STATE'S SELF-DEFENSE
JULY 3, 1934

The Reich's government has decreed the following law which is hereby announced:

Single Article
The measures for suppression of the highly treacherous attacks on June 30, July 1, and July 2, 1934, are justified in the name of the state's self-defense.
Berlin, July 3, 1934.

THE REICH'S CHANCELLOR
Adolf Hitler

THE REICH'S MINISTER OF THE INTERIOR
Frick

THE REICH'S MINISTER OF JUSTICE
Dr. Gürtner

This law is based on the notion that a state's dictatorship and those who rule within it are entitled to unchecked privilege. And from this, Carl Schmitt, the leading National Socialist legal authority and Berlin professor, who became a state counsel and crown jurist under the Nazis, developed the following thesis: the foundation for the German law that existed during those years lies in the principle that the Führer was always right and that he stood outside any legal control from above. Thereby numerous murders were allowed.[1]

In order to reach this goal more easily, a law dated April 24, 1934 (RGBI I 341), created a new apparatus of destruction, the Volksgerichtshof [People's Court; Am. ed.]. This was done because Hitler and his accomplices thought that the Reich's court, which was the highest court within the Weimar judicial structure, was too lenient. Thus by 1934 everything in regard to the allowance of murder was in place. The pogroms of 1938 and the Holocaust that followed were now possible. The fateful aspect of this development is that the murders which were perpetrated on the night of November 9 and 10, 1938, and which were already prescribed since 1934, were inevitable. A regime which firmly associated itself with the promotion of criminal acts as early as 1933 and 1934 had no inhibitions toward the growing expansion of the use of murder both inside and outside the concentration camp. The Volksgerichtshof was a willing instrument for this policy. It was characterized by the appropriate yet much too late *Resolution of the German Bundestag of January 25, 1985,* which, by the way, was a resolution of all parties—"as an instrument of terror for the purpose of enforcing arbitrary National Socialist rule."

The People's Court was, thus, not simply a newly established court but a new tool for the allowance of murder under the guise of supposedly orderly justice. Appropriately, the often-quoted and important phrase in regard to Nazi justice in its entirety—not only in reference to the People's Court—was coined at the Nuremberg jurists' trial: "The knife of the murderer was hidden under the gown of the jurist."[2] It is shameful that among the murderers who wore the gown of the People's Court, which issued more than five thousand death sentences, no judge was ever sentenced after 1945. Only one prosecutor who worked for the People's Court, Reich's attorney Ernst Lautz, was punished—and that by an American court in Nuremberg.

In the same fashion, the development of the model for permissible murder could be seen three years prior to the pogroms of 1938 only indirectly in the decree of the racial laws. Points of inhibition were removed through the *Reich's Citizen Law* and the *Law for the Protection of the German Blood*, which were both issued on September 15, 1935 (RGBI I 1146). They are often referred to as the Nuremberg Laws, which decreed the radical disenfranchisement of the Jews. The decisive Paragraph 2 of the *Reich's Citizen Law* determined that only those people of "German or related blood" could be citizens. The permission for murder can be indirectly deduced, in particular from the *Law for the Protection of the German Blood*. First, one has to look at the preamble of the Blood Protection Law, which refers directly and indirectly to primitive prehistorical tribal images:

> Recognizing the fact that the purity of the German blood is a necessary condition for the further existence of the German people, the German Reichstag, motivated by the tremendous will to secure a German nation for all future time, has decided unanimously on the following law which is hereby announced.

The same primitivism is also reflected in Paragraph 5 of the punitive law for "racial disgrace":

> The man who acts against the prohibition of Paragraph 2 (where extramarital relationships between Jews and "citizens of German or related blood" are prohibited) will be imprisoned.

The National Socialist publications found other smaller distinctions. After all, such a man could also be an Aryan man in the sense of the Nazi terminology. And, while the crime of a Jewish perpetrator was called "racial disgrace," the crime of a non-Jewish perpetrator (since only men were referred to in this dark legislation) was called "racial treason." The Aryan man has betrayed his race, while the Jewish man has disgraced the Aryan race. The perversity of this regulation is especially evident in such "linguistic creations." As punishment "only" imprisonment was envisioned. In spite of this, there was only a short path between this law and permitted murder, since sentenced Jews were removed from the normal due process—from prisons and penitentiaries—and quickly "turned over" to the SS. They were then sent to the concentration camps and, shortly thereafter, were murdered there as victims who were particularly hated.

After this development, a further step toward the pogroms of November 1938 was not far away. If one remembers the events of November 9 and 10 of that year, one would think, first of all, of the barbaric burning of synagogues and the destruction of Jewish stores. As one can see from the report of Supreme Party Judge Walter Buch of February 13, 1939, to Hermann Göring, the fanatic racial hatred and the concept that murdering Jews was permitted were in the meantime so solidified that more than ninety murders were committed in conjunction with the pogroms of those days. Moreover, the murders

of those people deported to concentration camps on November 9 and
10, 1939, are not counted here. These murders went unpunished. The
ordinary German courts did not deal with them, but the party did.
Thereby, immunity from persecution was guaranteed. In the above-
mentioned report, the last paragraph states:

> The report on the results of the investigations so far is being pre-
> sented, first, because the police investigations of the remaining (al-
> together ninety-one) cases of killings has not yet been completed,
> and second, because the results so far—particularly as far as the
> motives and connections are concerned—may provide an excerpt and
> an overview. This is the case especially, however, because the sen-
> ate may choose not to carry out legal proceedings in regard to the
> killings of Jews within the framework of the action of November 9,
> 1938, in the future, if police investigations find no suspicion based
> on selfish and criminal motives. The contents of this report substan-
> tiate this view. Moreover, as a result, the last major hearing in the
> case of Schenk (a Polish citizen), the first known case of the killing
> of a Jew was reported to the Reich's propaganda minister, party
> comrade Dr. Goebbels, on November 10, 1938, around two o'clock.
> Consequently, it was agreed that something had to take place in
> order to prevent the whole action from deteriorating to a dangerous
> level. According to the statement of the deputy local administrator
> of Munich, Upper Bavaria, party comrade Dr. Goebbels responded
> that the reporter should not get excited about one dead Jew because
> in the next few days thousands of Jews would be killed. At this
> point, most of the killings still could have been prevented by a sup-
> plementary decree. As this did not happen, it must be concluded
> from this fact, as well as from the statement, that the final result
> was expected or at least thought to be possible and desired. There-
> fore, the individual perpetrator not only realized the presumed de-
> sign but also correctly recognized the will of the leadership, even
> though it was not clearly expressed. He cannot be punished for this.[3]

In order, once again, to clearly recall the ever-frightening picture of
the permitted murders, the closing paragraphs of a report on an especially brutal pogrom murder which was committed in the early hours
of November 10, 1938, on the eighty-one-year-old Jewess Susanna Stern
in Eberstadt should be reprinted verbatim. The perpetrator, a local
leader (Ortsgruppenleiter) of the National Socialist German Workers
Party, declared for the records of the court at Buchen on November
10, 1938, that at six o'clock in the morning he was ordered by his
district leader (Kreisleiter) "to carry out an action against the Jews in
Eberstadt"[4]: "The district leader explained to me I could do with the
Jews what I wanted as long as there was no arson and no plundering."

Concerning the "action" itself the perpetrator reported the following:

After this we went to the house of the now-deceased Susanna Stern. I was accompanied by the cell leader responsible for this house, A. V., a peasant in Eberstadt, the treasurer C. D. in Eberstadt, and the SA troop leader E. F., a carpenter in Eberstadt.

First I knocked on the door. The widow Stern responded by looking through the closed window next to the entrance. I told Stern then that she should open the door. It took about three to four minutes till Mrs. Stern opened the door. When Mrs. Stern saw me standing at the door she smiled provocatively and said: "Already this morning, a high-level visit." I did not reply to this. Mrs. Stern turned around and went toward her room. I followed her closely up to the entrance of the room. I requested that Mrs. Stern get dressed. She, however, only walked around the room and smilingly refused my request. After about two minutes she sat down on a sofa which was located to the right of the entrance to the living room. In response to this, I asked her whether she was going to dress and follow my instructions. Stern replied that she would not get dressed and she would not come with us and that we could do whatever we wanted to do. We were planning to take Mrs. Stern to the City Hall; however, we did not tell her where we wanted to take her.

Mrs. Stern told us if we wanted something from her, we should call the police. She repeated over and over that she would not get dressed and she would not come along. I told her: "I'm telling you now, get dressed and come with us." She again declared: "I'm not moving from my home, I'm an old woman." I told her that I knew that she was going to the village every day in order to work in her vegetable garden. So there was no reason for her refusal to leave her home.

I then took my service pistol from my right pants pocket. Before I went to the home of Steinhardt I had turned my holster over to the propaganda coordinator N. O. From that point on I carried the pistol in my pants pocket. I did not want to run around early in the morning with the holster on my belt, and I tried to avoid any attention. I especially did not want to go to see the Jews with a buckled-up holster.

After I took my service pistol from my pocket, with the safety still on, I asked the woman five or six more times to get up and get dressed. Then Mrs. Stern screamed loudly, insolently, and scornfully into my face that she would not get up and she would not get dressed, and I could do with her whatever I wanted. At the moment when Mrs. Stern yelled I could do with her whatever I wanted, I pushed down the safety pin of the pistol and shot Mrs. Stern the first time. When I fired the first time, I stood about ten centimeters from the door. I aimed my pistol at the woman's chest. After the first shot Mrs. Stern fell onto the sofa. She leaned backwards and grabbed her chest with both hands. Right away I shot the second time, this time aiming at her head. As a result, Mrs. Stern slid off the sofa and turned over. She then lay immediately in front of the sofa with her head turned to the left, toward the windows. At that moment, Mrs. Stern was still showing signs of life. In short intervals her throat was still rattling. Mrs. Stern did not yell or speak. My comrade C. D. turned the head of Mrs. Stern, who was lying in front of the sofa, in order to see where she was hit. . . .

In order to make sure that Mrs. Stern was dead, I fired from a distance of about ten centimeters at the middle of the forehead of the prone woman.

It was recorded in the report of the police district of Buchen of November 10, 1938, that the perpetrator was "a decent and industrious fellow who had a good reputation in the community and lived a proper life-style." In contrast, the murdered widow Stern is described in this report: "The Jewess Stern is an obnoxious and notoriously insolent Jewess. It seems completely believable that she resisted the local leader's request that she follow him with typical Jewish impudence."[5]

The hearing initiated against the murderer was suspended (*Decree of the Reich's Ministry for Justice*, III g 10b-286/399 of October 10, 1940). The murderer committed suicide in 1951.

This and many other cases demonstrate that the permission to murder was apparently deeply anchored in the conscience of the fanatical National Socialists. And certainly it is justified to make the claim that the justice system under Hitler became an accomplice by not persecuting these murders and therefore permitting them. One must still ponder what the legal consequences of this terrible trend can be—not from the point of view of that time, but from today's point of view.

So much for this topic. It can follow through to the millions of murders that took place later. But that is not the purpose of this article.

WOLFGANG GERLACH

When the Witnesses Were Silent
The Confessing Church and the Jews

WHEN THE WITNESSES WERE SILENT: THE CHURCH AND THE "JEWISH
QUESTION" (1933–1945)

The facts are on the table. The witnesses of the time, who, during the
first twenty years that followed the war, made sure that the Confessing Church (Bekennende Kirche), at least, would appear sound and in
good shape, are now dead. W. Niemöller, in spite of a thorough knowledge of the records, noted briefly: the Confessing Church "took a firm
position" in reference to the "Aryan Paragraph" and never "became
soft in regard to this point."[1] Karl Kupisch, by critically observing the
evaluation and the selection of data that were customary after the war,
noted that it was "also strange that the first collections of documents
emphasized only the 'resistance' and 'strength' (of the Confessing
Church)."[2]

Replacing the witnesses, contemporary historians consequently have
an easier time uncovering the somewhat embarrassing statements made
by the professors and bishops in the records of the synod and in the
correspondence of the time.

From the abundance of existing documents, I would like to cite several examples of church-theological statements which reflect the climate and the spirit of all shades of Protestantism. The rostra, pulpits,
and synods were challenged, especially in 1933, to take a position against
the Jews, after the introduction of the Aryan Paragraph in the church,
which German Christians demanded. So in 1933, Adolf Köberle, the
Swabian theology professor, agitated with all the classic ingredients
in his sermon against the "secular Jews":

> Everywhere where something can disintegrate decomposed, can be
> destroyed, maybe marriage and family, patriotism or the Christian
> church, discipline and order, chastity and decency; everywhere where
> there is something to gain, he is involved there. He is mocking with
> his ingenious joking, with his smart and skillful talent, with his per-

sistent subversive energy. An atheist always acts destructively; but nowhere is the destructive force of this attitude as devastating as in the case of a Jewish person who wasted his rich heritage from the Old Testament and joined the swine.[3]

The general superintendent, Otto Dibelius, offered church-sponsored ammunition in his Easter message to the ministers in his district, a few days after the boycott of the Jewish stores on April 1, 1933:

> All of us will not only have understanding but total sympathy for the latest motives which evolved from the popular movement. I always thought of myself as an anti-Semite, although the term has taken a negative connotation in many ways. One cannot ignore the fact that Judaism is taking a leading role in all of the destructive manifestations of modern civilization.[4]

Two famous opinions characterize the theological situation in 1933. The University of Marburg Lutheran Theological Seminary (in this case, represented by Rudolf Bultmann and Hans von Soden) argued along the lines of the New Testament: the scriptures need to be preached universally to all people and races, and they make the baptized people brethren who cannot be excluded. An inequality in rights based on racial or nationalist reasons is just as much impossible as a segregation. Yet even the Marburgers seem to have been referring only to the Jewish Christians.

The theological seminary at the University of Erlangen, under the signatures of Professors Althaus and Elert, admitted that "no person may be excluded from the church" in view of the universal validity of the gospel. However, "the general filiation to God does not remove biological and social differences. Christians with a conscience need to recognize also that we cannot escape a biological bond to a certain nation."[4a]

Objecting to the National Socialist vocabulary which defined racism through "national characteristics," the Erlangers spoke of an Aryan super race and thereby continued what they had already claimed as "scientific" in the twenties.

This sphere of theological and pseudoscientific discussion culminated in glowing subservient addresses to the Führer. For example: "We pronounce a thankful 'yes' to this turn of history. God has given it to us," Marahrens, Kapler, and Hesse formulated in 1933. And Bishop Wurm wrote: "The gratitude for salvation from grave danger and the joy that a new state is acting for the sake of the people's well-being even overcomes the worry that the streamlining is taking place too rapidly. We urged the state in vain before and after the war to take this type of action."[5] Only Dietrich Bonhoeffer resisted this temptation. Already before the boycott of April 1, 1933, he was preoccupied with the subject of the church and the Jews. When he found out through his brother-in-law, Reich's Legal Counsel Hans von Dohnanyi, that new legislation concerning non-Aryans would be enacted on April 7 (the *Law for the Restoration of Professional Civil Servants*), Bonhoeffer again reworked his theses. Even though he was still caught up in a Lutheran attitude toward the state, which recommends noninterference in the state's authority, he recognized the necessity of immediate action right away. Contrary to the irritating and confusing verbosity which permeated the Lutheran churches in 1933, Bonhoeffer already saw an unjust state at work with Jews as some of its most prominent victims: "The church has an absolute responsibility toward victims of any social order even if they do not belong to the Christian community." His concept and support for *all* Jews (not only for the Christian Jews) can be characterized as unique at that time. Faithful to the old Jewish statement by the Jew Jesus in his Sermon on the Mount: "Not all who are saying 'Lord, Lord!' will come to the Kingdom of Heaven but those who are doing the will of my father in Heaven" (Matthew 7:21), he coined the famous statement in reference to the Christian support for the Jews: "Do good for everybody."

He also wrote the sentence which was included in the four statements of the Clergy's Emergency Council Declaration which appeared like a confession and indicated at the same time that the church's struggle began with the question to itself: What is your opinion toward the Jews? From the so-called Jewish question it became a Christian question which received the answer in the Clergy's Emergency Council Declaration: "I witness that there is a violation of the creed with the application of the Aryan Paragraph in the church."

This sentence was the result of Bonhoeffer's essay "The Church and the Jewish Question" to which every minister of the Emergency Council committed himself. It was a sentence that would soon become lost, although it was never retracted by the Confessing Church until the end of the war. After the "Brown Synod" of September 6, 1933, celebrated Werner Krause's anti-Jewish hate tirades and Wittenberg's National Synod of the German Lutheran Church on September 27, 1933, rejected the proposal which Bonhoeffer and Niemöller developed, it became clear to Bonhoeffer that their resistance against the Aryan Paragraph, which had been elevated only a few weeks earlier into the *status confessionis* with full support, had no chance for acceptance. The threatened resignations from various offices did not take place—they were deferred to "later dates which never arrived."[6]

Bonhoeffer faced the following alternatives: either to leave the church—but an earnest resignation from the church was denied foremostly by Karl Barth, especially because a man like Bonhoeffer was now urgently needed in the church—or his last option, "not only to heal the victims which fell under the wheel, but to throw oneself into the spokes of the wheel" (*Collected Writings* 2:58). He decided on the latter. He figuratively fell into the spokes of the wheel, between the wheels of the church and the state, and paid for his politically conspiratorial activities with his life.

The Aryan Paragraph finally got bogged down in the church bureaucracy, which declared on April 13, 1935, in the Church Law for Settling the Church's Position: "The annulment of the annulment will be annulled."

In the meantime, preparations were made for the synodical meeting of the Lutheran Church, which was to take place in Barmen. The clergy concentrated on a compromise between the Reformed and the Lutherans in a message to the German Christians, and there was no room for a seventh thesis which could have been directed in support of the Jews. Karl Barth, as the author of the *Theological Declaration of Barmen*, believed at that time—as he implored Dietrich Bonhoeffer in a letter—that the Aryan Paragraph was not yet central. A creed intended to unify the church at this moment should have been more important (compare *Collected Writings* 2:135). Only after thirty-three years, when Barth read Bethge's Bonhoeffer biography, he wrote to Bethge: "The fact that Bonhoeffer was the first one, starting in 1933, indeed almost the only one, who took the Jewish question as central and energetically dealt with it, was new to me. I have been feeling my guilt for a long time that in the church struggle . . . I, myself, did not also make it a deciding factor."[7] Barth certainly remembers correctly when he adds: "A declaration in which I would have done such a thing would of course not have been acceptable in 1934, either in the Reformed or in the General Synod, due to the spirit of the time, even among the 'Confessing.' However, it is no excuse, that because of other interests at that time, I did not at least fight for this cause with all means."

In 1935 Hitler issued the Nuremberg Laws "for the protection of the German blood and German honor," "the most devilish legislation that the history of Europe knows."[8] Two weeks later, to the horror of Bonhoeffer and his clergy from Finkenwald, the Confessing Synod of Steglitz remained silent when confronted by a quite obviously anti-Semitic thesis which was written by Albertz together with his "non-Aryan" collaborator Marga Meusel. In this case, perhaps, the Confessing Church failed to seize the last opportunity "to open its mouth for the silent ones" (Bonhoeffer).

After this, times became more difficult. With Hitler's successful foreign policy, the self-confidence of the state and party was growing. From July 1, 1937, on, Martin Niemöller was imprisoned by Hitler's personal order in a penitentiary. Consequently, the Confessing Church was significantly hurt. From then on the Confessing Church obviously fought more and more for its own survival and encountered all kinds of difficulties in supporting individual cases of "non-Aryan" Christians.

On November 9, 1938, the synagogues were burning, and the churches fell silent from paralysis and understandable fear. The police headquarters were amazed at the success of the dress rehearsal for the final, deciding action against the Jews. However, even the *Stürmer* had to admit that "the outraged and spontaneous anger of the people" was not everywhere: "There were some women and men who suddenly felt incomprehensible pity for the Jewish nation of criminals. There were some men and women who had no understanding for the justifiable anger of the people" (no. 48, December 1938, pp. 1ff.). And this even happened: "In a West German town a group of SS people refused to commit the crimes against the Jews which were ordered by their leader. Therefore, in that particular town, the Jews were saved from the pogrom."[9]

The church reacted to the Reich's Crystal Night in very different ways. ("Crystal Night" was coined by Berliners who understood the deeds of the Nazis and created this ironic verbal monstrosity, which contains just as many lies about the Nazis as truth. Today, the fact that most people believe that this word was a Nazi creation shows how successful this word was. The anti-Semitic cynicism is linguistically covered by an exposed cognition. According to Ernst Bloch, this is "the slave language" in a totalitarian system.) I have selected three reactions: the bishops' loyalty statements to the Führer, courageous sermons by individual ministers on the following day of penitence, and, finally, the beginning of personal support activities.

In writing to Justice Minister Gürtner, Bishop Wurm could not avoid emphasizing, while complaining about the acts of terror of November, "that there is no group in the society which is as free from Jewish influence as that of the Lutheran ministry." And by the way, the bishop "did not want to question the state's right to fight against Judaism as a dangerous element."[10] The German-Christian Bishop Martin Sasse from Thüringen edited a brochure for his ministers at the end of November 1938 with the title "Martin Luther and the Jews: Do Away with Them!" In it, he praised the November pogrom as a very fitting way to celebrate Luther's birthday of November 10. Sasse presented the late Luther as a glowing anti-Semite, as "one who warned his people about the Jews." He quoted extensively from Luther's thesis "About the Jews and Their Lies." In the document, while angered and despaired over the resistance of the Jews to conversion, Luther recommended "that their synagogues and schools should be burned, that their houses should also be smashed and destroyed. . . ."

And the general secretary of the Lutheran World Association, Dr. Hanns Lilje (later the bishop of Hannover), prepared a report during those days for the church's foreign office on his trip to America. He had refused to make any statements in the United States with regard to the Crystal Night's events in Germany because the protest demonstrations in the States were against the German Jewish policy and were clearly in the hands of skillful Jewish operators.[11]

Among the courageous ministers of the Confessing Church, two became especially known. The Swebian minister Julius v. Jan from Oberlenningen paid for his public criticism of the National Socialist terror with several months of jail, mistreatment, and finally banishment from his ministry. His bishop, Theophil Wurm, did not support him. Helmut Gollwitzer found a language which every member under him in the Confessing Church understood right away. He was not bothered by the Gestapo.[12]

An institution later known as the Grüber Office was initiated as the consequence of the pogrom night. Aid offices such as these were established in many cities in 1942. In their tolerance they assisted with the procurement of food ration cards, falsification of passports, arrangement of illegal hiding places, etc.

Precisely at that time the phase began which Gerhard Kittel had already mentioned in his 1933 essay "The Jewish Question." Kittel made a concession to the government's placing of the Jews into the legal framework of a state of apartheid; at the same time, however, he asked Christians to help the persecuted Jews in the spirit of the good Samaritan! He gave priority to the official Jewish legislation in order to preserve the German blood's purity ahead of Christian neighborly love.[13]

Unfortunately, no one sufficiently investigated the support efforts of small groups, individual Christians, and especially women, which were innumerable. Nevertheless, they do not change the fact that the aid only began at that moment when people dealt with individual Jewish fates. This, in turn, made the officially instituted anti-Semitism, an ideology which depersonalized individual persons, look relatively insignificant. The efficacious propaganda about "destructive Judaism" collapsed at the moment when individuals had to help people who wore the Star of David—people who sat next to them in prayer—to steal food ration cards "directly from the district offices." In the Dahlem parish Gertrud Staewen organized an illegal means of escape. She dressed persecuted women as prototypes of "German women." For this task, she collected motherhood medals [Nazis encouraged large families. Mothers with many children were decorated; Am. ed.]. "Sometimes, it was quite funny to see a Jewish virgin drive away with five children around her neck."[14]

Beginning in October 1941, the trains rolled in the direction of Auschwitz, which was "opened" on September 23. The political resistance was informed about the deportations from the beginning, and therefore the Confessing Church circles, as often as they were in contact with the opposition, also knew everything. Kurt Gerstein (according to Eberhard Bethge) informed about one hundred members of the Confessing Church, Dibelius included, but no one wanted to believe him about the gas chambers. On December 17, 1941, one month before the Wannsee Conference (January 20, 1942), the national church leadership of Sachsen, Nassau-Hessen, Mecklenburg, Schleswig-Holstein, Anhalt, Thüringen, and Lübeck made a declaration on the church's position toward the evangelical Jews, stating that "the strongest measures are to be taken against the Jews, and they should be expelled from German lands." "Racially Jewish Christians have no room and no rights in the church."[15]

The crowning event took place two days before Christmas when the German Lutheran Council sent a memorandum in which it spoke about "the breakthrough of racial conscience in our nation" that would result in "the elimination of Jews from the German community." The highest church officials were asked "to take proper measures so that non-Aryans would stay away from the spiritual life of the German community."[16]

Here, the church sermon on the final *salvation* degenerated before Christmas and became completely subservient to the state's "final *solution*"!

WHY THE WITNESSES KEPT SILENT: THE CHURCH AND ITS IDENTITY

The history of anti-Judaism in the church is a history of the institution's constant struggle with its own identity. The church's course began with the Jewish-Messianic sect which thought of itself as "better Jews." From the "better" came the "true" and the "only," the "new Israel," as the church called itself. The claim of the monopoly on the truth became the agent for stimulating hatred toward the Jews. "It is a sad truth in religious history that one can find the special aggressiveness that leads to accusations of devilishness and damnation only in rival groups which, within the same religious system, make competing claims for absolute truth."[17]

The early Christians perceived that the crucified Jesus and the res-urrected Christ was a prophet/son-of-man/king who had now appeared as the Messiah and healer, as the prophets had announced. The Jews, on the other hand, due to a continuous history of human cruelty, were not able to see any signs of an already existing kingdom of peace. Therefore, they rejected the claim of a Messiah which the Christians imputed to their fellow Jewish brethren and rabbis. The Christians, on their part, attempted to resolve their need for proof, considering the incongruity of the salvation which had arrived, and the empire of peace which was still not apparent by interpreting the act of salvation as one of anticipation made possible by the man from Nazareth. Thus an advance on the time of salvation was taken, so to speak, as the first installment on a down payment for that which would actually happen later. Or, in other words: "The gift of salvation is an aperitif which precedes the banquet at the end of the day and which makes us impa-tient with the bread of tears, which is being offered to us in these days of injustice."[18]

If, in the beginning, the Christian mission was a message opposed to Israel (analogous to Jesus' statement that he came to the "lost sheep of Israel"), then "the exclusion of the church from the Jewish religious community caused a new crisis within Christian identity."[19]

Since Christianity was thus deprived of its Jewish roots, or deprived itself of them, it distanced itself at the same time from its Jewish memo-ries and the related historical deeds which God performed for his chosen people. It removed the continuity of its Jewish heritage by replacing the memory of God's healing places with a design for a future which had already begun with Jesus' deed of salvation as the Christ. If only the Jews would join this non-Jewish, more Hellenistic way to believe they could reach salvation. Otherwise, they would have to count on disaster.

Figuratively speaking here, the younger brother challenged his older brother by questioning his stay in the home of their common father, although one can read differently, for example, in the letter to the Ephesians. There the Christians are being called "co-inheritors," "part-ners," and "fellow comrades." The younger brother began to present his co-inheritance as a sole inheritance early on, and thus deprived his older brother of his inheritance. We can see in the letter by Barnabas in the second century: "The testament actually belongs to us; they (the Jews) lost the testaments which they received from Moses at the time."[20] Adolf v. Harnack belabors exactly this form of deprivation of inheri-tance by interpreting the early heathen church as a community which was convinced that

the Jews have no business at all with the Old Testament. They insolently and illegally grabbed it, occupied, it, and tried to keep it away
from its sole owner. . . . Therefore, every Christian must reject their
claim of ownership on the Old Testament; a Christian, who says
that this book belongs both to the Jews and to us, has sinned; the
book belongs and has belonged from the beginning, now and forever, only to the Christians.[21]

One could define Christianity as a legitimate cuckoo egg laid in a nest
of Jewish tradition; once it was hatched, it grew into a glutton who
gradually threw out the "original" inhabitants of the nest one by one.
According to Friedrich Heer, the Old Testament became "the booty of
the church," and the new Israel—"the untouchable inheritance of the
church"—through the "greatest robbery of world history."[22]

This strategy, in the meantime, has been exposed by Christian theolo-
gians as "the theology of the deprivation of inheritance." After Shoa, the
Christian identity can be found only in a theology in which the church
is not confronted by "the *Jewish question*" anymore but "by the question of Christian relationship to the Jews and thus the *question of Christ*."[23]

The answer to the question of why the witnesses, why the church,
even the Confessing Church, kept silent—*horrible dictu*—must be because anti-Judaism was a part of the church's identity and is probably
still a part of it. People who do not allow themselves to be converted
have learned, according to Martin Luther's fateful quotation, "that one
should burn their synagogues and schools, . . . that one should do the
same to their houses, thus destroying them, . . . that one should pro-
hibit their rabbis under the threat of a death sentence to teach," etc.
People who are accused, contrary to all historical sources, of having
nailed the God of the Christians to a cross are given the dignity of the
just punishment of God, whereby the church proclaims itself as a legitimate judge and executioner of God's grace toward the Jews. The
German Christians did not keep silent. On the contrary they revealed
themselves, in that sense, as those who would bring the infamous Jewish
people to their proper punishment. And the Confessing Church, caught
up in centuries of this cultivated theology, may have viewed it as the
most humane behavior to keep silent, as its theology actually taught
that it should participate in the divine judgment against the people of
Israel with all of its strength!

Therefore, it should not be surprising that after the war one could
also hear similar Christian voices: so, for example, after 1945, Gerhard
Kittel, a world-renowned scholar of the New Testament confessed his
political guilt; "however, he insisted that his attitude toward the Jewish question during the Third Reich was determined by a 'Christian

anti-Judaism' which he found in the New Testament and in the tradition of the Christian church."[24]

For the same reason, the confession of guilt by the church in Stuttgart in 1945 could also only appear insignificant. Here, one admitted guilt in general terms, by using lofty comparisons, before the guilt was really perceived. The church would discover, decades later in a laborious and painful process, that the actual guilt lay not only in its keeping silent but in its totally misplaced theological statements. Only in retrospect, when the church recognized that within the church struggle it was primarily interested in its own survival, did the church understand the full weight of Jesus' statement: "Whoever finds his life, will lose it, and whoever loses his life for my sake (thus also for the sake of my being a Jew) will find it" (Matthew 10:39).

Also in 1947, the church did not say a single word about the Jews in the entirety of its distinguished "Darmstädter Wort." And the Synod of the Lutheran Church in Germany repeated, in Darmstadt in 1945, the old classic stereotypes about the rejection of Israel and the selection of the church, which had to deliver to "the mistaken children of Israel" the message on salvation through Christ, if it did not want to make itself guilty before God.

In 1950, in Berlin-Weißensee, the Council of Brethren of the Lutheran Church in Germany issued a "Word Concerning the Guilt toward Israel." "We declare that we became accomplices by not acting and by keeping silent before our God of Mercy in the sacrilege which was perpetrated by people from our nation on the Jews." With the term "accomplice" the first step was taken toward an understanding. However, the church is still far away from the understanding that its own announcement is rooted in anti-Judaism and that, therefore, its guilt does not reside in ethical failures but in its dogmatic oratory sins with implications and effects which it still does not comprehend.

Dietrich Bonhoeffer, as early as 1940, right after Hitler's victorious campaign against France, understood much more, when he wrote in his *Ethik* in the chapter on guilt: "The church was silent where it had to cry out loudly because the blood of the innocent screamed toward the heavens. It did not find the correct statement in the right fashion at the right hour." And since in order to become guilty one only had to look and observe without reacting, he continues:

> The church confesses to have seen the arbitrary application of brutal force, the physical and spiritual suffering of uncountable innocent people, suppression, hate, and murder without speaking out against them, without finding ways to rush to help. It became guilty in regard to the weakest and most defenseless brothers of Jesus Christ.[25]

In the history of the church, it is a new, monumental understanding that all Jews belong to the brotherhood of Jesus Christ (because, according to a statement by Martin Buber, Jesus was also the brother of the Jews).

Such a recognition has nothing to do with the fact that an anti-Judaist as well as an anti-Semite was and is able to help an individual Jew, because "such individual help and expressions of sympathy did not exclude fundamental anti-Semitic convictions."[26] One may name two examples: Dibelius, who called himself an anti-Semite,[27] wrote in a personal statement of January 23, 1965: "It was always a great pleasure for me that I succeeded in saving two Jewish families throughout the entire time of persecution, while endangering my own freedom."[28]

Also, the former state church office president from Kiel mentions two "prominent" Jews whom he saved. That same Ernst Kinder was a co-signer of a decree on December 17, 1941, which recommended "the strongest measures against the Jews" and "throwing them out of German lands." He had the gall to hypocritically justify himself after the war, apologetically, with reference to the Confessing Church, because he did not help the Jews with "words, gestures, and protests" but "with deeds."[29]

His left hand sent thousands of people to death with his signature, and his right hand offered two of them his help. Apparently, there are two different processes: First, a man who had committed himself to the depersonalizing ideology of anti-Semitism can be touched by normal human feelings in the face of individual destiny. Second, after a better understanding of the madness of an ideology, the need for justification grows. This need created the "Jew of conscience," which was appropriately named by Carl Zuckmayer [German writer; Am. ed.]. Thus General Harras said to his old friend Olivia:

> Now we want to look into the mirror and be struck by the fact that we are noble people. This is the way we appear. Everyone has his Jew of conscience, or several, so that he can sleep well at night. However, one cannot buy a way out with this. This is self-deception. Therefore, we are still guilty for what happens to thousands of others whom we do not know and whom we do not help. Guilty and damned in all eternity. To allow the meanness is worse than to do it.[30]

An Argument for a Theology after Shoa; or, The Church's About-Face

In the last twenty years there has been an accumulation of knowledge on the origins of the theology before the Holocaust. It is being uncovered as a theology that led straight to the Holocaust. It has been undressed as a "a theology of denying the inheritance" with all its seductions and mistakes. It was called "substitution theology" in which the church attempted to do away with the real Israel, calling it an old concept and replacing it with the claim of a "new Israel."

After these discoveries, further understandings of theological errors subsequently follow. The thesis is no longer valid that the nation of Israel is guilty for the death of Jesus on the cross; the thesis is no longer valid that there is a revelation of God's judgment in the persecution and suffering of the Jews; the thesis is no longer valid that the Christians are not allowed to rest till they convert all the Jews to Christianity.

This recognition has uncovered a confessional character in the centennial decision of the church which the Synods of the Rheinland adopted in 1980. Here a theology of "return and rejuvenation" is formulated which represents the church's actual 180-degree turn by its removal of the traditional anti-Judaisms—namely:

- Turning away from those teachings which empowered the church to deprive Israel of its inheritance and to replace them with a focus on a common theology of hope and promise.
- Turning away from the church's triumphalism toward a recognition that the suffering of Israel and the suffering of the crucified belong inseparably together.
- Turning away from the anti-Jewish interpretation of the New Testament toward an egalitarian testimony of faith by Christians and Jews with the goal of a common responsibility for the world.

The protest against this decision from various pulpits and lecterns revealed that for many such a 180-degree turn threatened the identity of the church and the Christian faith, especially when one asks whether anti-Judaism belongs to the foundation of the church's beliefs. And this question proves to be rhetorical if one looks into how great the danger still is of Christians arriving at an anti-Jewish biblical interpretation. I would like to give only three examples:

- Ulrich Wilckens, a scholar of the New Testament and the bishop of Lübeck, answered David Flusser's criticism of various anti-Judaic statements (which Wilckens's translation of the New Testament includes) in this way: "The *anti-Judaic* motifs in the New Testament are essential from a Christian theological point of view, because Christianity not only evolved, from a religious-historical point of view, from Jewish religious tradition but also developed its own identity against Judaism."[31]

- Sigo Lehming, in his position as a military bishop, interpreted the text of Acts 13:45ff. on Israel Sunday in 1978 in the following fashion: "God's word, the gospel, which was announced by Saint Paul and Barnabas, is being ridiculed by the Jews out of envy because they make it a subject of discussion due to their objection to it. This of course is nonbelief, and nonbelief will be judged by the gospel.

  "By choosing between the risk of the belief and the security of the religion, they (the Jews) chose, as a rule, their religion—and that means they chose against the life. Therefore, the gospel, due to its inner law, aims at others, the heathens, who are more willing to be rewarded."[32]

  In contrast to Wilckens, Sigo Lehming may not have even noticed that he expressed himself in an anti-Jewish fashion here. A request for a clarification of his position went unanswered.

- Ako Haarback, the state superintendent of the Reformed Lippic Church, referred to his interpretation of Cain and Abel in reference to Hebrews 12:24 "The Blood of Christ Speaks Better than the Blood of Abel." Later, he again used this comparison in the following assertion: "The Christians can solve their conflicts and problems in life easier than other human beings."[33] Such comparisons make a claim that one has selected the better position, it shows a sense of exclusivity, and, in a debate, it humiliates your partner who is of a different faith.

Finally, the latent disassociation of the Christians from their Jewish roots can also manifest itself in the exclusion of Jews; in other words, the text of the Hebrew Bible becomes Christian booty. The motto of the Lutheran Church in Germany in 1986 was "I am the Lord your God, you shall not have other gods beside me." As referenced, one usually cites Deuteronomy 5:6ff. The complete citation, however, is as follows: "I am the Lord your God who has led you from Egypt, from slavery. You shall not have any other gods beside me." The short quotation, as we know it from Luther's Small Catechism, introduces God with his sole claim to power. In the original text, God introduces himself as that divine power which has liberated Israel from slavery and has selected the Jews as his chosen people. He speaks to the whole nation. Luther's translation has a Western individualistic connotation. Finally, Luther's shortened version does not give the impression that the God of the Hebrew Bible is speaking here. We are only part of that belief because this Hebrew tradition has been transferred to us through the Jew Jesus. Through the condensed version, the so-called New Testament is separated from the old one consciously or unconsciously. In any case, by compromising a responsible handling of biblical texts, the umbilical cord to the Jewish people is being cut by the

Christians. The apparent harmlessness of these observations may certainly be misleading in light of the heavy implications with which such text alterations are connected.

One should take, for example, the Lutheran Church in the Rheinland which has, in the meantime, thoroughly changed its platform. It cancelled its missionary activities in Israel and now encourages a dialogue with the Jews instead. However, sentences from the Lutheran Church hymnal which cannot be sung anymore since Auschwitz should also be weeded out. In Song No. 216 of the hymnal ("Wake up thou spirit of the first witnesses"), the seventh stanza reads: "O correct the wild bridges of Zion," and the sixth stanza reads: "Awake also soon Israel." The Christian identity is inseparably tied to Judaism. This attitude is starting to gain popularity and is also leading the way back to the origin (according to St. Paul's message to the Christians: you are not carrying the root, but the root—the Jewish tradition—is carrying you; quoted in Romans 11:18). The Protestant theologian Wolfgang Huber says: "By persecuting the Jews, they (the Christians) damaged their own identity."[34] And the Catholic theologian Johann Baptist Metz says: "The Christian theology after Auschwitz must recognize once and for all that the Christians can formulate their identity and sufficiently understand it only by considering the Jews."[35]

Furthermore, Dietrich Bonhoeffer was the one who, in 1940, introduced a thorn into the side of the self-confident church theology with the phrase "The Jew keeps the question of Christ unanswered."[36] The *Breslau Christian Weekly* had already provocatively turned this into a humorous parody in October of 1933:

Vision

A church Service. The first hymn has been sung. The minister stands at the altar and begins:

"The non-Aryans are being asked to leave the church!"
No one moves.
"The non-Aryans are being asked to leave the church!"
Everything remains quiet.
"The non-Aryans are being asked to leave the church!"
To this Christ steps down from the cross on the altar and leaves the church.[37]

The "vision" of a correct estimation of the present situation can be seen in Ernst Lohmeyer's letter to Martin Buber, a letter the Protestant scholar of the New Testament wrote to the Jew after reading the exchange of correspondence between Buber and Gerhardt Kittle. Lohmeyer wrote that he was deeply "ashamed" because "his theological colleagues could think and write as they did, that the Lutheran Church can be silent and allow itself to be blown off course like a rudderless ship in the political storm of a presence that it still passing." Lohmeyer views the relationship between Jews and Christians as a network of insoluble "connections and differences," and, in agreement with Buber, he hopes

> that the Christian faith is only Christian as long as it carries the Jewish faith in its heart; I do not know whether you (Buber) would also agree to the inverse that the Jewish faith is also only Jewish as long as it can keep the Christian faith in itself. For the time being, no more should be said other than this, that the question of Judaism and Christianity cannot move back and forth as between a score and a counter score in music. On the contrary, it is an inner question of faith which should shake up one's own earnestness and one's own truth. For a Christian theologian, I would almost know of nothing else which should absorb him by the 'tua res agitur' as the question of Judaism.

Lohmeyer's vision also contains the hope which the Lutheran Church in the Rheinland realized forty-seven years later through its theological program of "about-face and rejuvenation." Lohmeyer is painfully conscious "that we were hardly ever as far removed from the Christian faith as we are right now. There only remains for us a silent hope for a rejuvenation of Christianity, just as you (Buber) are hoping for a rejuvenation of Judaism."[38]

Manfred Messerschmidt

The Difficult Atonement Toward Judaism

The Command Structure and Knowledge in the German Military

Hans Filbinger concludes his book of justification, *The Disgraced Generation*, with an "encouragement for the future," as he calls it. Quoting the *Economist*, he laments that the Germans "quietly endure while they are continuously blamed and defamed."[1] He seems to be especially annoyed that the military is being blamed as well; therefore, he cites a comment by the Italian historian Rosario Romeo made in the *Frankfurter Allgemeine* newspaper on April 12, 1986: "During the Second World War, the German military accomplished things which must be counted among the most extraordinary in military history." The military had no choice but to do its duty, since the foreign countries were not even able to see through Hitler's true plans. Filbinger lets us know that in 1936 Lloyd George called Hitler "the George Washington of Germany" and "the greatest living German." And foreign statesmen did not avoid playing up to Hitler at official events, even after the passage of the Nuremberg Laws against the Jews. For Germans, the greatest danger is not terrorism nor the philosophy of violence but "the tendency toward self-accusation and satisfaction from the accumulation of the greatest amount of guilt." Therefore, Filbinger welcomes the idea "that German historians are planning to create a remedy."[2] In the "dispute of the historians," these valiant warriors were busy at work. These reactionary scholars were convinced that the German historians of the past had followed the wrong path. According to the former navy judge, who quoted Thomas Nipperdey, the historian, the history is politically overtaxed.[3] It especially appears that the writings concerning military history are suffering. Filbinger, therefore, demands that the war generation be presented to the young people as it really was, rather than as a crowd that was obedient to Hitler and more or less willingly

83

tolerated the crimes or even participated in them.[4]

Up until now, no serious historian created such a picture of "the war generation." Filbinger studiously quotes Erich Schwinge, the jurist, who was playing around with history and had attempted to achieve precisely the opposite, i.e., to completely absolve the war generation and to blame Germany's war enemies as co-conspirators. In the case of the call for absolution, we are dealing with the most simple of arguments. This is also used in the historians' dispute, where Schwinge presents the thesis under the title *The Result of the War Generation.*[5] The book has become a kind of Bible for the military apologists.

Dealing with Filbinger and Schwinge leads us to the core of our subject. The jurists are not speaking coincidentally about the role of the military, which they frequently confuse with the whole war generation. These jurists tell us that in the Second World War, as far as the military was concerned, things were done properly. As a whole, German violations of the law were comparable to those of other nations. According to Schwinge, moreover, the German soldier had the additional responsibility of saving Western Europe from Bolshevism, and therefore he did not act according to a certain attitude or ideology but in defense of his homeland. The circle of confidants who knew Hitler's true intentions was very small.[6]

All these statements make sense only within a framework of an intentional justification strategy. They are basically rejected through scholarship. After all, the essential point is not whether the military leadership was directly informed about Hitler's goals in the East but what it really knew, to what extent it observed, accepted, or participated, and for which reasons it did this.

Furthermore, still more significant is the question of how many officers and soldiers beneath the level of the commander gained an understanding and participated in part. This question concerns not only the measures taken for the extermination of the Jews but all of Germany's activities in the East. However, the deeds directed against the Jewish population represent those which were ideologically and propagandistically prepared for the longest amount of time. They were also the most focused actions in the so-called war of ideology.

Hitler's speech of January 30, 1939, which refers to "the annihilation of the Jewish race in Europe" as the result of a new world war, is viewed by some scholars as a very essential document which is significant in helping to clarify his military goals. We do not have any knowledge of any discussions of Hitler's statements within the military leadership. It is difficult to evaluate this silence; however, the acceptance of these pronouncements, albeit in weakened form, through

a document from the Army's Supreme Command has important implications. Therefore, it was agreed that Germany's energy would also
be devoted to freeing Europe from the Jews in the forthcoming war.
The war against the Jewry was proclaimed as a future military goal.
During the Polish campaign and for some time after that, several generals voiced objection to the atrocities committed by the police and
the SS. But at the top, in the Supreme Command, a change of tone
which advocated the racial political extermination activities in the East
was already noticeable at the beginning of 1940.

The opposition to the Eastern policy was even more apparent since
various commanders expressed their opposition, in the winter of 1939–
40, to opening an offensive in the West by referring to the practices of
the SS and the police in Poland. Colonel-General von Leeb wrote that
these activities were unworthy of a cultural nation. Colonel-General
Blaskowitz, the supreme commander in the East, spoke about a blood-
thirsty police in the East. His concerns reached Hitler's desk, but, since
the Manstein plan for the western campaign was under discussion and
the chances of success against France kept improving these protests
had no effect on the Army's Supreme Command and the chief of the
General Staff. On February 7, 1940, Brauchitsch gave the supreme army
commanders the order which, in typical fashion, regulated the relationship between the army and the SS in regard to the "national struggle"
in the East: he affirmed the brutal policy of extermination which mocked
every international law. The troops should not get involved in this.
According to the Supreme Commander of the Army, the events and
activities expected in connection with the national struggle would be
damaging to the spirit and the discipline of the army. Therefore, the
troops were not to be exposed to them. In fact, the military leadership's attitude toward the murderous practices in the East could not
have developed any less problematically for Hitler. Discipline was the
highest virtue, but the rest were to keep their eyes closed.

In March of 1940, Brauchitsch asked Himmler to give the generals
and officers a lecture on the duties of the SS in the East. General von
Tippelskirch, who transmitted the invitation, signaled to the SS chief
that the army was not averse to the brutality which was applied in
Poland but it worried about "the danger of the brutalization" of their
own people. Heydrich had already explained to the General Staff in
September 1939 who was to be affected by the "field clearing" in the
East: Jewry, intelligentsia, clergy, and nobility. The General Staff ordered individual army headquarters not to get in the way of the or-
gans of the Reich's Führer's SS. The army still remained an informed
spectator, which, through its presence, made the activities of the SS

possible. Numerous protests were sent to the Supreme Military Command. They all amounted to nothing.

Then, the next step took place in Russia and Serbia: direct participation in extermination. General Roettiger, the first army inspector of the Bundeswehr, who was the chief of the General Staff of the Fourth Army in Russia in 1942–43, wrote for his defenders, probably in November 1945, that he became conscious at that time that the final goal of the partisan war in the East was to involve the army in the termination of Jews and other undesirable elements. Apparently Hitler convinced the military leadership of the necessity of this war and the mode of carrying it out, by conjuring up the old stereotypical images of an enemy in Jewish Bolshevism. He did this in order to give the German war plans a sense and purpose. While preparations for the institution of the Supreme Command's criminal orders were still aiming toward the proper ideological phase, Halder, the chief of the General Staff and temporary head of the opposition in 1938–39, ordered the army on April 2, 1941, to cooperate with the security police and the security services in the Balkan campaign by targeting Communists and Jews as enemies who must be fought against.[7]

Consequently, Halder exceeded the agreement which General Wagner reached with Heydrich on March 26, 1941, and which Brauchitsch was supposed to release as an order on April 28, 1941.[8]

The relationship between the two orders should not be understood in such a way that the chief of the General Staff for Yugoslavia and Greece advocated more energetic proceedings against the Jews. At the beginning of June 1941, shortly before the attack on the Soviet Union, the chiefs of General Staffs of army groups, armies, and tank groups were notified that Brauchitsch and Himmler agreed that the dispute between the army and the SS concerning the murders in Poland was "settled forever." The indignation of numerous commanders and attempts to proceed with court-martials against those who were guilty of excesses were thereby dismissed by orders from above.

This agreement incorporated the fundamental attitude of the military leadership toward the activities of the security police and the security service against the Jewish population. The Supreme Commander of the Army judged the predictable practice of murder from the point of view of his previously mentioned order of February 7, 1940. As long as it was guaranteed that the soldiers would not become unruly murderers, the military leadership would not criticize anything that was taking place in accordance with the will of the Führer.

However, in June of 1941 such an attitude did not just mean a voluntary retreat into the position of spectator. Hitler demanded, no later than March 1941, that the army had to cooperate actively in the planned extermination project.

As essential proof of the military command's willingness to cooperate one can look at the pertinent orders which were issued by the Supreme Command of the Army and the Supreme Command of the Military before the beginning of the war, especially the Decree Concerning the Exercising of Court-Martial in Regard to the Sphere of "Barbarossa" and the Special Measures by the Troops of May 13, 1941, and the Directions for the Treatment of Political Commissars (the so-called Commissar Decree) of June 6, 1941. They opened the door which allowed crimes against Jews to go unpunished, even though nothing was specifically said about the treatment of Jews. The many references to encountering the main enemy, namely the Jewish Bolsheviks, categorized the Jews from the beginning as the suspected group. Thus one must read the paragraph of the exemption from court-martial which dealt with the regulation of German soldiers' crimes against a country's inhabitants: "In evaluating such acts, one needs to consider in every case that the collapse of 1918, the suffering of the German nation that followed, and the struggle against National Socialism which resulted in numerous victims of the movement were decidedly due to Bolshevik influence, and no German has forgotten this."[9]

In the case of the Brauchitsch directive of February 1940, it was decreed that an intervention by a military court should take place only "when required due to a need to maintain the discipline or safety of the troop." One can list in such a case "signs that the troop is in danger of becoming unruly." This statement makes it very clear which methods the military command was already relying upon before the attack. Thus, in general, the murder of Jews represented at best, a disobedience which needed to be handled by disciplinary means.

On March 30, 1941, Hitler explained to the assembled generals the task of the military: This is a struggle between two ideologies, National Socialism against the antisocial criminality of Bolshevism. The struggle is directed against "the poison of decay." This question does not concern the military courts. Therefore, the troop needs no guidance from leaders, but it needs to demand sacrifices from itself in order to overcome any obstacles.[10] In clear language that meant: now you have to participate, the maintenance of discipline will not be much of a problem.

Accordingly, the military prepared itself for its task. With his supplementary directive for exemption from court-marital, Brauchitsch clarified that a soldier is not allowed to proceed on his own against civilians. Actions against local inhabitants should be determined by officers. Overall, however, the Supreme Command of the Army ordered that "the general attitude" of the population "and the degree of its agitation" need to be considered.[11]

All these formulas offered a suitable foundation for the persecution of Jews, whom one could accuse of "undermining" and "agitating without difficulty." Apparently no one needed proof that they were Communists. Thus in May 1941, Lattman, the top jurist at the Army Supreme Command, explained to the officers who were to be briefed on the Commissar Decree and the Exemption from Court-Martial Decree that "many of the non-Jewish commissars are doubtlessly only fellow travelers who were not influenced by Communist ideas."[12] Lattmann was in the judicial section of the Supreme Command of the Army under Lieutenant General Eugen Müller, the person responsible for the formulation of the Supreme Command's proposals for criminal orders. However, the chief of the General Staff himself was mainly responsible for the suggestions which came from the Supreme Command, and Müller was directly subordinate to him in all judicial questions.

It is a fact that the Supreme Command was the source of more serious recommendations—recommendations which were particularly aimed at Jews. So, for example, on May 6, a preface was added to the draft for the Exemption from Court-Martial which was presented to the Supreme Military Command. The rationale clearly states: "In contrast to earlier campaigns, the troop will not only be confronting guerrillas but particularly a dangerous and order-destroying element from within the civilian population which is the carrier of Jewish-Bolshevik ideology."[13]

In addition to cooperation with the special units and commandos of the security police and the security services which were mandated within the Army's operational area by the "Instructions for Special Areas of Decree No. 21 (the Barbarossa Case)" and the Brauchitsch order of April 28, 1941,[14] the Supreme Military Command also planned ahead for direct military operations against the Jewish population which included a generous tolerance for excesses.

Therefore, the army had allowed itself to become, and also caused itself to become, the hardened center of this type of warfare. Its concern with troop discipline did not represent a defensive reaction, but contributed to the efficiency of the whole procedure even more, which, of course, was to Hitler's liking.

For the time being the common soldier was only familiarized with the planned method of warfare in general terms, namely through the Instructions for Troop Behavior in Russia.[15] This order, however, was written in a fashion which characterized the imminent war from the beginning as a conflict beyond internationally recognized rules, as a war of ideology. The powerful wording in reference to the Jews is enlightening:

1. Bolshevism is the deadly enemy of the National Socialist German nation.
   Germany's struggle is directed against this destructive ideology and its supporters.
2. This struggle demands scrupulous and energetic action against Bolshevik agitators, guerrillas, terrorists, and Jews and a thorough removal of any active and passive resistance.

The guidelines demanded concentrated action against the aforementioned groups, as well as the Jews. The Jews, however, were especially targeted as an enemy which had to be destroyed. The Military Supreme Command, thereby, tried to seek understanding for the practices of the special commandos and also attempted to prepare the army for direct action within the framework of the ideological war. The military commanders took it upon themselves to ready the soldiers accordingly. One should remember the order of Colonel-General Hoepner, the commander of the Fourth Tank Group, who was also one of the officers of the military opposition. He had already formulated this instruction at the beginning of May 1941. In this order which concerned the eastern war effort of May 2, 1941,[16] he discussed "the defense of European culture against the Muscovite-Asian flood" and "the resistence against Jewish Bolshevism." In the autumn of 1941 the Supreme Military Command rules in regard to the necessary considerations for exacting of vengeance appeared in several orders of various commanders who tried to incite the soldiers against the Jewish population.

On October 10, Reichenau mentioned the campaign "against the Jewish-Bolshevik system," in which the soldier has to be "the carrier of an uncompromising national idea" and the avenger for all the bestialities that were suffered by Germans and related peoples. Reichenau demanded the "merciless extermination of foreign deceit and brutality"; only through this could the German nation "be liberated from the Asian-Jewish danger once and for all." He advised his soldiers that this was the historical task of the German military.[17] Following the instruction of the Army's Supreme Command, the general-quartermaster had this order, which Hitler considered to be excellent, distributed to the commanding authorities as a model.

Colonel-General Hoth, the commander of the Seventeenth Army, spoke in his order of October 17, 1941, about "the necessity for rigid measures against antisocial and foreign elements" which had to be understood especially by the soldiers.[18] Colonel-General von Manstein expressed it more clearly on November 20, 1941: "The Jews are the middlemen, between the enemy in our rear and the remainder of the Red Army and the Red leadership which is still fighting."[19] Thereby the Jews were assigned a central role in the guerrilla movement. This did not pass without consequence. Manstein demanded that the soldiers understand "the necessity for hard vengeance against the Jewry."

Considering these and other orders, the Jews who came into contact with the German army had little chance to escape. Many were imprisoned, perhaps some were not even identified as Jews. In order to turn these people over to the security police and the security services, Heydrich and the Supreme Command of the Army agreed on the guidelines of July 17, 1941, whereby the security police and the security commandos were to search the prison camps for various groups of people who were sometimes specifically identified, including all Jews.[20]

Accordingly, this was included in the Supreme Military Order of July 21, 1941, for all prisoner of war camps in the operational area.[21] For the time being, however, the army was not prepared to permit Heydrich's agencies to do whatever they wanted to. General-Quartermaster Wagner prohibited independent activities by the special commandos in the prisoner of war camps in the operational area with his order of July 24, 1941. Wagner apparently did not look upon the Jews as politically intolerable and basically suspect elements, and therefore wanted to use them for labor assignments. As it became clear later, in the end, the Supreme Military Command had not succeeded in implementing its plan for the troops. The collaboration between the commandos did take place, and the commandos did gain access to the camps.[22]

The "Activity Reports: USSR" of the Reich's Main Security Office[23] repeatedly refers to positive cooperation with the army's command structures. The details concerning the function of the commandos in the rear of the army's operational area, which Wagner and Heydrich had agreed upon, were pushed aside more and more. Therefore, the commandos eventually gained a huge opening within the entire area behind the fighting units. Already by July of 1941, there was an agreement with the South Army Group which stated that all special commandos "would move as close as possible to the fighting units."[24]

The entire range of these commandos' activities has been treated exhaustively by Krausnick-Wilhelm. The work documents the beginning of the annihilation process which was employed against the Jews. This process took place in front of the army's eyes, and often received its support. Commando units were often requested by the army branches. They often entered towns and villages along with the fighting units. It could no longer be said that the special commandos in the rear were safeguarding the materials and objects of hostile organizations and "especially important individuals (leading immigrants, saboteurs, terrorists, etc.)" as outlined by the Supreme Military Order of April 28, 1941. Already by that time, members of the army recognized that the goals of the commandos went beyond this.

Some accounts in the activity reports spoke of a lack of understanding on the part of the army for measures taken against the Jews. Overall, however, one can agree with Helmut Krausnick that the "supreme commanders of armies, commanders of the rear areas, and commanders of the middle and lower chains of command increasingly intensified their cooperation with the 'Jewish question,' beyond the original level, without considering their own jurisdiction." The army command posts were informed not only about specific activities but also about large-scale massacres, such as, for example, the activities of Special Unit C at Kamenez-Podolsk, where more than twenty thousand Jews were liquidated in a few days.[25]

The direct cooperation with army authorities took place in the following manner: special unit—army. For example, Stahlecker joyfully reported on the spirit of cooperation between his Special Unit A and the armies of the North Army Group. Major von Gersdorff noted in his combat travel log for the central front area on December 9, 1941,[26] that the combat officer corps was fully informed about the facts concerning the execution of Jews.

Various commanders prohibited their officers from criticizing such actions; others cooperated closely with the special commanders in the liquidation of the Jews. It was little help that individual commanders prohibited freelance murder by soldiers and officers. For example, General von Roques, the commander of the rear of the South Army Area, asked his officers to intervene in order to prevent the troops from degenerating into a "horde."[27] According to Roques, executions of this sort should only be performed by forces of the higher-ranking SS and police commanders. The general had thereby precisely described the position of the military leadership: basic agreement, on one hand, and, on the other hand, an effort to restrict the army to the role of passive spectator as much as possible.

This role could not continue. Fundamentally, Manstein, Reichenau, Hoth, Hoepner, and other high commanders undermined this formula with their ideological servitude orders to which individual commando leaders pointed with great pleasure.

The real cooperation which was encouraged by further orders from above occurred in a variety of forms: for example, Keitel's demand to proceed "primarily against the Jews, the main carriers of Bolshevism";[28]

furthermore, the exaggerated hate propaganda in the military newspapers.[29] Moreover, it came about through orders from above that the army should cooperate by closing off areas where liquidation activities took place and by turning over Jewish civilians to the security services. Local town commanders especially participated in these actions. In Luck 1,160 Jews were executed with the help of an infantry detachment; in Slibomir army soldiers participated in the execution of more than five hundred Jews.[30] The liquidation activities were planned jointly by the special commanders and the army field commanders. The army provided the transportation. The mass murder of more than thirty-three thousand Jews at Babi Jar close to Kiev was preceded by an agreement between Special Unit C and the city commander. In order to prepare for the capture of Jews, the political unit of the Sixth Army produced two thousand wall posters in its printing shop. After the completion of the massacre, a pioneer unit concealed the activities by blowing up the area. In the town of Belaja Zerkov, a field commander of the Sixth Army requested Special Commando Unit 4A to liquidate the numerous Jewish women and men who he had registered and detained.[31]

This small glimpse into the army groupings' cooperation activities already demonstrates that the army leadership was not able to realize its concept of preserving discipline, in any case not in the fashion it desired, i.e., by keeping the soldiers far away from the murderous activities and by preventing any involvement or witnessing. The logistical support which was permitted for the commandos led to organized and wild participation of various kinds.[32]

Therefore, it had to come to a test of the court-martial decree. It is known that the Supreme Command of the Army viewed the so-called wild participation in massacres and murders by individuals as an activity which endangered discipline and had to be dealt with in military courts. But how, and with which intention, could this be dealt with by a military leadership which agreed to support organized murder activities and which agreed to the principle that the commandos were the appropriate executors of the so-called clearing of the field? Murder is murder. This equation did not work out according to the schizophrenic attitude of the Supreme Military Command and various commanders. Therefore, murders perpetrated by individual soldiers were, in most cases, reduced to disciplinary transgressions, and therefore were never introduced in military courts. General von Roques gave the appropriate support for this with his decree on September 1, 1941:[33] "If judicial interference is not necessary, one should treat every willful execution of local inhabitants, Jews included, by individual soldiers as well as participation in execution exercises of the SS or the police forces as a disobedience to at least be dealt with by disciplinary means." Murder = disobedience: this formula circumscribes the practical application of the Court-Martial Decree. It is significant that in his decree, Roques still found it necessary to make the distinction between Jews and other local inhabitants. The procedure of the military courts corresponded to this if a rare case involving the murderer of a Jew was judged. For example, there is the case of officer Karl Schu, who faced the court of Division No. 187. In spite of his admitting the crime, the trial judge did not even order an indictment. The officer was quoted in the court proceedings:

> I concluded that I was justified to have the Jew shot, because, as far as I know, all the Jews in the East were being killed. In all of the larger cities ten thousand or more Jews have been killed. If a man claims that he is a Jew three times he should be eliminated. If I had brought him to the proper authorities, he would have been killed there.[34]

On a few occasions minimal sentences—never for a murder—were decreed, which were usually not even carried out.

Apparently, the army did not take its own weak recipe for prevention of the soldiers' brutalization seriously. The military courts made a farce of factual events.

The situation in the Balkans was no different. In Serbia, a chapter of the Holocaust took place with the direct responsibility of the German army. The army, the SS, and the Foreign Office worked closely together here in 1941 implementing a program for the extermination of the Jewry. Around that time, the male Jews became victims of the "final solution."[35] In 1942 in Croatia, in direct sight of the army, the Jews were brought to the Jasenovac concentration camp; in Greece, the army and the navy command structures took care of the capture and transportation of Jews on the mainland and on the islands. Individual attempts to halt this process were quickly nullified via radio transmission. Usually, only a mere call from Army Group E was enough. According to an entry of May 12, 1942, Army Group E had no objections to transporting the Jews from the islands of Corfu and Crete. The cooperation with admiral Ägäis went perfectly.[36] On the island of Corfu, the corps group Joannina took the initiative with a report to Army Group E:[37] "In order to settle the Jewish question, the corps group requests the security service to take action." The Italians described the measures taken by the army on the island of Rhodos as barbaric.

The army participated in the extermination process from 1941 until 1944. On one occasion, Himmler spoke at a Nazi officers' conference in Poznan (Pasen) in front of about three hundred generals and staff officers about the "complete solution" to the Jewish question in the occupied territories.[38] He was met with approval here. One has to ask whether the conscience of the accessory played a part in this case. Going beyond the answer to this question, was there a general explanation for this complicity? We must certainly assume various types of motives for the individual officers and commanders. Many were convinced that the Jewish question had to be solved, a view which was also held by the civilian members of the opposition. Many also equated Bolshevism with Judaism. Others were simply conformists. Many people combined motives and convictions. The most plausible motive, however, was probably the persuasive power of the image of the enemy— a familiar concept, since the stab-in-the-back legend. Such an image was also in the mind of the conservative former Supreme Commander of the Army, von Fritsch, who, in 1938, was known to have viewed the struggle against the Jews as the most difficult battle to be fought.[39] The army leadership only articulated what many people thought, when it called the so-called existential struggle of the German people just and necessary and tried to explain to the officer corps that the "justice" of the war in the East was part of the "aim" and within "the great course" which Hitler demanded.[40]

Without a doubt, the attitude of the army in the East was also a product of the political and social convictions of conservative and bourgeois conformance. However, this alone does not explain the transgression into criminality—the participation in the darkest chapter of German history. The whole thing is incomparably out of line with the traditions of the often evoked Western values which Hitler's followers pretended to salvage. The historians' dispute has shown how little the historians have understood this. Is it surprising then that Hitler's chief of General Staff, Colonel-General Zeitzler, around 1950 expressed his concern in anticipation of West German rearmament: "We cannot neglect forever our duty in regard to Europe and the Western world for the preservation of Western culture and civilization," because we "probably have the strongest fighting morale of all of European peoples today, due to our close contact with Bolshevism."[41]

The denial of complicity on the part of the army combined with a new feeling of strength: does this not sound familiar? This new self-confidence is dependent upon forgetting, glossing over, and a new "outlook." The dispute of the historians has made this apparent again. We still remember the statement by Professor Nolte whereby he said that Katyn is more symbolic for the strategy of annihilation than Auschwitz [Stalin ordered the execution of captured Polish officers at Katyn; Am. ed.].

Nothing more probably needs to be said in opposition to this. I would only like to point out that the army did not only participate in one "Katyn," but one can also mention, among others, the massacres of Kraljevo, Kragujevac, Kozara, Kefalonia, and Kalavrita [infamous executions of civilians by the German army in Yugoslavia and Greece; Am. ed.].

Hitler once called the army the column which, together with the party, carries the Nationalist Socialist state. Who will deny that until the end the army proved that this statement was true?

ERNST PIPER

National Socialist Cultural Policy and Its Beneficiaries

The Example of Munich

Dedicated to Martina Petrik

Max Liebermann, the greatest enemy of the German identity, endeavored to carry out, through his connections to the media and especially as president of the Prussian Academy of Fine Arts, a poisoning of German artistic life to such a degree that without the National Socialist rejuvenation the German identity and the German spirit would have soon come to an end. Liebermann, the true embodiment of the sinister international left, knew how to undermine a nation in the deadliest way. Accordingly, he took all necessary measures. First, the artists themselves were fragmented again according to the principle "Divine and conquer!" Then, conspirators, who were compliant as well as internally and externally dependent, were placed in all influential positions in the art schools and museums. They were appointed as chairs in art history at the universities, including all official positions influencing purchases, commissions, and stipends.

These were the words of Hans Adolf Bühler in his essay "Art in the Third Reich in 1937."[1] At the same time, he articulated several themes on National Socialist art and art policy. Among them for example is the conviction which originated in National Socialist racial teachings that everything Jewish is non-German. A fundamental contrast between the Aryan German and the Jewish race is established. The semiofficial handbook of the Nazis entitled *Global Decision in the Jewish Question* states, "The Jew cannot change his heredity, no matter how much he tries to assimilate or to camouflage himself as a German."[2] "Jewish" is contrasted to the terms "German," "national," and "people's conscience." A second theme is internationality. The Jew was not only non-German but also an agent of sinister forces, a representative of world Jewry

which worked against everything righteous with all its power. Therefore, it was not surprising that he was trying to gain influence everywhere through conspiracy. In the third theme, Bühler's keywords are
"media," "academies," "museums," "university chairs," and "purchases,
commissions, and stipends," as well as "conspirators." One should note
that Hans Adolf Bühler was also a painter and even the deputy chair
of a "German Art Society"; only his fame remained noticeably behind
that of Liebermann. However, the Nazis thanked him for his involvement and right after the so-called power grab, made him the academy
and gallery director in the city of Karlsruhe [i.e., in 1933; Am. ed.].

Against such a dangerous enemy, as Bühler describes him, the most
drastic defensive measures, of course, are allowed, even recommended.
The keyword is "dejudaization" (Entjudung). "Dejudaization of the German cultural life" was "a task which was carried out essentially within
a few years, under the direction of the Reich's Ministry for National
Education and Propaganda of the Cultural Chamber with the thorough-
ness and care which merits the great responsibility for our German
culture."[3] This is what happened according to Erich Kochanowski, an
official in the Propaganda Ministry in 1939. The "dejudaization of
German cultural life" which was part of the cultural political concept
of the National Socialist state, and its consequences, are our subjects
for discussion.

In 1932 Hitler told Goebbels:

> Goebbels, think about how to put an end to this menace, when you
> have to restructure the whole propaganda apparatus in the Reich's
> government someday. Art has nothing to do with propaganda—it is
> the deepest expression of the truest soul of a nation. This soul, how-
> ever, has been stained, misled, and made irrelevant by Jewish and
> secessionist propaganda. . . . Therefore, it is the task of propaganda
> to help the healthy national sentiment to find its freedom and its
> power again.[4]

On March 15, 1933, ten days after the last relatively "free" Reichstag
elections, Goebbels was named the Reich's minister for National Education and Propaganda. This was the only ministry that was newly
created by the Nazis at that time. Due to his position, the propaganda
minister was also the president of the newly created Reich's Cultural
Chamber with its seven subchambers. In addition, all the permit-granting
and controlling agencies for the cultural realm were under his aegis.
The first procedural decree of the Reich's Cultural Chamber Law of
November 1, 1993 was critical. It stipulated obligatory membership in
a particular chamber. This translated into a professional ban for all

those who were rejected or who were later expelled. For the time being, there was no formal prohibition against admitting Jews. Due to the strong position of Jews in certain cultural areas, for example, in the art trade, one would have had to worry about economic losses. The Reich's economic minister was, therefore, the only one who had a legal right to participate in the decisions made by the Reich's Cultural Chamber. The goal was to eliminate the "spiritual and material influence of the Jewry" without "loss of economic value."[5] That was an argument which was brought up by critics of the pogroms within the leadership of the National Socialist German Workers party after the destruction of Kristallnacht.

The National Socialists aimed toward the "liquidation of the momentous emancipation of Jews";[6] therefore, the first stage of anti-Jewish policy was primarily of a logistical nature. The Law for the Restoration of Professional Civil Servants was passed on April 7, 1933, which demanded an official proof of Aryanhood for all officials and, naturally, also became valid for the states' and cities' cultural institutions. The Reich's Cultural Chamber Law and the Editor Law followed in the same year. The Nuremberg Laws in the fall of 1935 "finally established in practice the proven racial political measures for the solution to the Jewish question on German soil with definitive results."[7] Goebbels explained in February 1935: "Basically, all the non-Aryans [Jews] should be removed from the individual professional associations of the chambers."[8] Thus, a year later, the stage was attained where the members of the Cultural Chamber were also asked to give proof of their Aryanhood.[9] At this point, only a few were affected. In the Reich's Writers' Chamber, for example, as of the end of January 1936, 447 Jewish and four "Jew-related" authors had already been excluded, so that only eight Jewish and thirty-five "Jew-related" authors were still members of the chamber.

The formation of the National Socialist state developed very quickly especially in the area of culture. Artists were merely a small group without a powerful lobby, and the Nazis could count on the broad approval of the population in regard to the Party's attack on modern art. By April 11, 1933, the Bauhaus was already closed; on May 10 the infamous book-burning took place; and six days later, the first List of Prohibited Creative Literature was published. Lists of prohibited "deleterious and undesirable writings," supplemented by lists of recommendations, were published periodically. There were three reasons for banning an author: race, emigration, and political orientation. On July 24, 1936, the first "cultural-political press conference" took place; from then on, such conferences published uniform "language directives" for reporting cultural events.[10] The Decree for the Formation of the New German Cultural Life[11] was issued on November 27, 1936. It generally prohibited any art criticism and allowed only the viewing of "positive art." Alfred-Ingemar Berndt, the ministerial official from the Reich's Cultural Senate, explained:

> The Jewish critic was, in a manner of speaking, the intermediary who fixed prices for the businessmen, who praised what should be sold, and damned what was to be bought cheaply. In this fashion, the most grotesque pictures by Jewish painters were sold at crazy prices to the museums of the Reich, the lands, the communities, etc. up until 1933. The good German artist was starving while prices which amounted to tens of thousands of marks were paid for cubistic smears.[12]

Here a further argument against Jews in the cultural sector was being articulated, namely, that they were enriching themselves with hard-earned German tax money. This accusation was repeated later in the lowest manner of propaganda in the "Degenerate Art" exhibit. Here the purchase prices of paintings from public collections were quoted at the level they had attained during the inflationary era and thus the suggestion was made that these were the actual prices in present-day Reichsmarks.

One of the favorite themes of National Socialist propaganda was that the German artist was undermined in his work and success by sly Jewish machinations. In this manner, the Nazis hoped to win those who felt mistreated over to the side of National Socialism. Already by 1930, Hans Severus Ziegler, in his dogmatic manual, *Cultural Work in the Third Reich*, emphasized that the only thing that mattered was to free the museums from "Bolshevik-Jewish incompetency and inferior racial traits." Therefore, the state, the communities, and also the churches should have bought works by German painters and sculptors on a regular basis. This proposal was gladly supported by those affected. Nine years later, the official in the Propaganda Ministry who was already quoted above stated with satisfaction:

> The cultural effect of this successful dejudiazation was amazing. German cultural life bloomed faster than anyone would have expected. German artists obtained bookings and contracts, theaters and concert halls were filled again, the German movie industry—previously completely in the hands of Jews—was honored with international awards. Already within the six years of National Socialist leadership, exhibits in the House of German Art, distinguished buildings of the Third Reich, and many other great achievements were testimonials to the blessed liberation of German culture from the pressure of Jewish alienation.[13]

Even the Nazis rarely lied in such a shameless manner. At the same time, it became apparent in this regard that they had made their self-image in the cultural sector a high priority.

In September of 1933, at the First Party Congress of the National Socialist German Workers party after the power grab, there was a separate cultural meeting at which Adolf Hitler gave the keynote address. He also did this in the years to follow. The focal point of this First Party Congress, which celebrated the Nazis' newly achieved power within the state, was the theme of ideology. This was also true of Hitler's speech at the cultural meeting, which was entitled "National Socialism as Ideology."[14] His speech contained a sentence which would later be placed above the entrance of the House of German Art: "Art is an elevated mission which obliges fanaticism." In his speech, Hitler also returned to his theory, which was already developed in *Mein Kampf*, that humanity should be divided into founders of culture, carriers of culture, and destroyers of culture. The only founders of cultures were Aryans, while the Jews, of course, had to be counted among the destroyers:[15] "Every clearly developed race has its own handwriting in the book of art, unless it is completely unable to produce its own art as in the case of the Jewry."[16] If Hitler restricted this speech to general thoughts and references, he later became much clearer at the cultural meeting in the fall of 1936 after the successful completion of the Olympic games, which up to then had motivated his restraint. This time the title of Hitler's speech was "The Forces of Order against the Spirit of Chaos." Hitler now announced that the power achieved through struggle and strength could only be maintained in the same fashion. His main enemies were the Jewry and Bolshevism, a Jewish creation, whose goal was "to destroy the existing organic national leadership based on blood and to replace it with a Jewish element which is foreign to the Aryan peoples."[17] The Jewry, which stood against any national community, was always "fermenting decomposition." Its activity in the economic and cultural area was destructive in the same way. In cases where Jewry appeared to support culture, there was really "cunning economic exploitation."

There were in fact quite a number of Jews among the gallery dealers who promoted modern art. In contrast, there were relatively few significant Jewish painters, such as Max Liebermann, Lesser Ury, Jankel Adler, and Felix Nussbaum. On the one hand, this had something to do with the traditional Jewish ban on image-making which Jewish artists transcended only after the Enlightenment. On the other hand, however, many Jewish entrepreneurs were pushed into the trade by exclusion from most of the other sectors of production. Jews owned a number of department stores as well as textile and jewelry shops and even galleries. Some Jews also owned a few publishing houses, the last of which were Aryanized or dissolved after Kristallnacht. It is evident that these gallery owners were a special irritation to Hitler, the "picture-postcard" painter, who rejected all modern trends in painting with extreme radicalism. Hitler, therefore, clearly expressed that instead of free enterprise, the "time of unified performance and unified resurrection"[18] had now begun. The period of "Bolshevik art foolishness" was over:

> Therefore, National Socialist art can no longer tolerate manifestations of the decadent world which is behind us, whose democratic destruction obviously carries over to other cultural areas as well. We love what is healthy. The best kernel of our nation which is measured by body and soul should raise the yardstick of determination. In our art, we wish only its glorification.[19]

The goal was a style "of mutually supportive and elevating communal creation." At the end, Hitler pointed, in this regard, to his great building plans, to "Nuremberg of the Reich's Party Days," to "restructuring of the capital of the movement," and to the "new construction of Berlin."

Munich, that "most beloved spot on earth,"[20] as Hitler wrote in *Mein Kampf*, was not only "the capital of the movement." Its other honorary title, given by the National Socialists, was "the capital of German art." This name was given to the city by Hitler on October 15, 1933, during the laying of the foundation stone for the House of German Art. In the Nazis' opinion, this exhibition hall was the largest and most beautiful in the world.[21] It was the only significant museum founded during the Nazi era. It was inaugurated on July 18, 1937, with the first Great German Art Exhibit, which from then on offered an annual overview of the art that was tolerated by the Nazis. A day later and only a few hundred meters away beneath the arches of the courtyard, the "Degenerate Art" exhibit, which was looked upon as a deterrent, was opened.[22] The dress rehearsal for the former was the exhibit "Great Germans in Portraits of Our Time," which was shown with great publicity during the Olympic games in Berlin.[23] The counterexhibit also had forerunners which went back to 1933. The former had already taken place in April of 1933, when the newly appointed gallery director Bühler organized the show "The Art of the Government from 1918 until 1933" in Karlsruhe. However, this tortune chamber of 1937 overshadowed everything and robbed German museums of the most significant twentieth-century art works in an unparalleled storm of art thefts. Altogether, the public collections lost about seventeen thousand works of art. The target of this iconoclasm was "german decadent art since 1910,"[24] as it was called in Goebbels's authorization for the "theft commission" which cleaned out fourteen museums in a few weeks. The members of this commission, which made an important contribution to what Hitler called the "relentless cleansing war . . . against the last elements of our cultural displacement,"[25] were led by the painter Adolf Ziegler, the president of the Reich's Chamber of Fine Arts. Among the members were Klaus Graf Baudissin, the director of the Folkwang-Museum; Hans Schweitzer, the Reich's representative for artistic creation (whose professional name was Mjölnir); Wolfgang Willrich; and Franz Hofmann.

The "Degenerate Art" exhibit had the declared goal of illustrating the danger of a "development which was guided by a few Jewish and politically Bolshevik spokesmen."[26] It was divided into nine sections:

1. Barbarism in presentation
2. Religious content
3. The political background of art deviation
4. Political tendency
5. The moral side
6. Planned destruction of the last remainders of any racial conscience
7. The idiot, the cretin, and the paralysis of spiritual ideals
8. A small sample from the numerous lazy Jewish concoctions
9. Perfected madness

A flyer printed on magenta paper was added to the exhibition guide on which there was an appeal to visit the exhibit:

> Tortured canvass—spiritual wasteland—sick fantasies—crazy incompetent individuals, who were rewarded by Jewish cliques and praised by writers, were products and producers of an "art" for which the national and municipal institutes diligently threw away millions of marks of the German people's resources while, at the same time, German artists starved. Thus, just as that "state" was, so too was its "art."[27]

Here we again meet the previously introduced National Socialist buzzwords concerning the Jewish manipulation of the art market, the squandering of tax monies, and the suppression of German artists. The "Degenerate Art" exhibit was shown in Munich until the end of November; in February of 1938 in Berlin; in July of the same year in Düsseldorf; and in July of 1939 in Frankfurt am Main. Altogether more than 2 million people visited the exhibit. In addition, there was also direct political propaganda, such as an "Anti-Bolshevik Show" which opened in the summer of 1936 in Munich and subsequently toured the German Reich. The third large traveling exhibit was named "The Eternal Jew—The Great Political Show." It opened almost a year before the day of the Kristallnacht, on November 8, 1937, in the library of the Deutsches Museum (Munich). It attempted to demonstrate that "in all countries and at all times, one must lead a defensive struggle against Judaism and the Jewish plague."[28]

Munich was not named "the capital of German art" only because Adolf Hitler lived here. Earlier, in the course of the First World War, a very strong anti-Prussian sentiment developed, and Munich became the capital of the "Regulation Cell of Bavaria" (Ordnungszelle Bayern). After the repression of the revolution of 1918–19, it not only became the refuge for anti-Prussian and anti-Semitic sentiments but also a meeting place for nationalist desperados, the Freikorps, citizens' militias, and revolutionaries. Public life was characterized by an antidemocratic, antirepublican, reactionary bourgeoisie, as Lion Feuchtwanger described it so masterfully in his novel *Success* (*Erfolg*). Hitler's failed coup made no difference. The National Socialist German Workers party was prohibited for a time, but the People's Alliance (Völkische Block), which was controlled by it, received 50 percent of the vote in Munich in the local elections of April 1924.[29] A few months later, Hitler's prison sentence was reduced to probation. In 1933, the National Socialist art ideologist Hans Kiener was able to note with satisfaction: "In the last few decades, Munich defended itself with a bitter and prolonged struggle against the influence of destructive ideas, frequently but not always victoriously; and, in response, the left screamed about Munich's downfall as an artistic city."[30] Already by this time, a clearly pleased Rudolf Oldenbourg wrote in the *Munich Art Annual* which was founded at the end of the First World War, that "Munich's unique tradition—in contrast to Berlin—offered tenacious resistance against the penetration of Impressionism."[31] At the end of the nineteenth century, the influence of French Impressionism was especially strong on German art. The fact that the most significant German Impressionist was Max Liebermann, whose "dangerous" influence we had heard about at the beginning of this paper, certainly did not help the cause. Oldenbourg, of course, did not view the envy of the above-mentioned and suppressed German artists who were cheated out of their success as the reason for rejecting Impressionism. He focused on the "artistic character" of Impressionism, which was not able to satisfy "our race's need for artistic expression." Expressionism "with its strong emphasis on ideal content" better satisfied "the natural inclinations of Germans."[32]

With this statement Oldenbourg, without a doubt, touched upon the right point. Expressionism, with its tendency toward idealistic madness, exaggeration, superlativism, and brute force, could have been quite suitable as the showpiece of Nazi art, just as much as Futurism found its support among the Italian fascists. The national revolutionary publication *Uprising* (1931), for example, was illustrated mainly by the "visionary ecstatic artists" Ernst Barlach and Emil Nolde. The dispute in regard to Expressionism continued within the National Socialist German Workers party for a long time. It was settled only by Hitler, the picture-postcard painter, who rejected any art which was not absolutely naturalistic. Nolde, Kirchner, Pechstein, and others who were always ready to participate in anti-Semitic activities were deeply disappointed later to find their art in the "Degenerate Art" exhibit. When Kirchner was asked in July of 1937 to give up his position in the Prussian Academy of Art, he responded: "I sincerely wish that a new beautiful and healthy art would grow up in Germany. I myself and many other older artists have honestly and faithfully worked for this; sooner or later someone will recognize this."[33] Nevertheless, Kirchner was represented in the "Degenerate Art" exhibit with thirty-two of his works. In light of this, he wrote: "I have always hoped that Hitler would support all Germans, and now he has defamed so many truly serious and good artists of German blood."[34] Nolde even joined the Nazi party after the so-called power grab; his application for the Fighting Association for German Culture was, however, rejected. He saw himself, as he wrote to Goebbels in July 1938, "as almost the only German artist in open struggle against the alienation of German art."[35] Therefore, it must have hurt him even more to see his work at the center of the "Degenerate Art exhibit."

The supporters of the nationalistic direction who stood against Expressionism met primarily in the Fighting Association for German Culture, which evolved from the National Socialist Association for German Culture which was founded in 1927. The leader of the Fighting Association was Alfred Rosenberg, more or less the Nazis' chief ideologist and at the same time the editor and chief of the *Völkischer Beobachter* (People's Observer). The architect and later president of the Reich's Chamber of Fine Arts, Eugen Hönig, represented the Association of German Architects on the executive board of the Fighting Association. Other prominent members on the executive board were Buldur von Schirach and Robert Ley. The Fighting Association was supposed to unite all "national forces" against "the deviation, destruction, and judaization of German cultural life," and it agitated wherever it could. Up until 1933, the organization had only about six thousand members, but the membership had already increased by the end of the same year to more than thirty thousand, since the drive to "join the victorious battalions" was always very strong. One of the co-founders and main orators of the Fighting Association was Paul Schultze-Naumburg. The titles of his books speak for themselves: *Art and Race* (1928) and *Art from Blood and Soil* (1934). However, in his *The Flat and the Inclined Roof* (1927), he already announced his struggle against the "Bolshevik-Jewish flat roof."[36] Only a malicious person may have recognized as the motive behind all of this a poor business situation for the architect who was committed to the neo-Biedermeier style. In any case, the Nazis took care of their own and made Schultze-Naumburg the director of the National Art Institute in Weimar in 1930, when they governed Thuringia for the first time.

Another beneficiary of the barbarism organized by the state was Wolfgang Willrich. Willrich was originally a painter:

> As an artist, Willrich had already tried to formulate racial ideas in an artistic sense since 1920, in clear contrast to the then common conception of the human being as a miserable creature which became sufficiently known to us through the writings of the cultural Bolsheviks Schmidt-Rottluff, Heckel, Kirchner, Kokoschka, Dix, Grosz, and Hofer. Such attempts to emphasize the healthy human being of the Nordic race as an artistically valuable goal for artistic creation in its entirety were unfortunately in no way frequent during the dark Marxist-liberal, completely Jewish-contaminated period from 1918–1933.[37]

After 1933, Willrich became known as the portrait painter of SS men (*On the Family Tree of German Art*, preface by Heinrich Himmler) and, especially, as the author of numerous hateful writings. In 1934, he was called to Berlin by Darré, the leader of the Reich's peasants, "in order to artistically create the national idea of blood and soil." In 1937, his pamphlet "The Cleansing of the Temple of Art" appeared, which coined the concept of the "Degenerate Art" exhibit. Ziegler "half-jokingly" made the suggestion of creating a museum from the exhibit and appointing Willrich as its director. Then he would be taken care of, and the Reich's Chamber of Fine Arts would have gotten rid of him.[38]

Another member of the commission for the exhibit on "Degenerate Art" was Franz Hofmann. Since 1931, he had been the main art critic at the *Völkischer Beobachter*. In June of 1934, he was appointed as the new director of the municipal gallery in the Lenbach-Haus (Munich). Since he was unusually weak as an art critic, even by National Socialist Standards, the city gave him only very limited duties. He was free to make purchases only up to two hundred Reichsmarks. He referred

to himself as an "old fighter" [Nazis who joined the right-wing movement in its early stages; Am. ed.]. The *Angriff* (Attack) honored Hofmann
the artist on January 11, 1939, by reproducing one of his drawings
and allowing him to say a few words as well:

> After the contemptible peace, I participated in the storming of my
> home city of Munich with the Epp Freikorps. . . . Thus, on Novem-
> ber 9, I stood in the right place. Today, this appears to me as the
> symbol of my own inner revolution; I became a journalist, and for
> several years I was in charge of the art section at the *People's Ob-
> server*. The young movement had to fight against a formidable op-
> ponent in the field of art! The municipal gallery of Munich allowed
> me, as its director, to organize contemporary art with the art of the
> past. Through this process, degenerate art was eliminated, and the
> great cleansing which was instigated by the Führer in 1937 there-
> fore, did not, affect my gallery.[39]

Chamber President Ziegler indeed noticed, during an inventory before the "great picture storm," that of all the German museums, the
gallery in the Lenbach-Haus was the "most immaculate." This of course
also demonstrates the acquisition policy of Eberhard Hanfstaengl, who
administered the gallery from 1925 to 1933 and in whose planning
there was no room for modern art.[40] In any case, the status of the
gallery qualified Hofmann to become a member of the "robbery commission" (Raubkommision). For this purpose he was given a three-
month leave, and after completing work, on January 1, 1938, he was
promoted to the directorship of the Fine Arts Section in the Propaganda Ministry.

The year 1933 was also a decisive time for careers in the area of
architecture. One of the most renowned modern architects was Robert
Vorhoelzer, who first worked for the railroad system and then, from
1920 on, for the post office. In 1930 he became professor at the Technical Institute in Munich. The post offices and the package delivery
office which were built by Vorhoelzer were declared "Communist post
office structures," in 1933.[41] Vorhoelzer was then removed from his
professorship in October of the same year, after an intensive hate campaign. The reason which was given for his dismissal, according to the
Bavarian Cultural Ministry, was that his taste in art stood "in conflict
with the principles which are exclusively valid and which have been
determined in the new Germany, as it is known, by the Führer himself."[42] Also in the same year, Lösche, a cultural administrator at the
ministry, informed the public that it was also necessary to "terminate"
the sculptor Karl Knappe, who had a sculpture teaching position at
the Technical Institute.[43] Instead, reliable conservative architects and

opponents of the "new building style," such as Roderich Fick, Friedrich Gablonsky, Alexander von Senger, and—on Hitler's special request—Julius Schulte-Frolinde, were appointed professors to an extent without appropriate proceedings. These personal political decisions took place against the background of the dispute between the Munich Association, which represented the position of the German Work Association in Bavaria, and the Fighting Association of German Architects and Engineers, a dispute which ended with the dissolution of the Munich Association in February 1934. Only fourteen of the more than 260 members dared to attend the last membership meeting.[44]

In the same year, 1934, an independent Municipal Cultural Office, directly subordinate to Lord Mayor Karl Fiehler, was created. This office was supposed to help with the process of the National Socialization of cultural activities. Fiehler declared openly: "At the present time, it is much more important for me to have absolutely unwavering National Socialists in these positions than some dilettantes who may have well-known names as artists."[45] Hans Zöberlein, who had a party career similar to Franz Hofman's, became the director of the Cultural Office. He was a writer, and he received the Literary Prize of the City of Munich right after the power grab for his book *A Belief in Germany*. The former military officer Max Reinhard, the painter Hans Flüggen, and the unemployed bandleader Franz Adam became the supervisors of the sections for literature and theater, fine art and music, and film. Additionally, Götz Mayerhofer was appointed as the municipal music official. Mayerhofer was the director of the music library and an official in the working circle of National Socialist composers, but his compositions were not performed.

Overall, the work of the municipal cultural office was not very successful, as the example of the Kammerspiele (theater) will demonstrate.[46] The year 1933 brought a significant loss to the cast of this prestigious stage. Several of its most important members, especially the Jewish ones, for example, Julius Gellner, Therese Giese, Kurt Horwitz, emigrated right away. The demand that Jews should no longer be employed could not be ignored forever. Although the theater, which remained under the direction of Otto Falckenberg, was repeatedly attacked by the conservative media before 1933, the Kammerspiele proved to be irreplaceable if the "capital of the German art" were to have any chance of competing with Berlin in the realm of theater. The theater saved itself by programming increasingly apolitical entertainment; explicitly National Socialist dramatists were hardly ever performed. It even halfway circumvented the demand to perform a play by Dietrich Eckart for his seventieth birthday by staging only his version of *Peer*

Gynt. The Bavarian Staatsschauspiel was much more in the regime's service. The theater's director from 1938 on was Alexander Golling, who declared his loyalty to National Socialism early on. The relatively peaceful position of the Kammerspiele became endangered in 1938, when under pressure from Fiehler, the notorious troublemaker Christian Weber, "a businessman and cattle salesman," a Nazi from the very start, and an official in numerous party offices, became the president of the administrative council who appointed the SS-Sturmbannführer Paul Wolfrum as the chief administrative official. The new bosses' performance, however, was so incompetent that they were soon replaced upon Hitler's personal initiative. The Kammerspiele company was completely dissolved, and the theater was absorbed by the Stages of the Capital of the Movement in January of 1939. Falckenberg, who was also recruited by Goebbels for Berlin, continued to have a certain freedom of action, and on Hitler's fiftieth birthday he was appointed as the theater's director. Despite this recognition, the Kammerspiele remained relatively far away from the National Socialist agenda. Dramatists who were rewarded with positions as producers, with performances, and with national book prizes after 1933 for their National Socialist ideology, hardly appeared in the repertoire of the Kammerspiele. Friedrich Bethge—who quickly became a member of the Nazi party on May 1, 1932, and, right after the power grab, took over as the chief dramatist at the Frankfurt Schauspiel, where he used his position in order to finally draw attention to his plays—was not performed at the Kammerspiele.

Even the president of the Reich's Document Chamber, Hanns Johst, and Curt Langenbeck, the chief dramaturg at the Bavarian Staatsschauspiel since 1938, each appeared only once in the program. The required quota of Nazi ideology was satisfied more with authors such as Alois Johannes Lippl and Richard Billinger, whose works were performed four and three times respectively. Billinger, the Austrian who received the most prestigious German literary prize, the Kleist-Preisfor, for his play *Rauhnacht* in 1932, also received recognition. Rosenberg, who was ultra-orthodox and who, in contrast to other National Socialist leaders, was highly interested in introducing ideology to the theater, considered Billinger a "schizophrenic phenomenon": "His mixture of crude sensuous ruralness and refined urban intellectualism is not very attractive."[47] But Rosenberg and his Fighting Association stood alone in this position, as they did in many other cases, because Billinger's peasant plays were well suited for the Nazi ideology. He received the Literary Prize of the City of Munich, the Grillparzer-Prize, and finally, in 1943, the Raimund-Prize of the City of Vienna.

Joseph Goebbels first organized the party's propaganda apparatus then that of the state, with brutality and skill. He was a true politician and he knew that it was important, in order to neutralize the citizens and to bolster the image of the regime abroad, to win renowned artists for collaboration in a National Socialist Germany. He was especially successful in the area of music. Richard Strauss, undisputedly the most significant composer of operas in those days, became the President of the Reich's Music Chamber. His deputy was Wilhelm Furtwängler, who, after a period of indecision, decided, in the spring of 1935, against emigration and instead actively participated in the German Reich. This decision, due to Furtwängler's international reputation, was a significant gain in prestige for the Nazis. This was also true to an even higher degree for Strauss, who, at the time of Hitler's appointment to the Reich's chancellorship, was already sixty-eight years old and had been working only as a freelance composer and conductor since 1925. He was deeply indifferent toward politics, and he was only interested in his glory, the reputation of his work, and his name. When Arturo Toscanini canceled his conducting of *Parsifal* at the Bayreuth Festival in 1933 in protest against the anti-Semitic policy of the Nazis, Strauss did not hesitate a moment to conduct in his place. On February 13, 1934, he gave the inaugural speech at the first meeting of the Reich's Music Chamber (Reichsmusikkammer). Once more the well-known refrain was heard about the "worsening of the economic situation for German musicians" in the recent past and the hope for a regulating hand from Adolf Hitler.[48] When the Gestapo intercepted a letter by Richard Strauss in which he confessed to having placed himself at the disposal of the Nazi regime only as a result of opportunism, he had to resign from his presidency of the chamber. This, however, motivated him to make a loyalty statement to Hitler, the "great all-around creator of German life."[49] Consequently, Strauss remained completely unaffected, and furthermore, he was allowed to preside over the Permanent Council for the International Cooperation of Composers, which was founded in 1934, after Germany's exit from the International Society for New Music. Strauss remained the opportunist he was, and in May of 1935, the manager of the Reich's Music Chamber was able to communicate to the manager of the Reich's Cultural Chamber, in a confidential spy report concerning Strauss's "house policy," that he preferred Clemens Krauss over Furtwängler, simply because the former was doing more for the performance of his operas.[50]

The composer Clemens Krauss, born in 1893, demonstrated early sympathies for the Nazis. In 1933, he, instead of the expelled conductor Fritz Buschtook, took over the conducting of the first performance of

Strauss's opera *Arabella* in Dresden. In 1935, he moved from the State Opera in Vienna to Berlin, and in 1936, he came to Munich. In Berlin as well as in Munich, Krauss profited from the political, racially motivated elimination of this predecessors Kleiber and Knappertsbusch. After Furtwängler's resignation, he became the deputy Chamber President; after the so-called Anschluß, [the 1938 absorption of Austria into the German Reich; Am. ed.], he became the director of the Salzburg Festival and the director of the Mozarteum [the world-famous music academy; Am. ed.], for which he offered thanks with the following words:

> In this position, I promise to provide leadership for this high-level art institution which has been entrusted to me with all the reverence that has been bestowed upon us artists in this city where Mozart had been a pupil, with deep respect toward the genius of Mozart, and toward the forward-storming and dignified master and artist, Adolf Hitler![51]

Clemens Krauss was highly valued by the "forward-storming" master, and in 1941 the Munich State Opera Orchestra was classified, as he requested, into the "Special Category of German Cultural Orchestras." The following letter by Martin Bormann of April 1, 1942, to the Munich lord mayor speaks for itself:

> Dear Party Colleague Fiehler!
> According to the decree of the Führer, general director Clemens Krauss will contact me whenever he has any desires in regard to the opera. Accordingly, on February 24, 1942, Clemens Krauss wrote that he was no longer able to obtain apartments in Munich for the newly contracted members of the Bavarian State Opera. I'm not surprised, because I am sufficiently informed about the Munich housing shortage by officials and political leaders who were transferred to the Party Office. Today I reported to the Führer about the correspondence from general director Krauss. The Führer wishes you to check one more time to see whether a few more Jewish apartments could be made available for the newly contracted members of the Bavarian State Opera.[52]

The lord mayor answered Bormann right away and stated that, unfortunately, it would be very difficult to rent the few "Jewish apartments," and that additionally, according to his own request, these would be distributed only in cases of special public interest or to the members of the Party Office. Only a few weeks earlier, he distributed, according to the wishes of the general directorship, six Aryanized apartments to three choir singers, two orchestra musicians, and one lead dancer.

Krauss also played a leading role in the "dejudaization activities" in the area of music.[53] At that time, librettos by Jews were purified en masse; sometimes even whole operas were rewritten. Nedbal's *Polish Blood* (Polenblut) was rewritten as *The Harvest Bride* (Erntebrant); a new concluding chorus was added to Richard Wagner's "Emperor's March" with a hymn to the Führer; etc. As this activity produced stranger and stranger creations, it became centralized in 1940 in the Reich's Office for Musical Creation (Reichsstelle für Musikbearbeitumgen). Clemens Krauss assumed the presidency of the executive committee. He was also available whenever the staffs of Foreign Propaganda Offices called. So, for example, he participated in army concerts in occupied Poland and in Paris.

After the "final victory," Clemens Krauss and Karl Böhm as well, were prohibited from practicing their profession by the Allies. Böhm, a year younger and Austrian, like Krauss, had directed the Dresden opera from 1934 until he moved to Vienna in 1943. His move from Hamburg to Dresden took place upon the "personal initiative of our Führer."[54] Böhm showed his gratitude when, under the title "The Musical Crisis Is Solved," he declared in response to the Reichstag's election force of March 29, 1936:

> It proved to be a great blessing for the cultural renewal of Germany that, all classes and professional groups were newly organized and strictly coordinated after Hitler seized power.... A musician, be he a freelance or a performing artist, a music educator or an orchestra musician, has to be tremendously grateful to Adolf Hitler. This is meant in a social and economic context—whereby many unemployed musicians received new work opportunities—in an ideal context as well![55]

The Salzburg Festival is another clear example of how the demotion of one helped the promotion of another. The festival was boycotted by the Nazis up until the so-called Anschluß, because of the "international Jewish influence" and because of its competition with Bayreuth, whose ceremonial seriousness was missing in Salzburg anyway. Hitler allowed only two "Reich's German artists" to participate per year. After the German armies entered Austria, an artistic power shift took place as well. Toscanini and Bruno Walter were no longer allowed to conduct anymore. They were replaced by Furtwängler, Böhm, and Krauss. Böhm declared in response to the "Anschluß": "Whoever does not affirm our Führer's action 'a hundred percent' is not worthy of having the honored title of German!"[56]

Hans Pfitzner also profited from the new situation. He was allowed to contribute an overture from Kleist's *Kätchen of Heilbronn* to the festival. The case of Pfitzner is especially interesting because he believed his compositions were boycotted during the Weimar Republic. This was only true in his imagination and in that of his supporters. This is contrasted with a renaissance after 1933, which, however, did not amount to much more than loud expressions of support. Pfitzner had also fought, just as Nolde had, for "German art" and "German music" against "new music makers" and the influence of "foreign, destructive elements." He viewed himself and his defensive struggle as part of Richard Wagner's legacy. Pfitzner is a memorable example of the embellishment of aesthetic positions with political slogans.

Pfitzner had already created the legend of his own suppression, which was "caused," in this case, by music critic Paul Bekker, who, as Pfitzner wrote already in 1919, "together with his powerful *Frankfurt* Newspaper manipulated the international Jewish movement in the arts."[58] When the *Journal for Music* made its first summary in May of 1933, Pfitzner was not missing:

> In the April issue we analyzed the intolerable situation at the State Opera in Berlin . . . in the essay "Hans Pfitzner Boycott in Berlin." In the meantime, the Fighting Association for German Culture made sure that Pfitzner would be invited during the Spring Arts Weeks as a guest conductor to the Berlin State Opera and that Pfitzner's *Palestrina* would again be part of the program. On the other hand, the general music director Otto Klemperer was fired.[59]

Otto Klemperer was a Jew.

In 1934, Pfitzner became the first composer ever to receive the Goethe Prize of the City of Frankfurt; in 1936, he was appointed to the Reich's Cultural Senate (Reichskultursenet); in 1941, he received the maximum state bonus of six thousand Reichsmarks from the Propaganda Ministry in spite of his very good income; and in the following year, he received the Beethoven Prize of the City of Vienna. As the "emissary of German musical culture,"[60] he traveled to the occupied territories of Poland, France, and Czechoslovakia. In gratitude, the "German fighter for music who was close in spirit to National Socialism"[61] received, during the third War Music Week in Poznan in 1942, the Wartheland cultural prize, for which he thanked the general governor by devoting the composition "Cracow Greetings" to him.

Finally, *Simplicissimus* must also be mentioned. This journal was founded in 1896 in Munich, and it soon became the most prestigious satirical German weekly. It was popular especially because of its criticism of certain tracts of the Wilhelminian era. After the outbreak of the First World War, however, the editorial staff changed to an explicitly nationalistic direction, after the termination of the journal's publication was discussed. However, during the Weimar Republic, the journal returned more to its critical position, even though a certain distancing from the new democracy was noticeable. National Socialism, as well as communism, was sharply criticized in many cartoons. Therefore, it was even more surprising to see its later quick adaptation to National Socialism. On February 12, 1933, a full-page cartoon—"1933: An Open View at Last!"—by Karl Arnold already welcomed the new situation.[62] Nevertheless, the journal's editorial offices were occupied and ransacked in March by the SA. Two issues were canceled, but in the April 1, 1933, issue one could read "that the temporary prohibition of our journal was retracted after we assured the government of our loyalty. The restructuring of the editorial board also went hand-in-hand with this assurance."[63] Behind the euphemism "restructuring," Schoenbergner's and Th. Th. Heine's escapes were hidden. As a Jew, Heine, although the most famous cartoonist of the journal, could not be tolerated anymore. Instead, Arnold and Gulbransson adapted even better to the new situation just as had Thöny, Schulz, and Schilling.

Karl Arnold adjusted so well to the regime that, at the beginning of 1934, he became temporarily became the chief editor of the journal, and in 1939 he received a professorship. Thöny had already been appointed by the Academy to a professorship *honoris causa* in 1934.

Simplicissimus now regarded it as its "patriotic duty" to serve Germany and "its great domestic and foreign goals" in its own way.[64] Little by little, the journal's loyalty to the regime became more disturbing, and it even intensified with the outbreak of the Second World War. Anti-Semitic cartoons, which had occasionally already appeared before 1933,[65] now had a field day. In September of 1944, the lack of paper put an end to its inglorious activity.

Let us summarize: it has become clear what the power grab meant: the uncompromising struggle against the avant-garde, the "purging" of artists who helped to establish the international appreciation for German contemporary culture, and especially "dejudaization." On the other hand, mediocre talents now made their careers only by putting the right phrases into their mouths. A gigantic apparatus of associations, chambers, and official channels was created. Whenever possible, they always carried the prefix "Reich" in their names. The Reich's Cultural Chamber organized about one hundred thousand people who were active, one way or another, in cultural life. In March 1933, the Steering Committee of the National Cultural Associations immediately distinguished itself with the memorandum "What German Artists Expect from the New Government"! All the programmatic suggestions are known to us by now:

- Removal of all "creations characteristic of the world bourgeoisie and Bolshevism"
- Firing of all museum directors who are guilty of "unscrupulous squandering of public money" and the purchase of modern art as well as the removal into storage of "truly German art"
- An exhibit of the diplaced art works with quotations of the sums of money for which they had been purchased and the consequent burning of them[66]

Such a program was quickly formulated and, by assuming the necessary tools of power, could easily be carried out. And it was consequently carried out. However, what was supposed to fill the vacuum that had been created? One could not sustain an internationally recognized cultural life only with artists of the third or fourth rank, even if one wished to do so. Nobody recognized this better than Goebbels. He was the reason that, for the time being, the Jewish libretto writers Hofmannsthal and Zweig were overlooked because the working circle of the National Socialist composers, in spite of all its efforts, had nothing comparable to the Strauss operas to offer. Exemptions for several Jewish movie actors, Olympic athletes, and others are also known to have existed. Significantly, in 1939, due to the war economy, the world-renowned journal *Simplicissimus* was not discontinued but the party's own *Brennessel* (Stinging Nettle) was. It was also Goebbels who stopped party fanatics from exposing Mozart as a Freemason, attacking Wagner because of his Jewish performers, and even expressing concerns about Goethe. At the cultural-political press conference of October 17, 1936, he declared: "From now on great Germans . . . are under special state protection . . . [because] the new period since 1933 indeed has nothing comparable to place next to these great works."[67] By reaching back into the "cultural inheritance," as one would say in the GDR, one could only partially conceal the dilemma that there was generally a lack of significant National Socialist contemporary art. On the walls of the museums there were no more "degenerate" works by Picasso, Beckmann, Chagall, Liebermann, Klee, Kokoschka, Kirchner, Nolde, and Kandinsky. And Ziegler, Padua, Bühler, Willrich, Kampf, Eber, and Kriegel had a difficult time convincing one to forget the losses. The report which Reinhard Piper gave in a letter to Ernst Barlach about the Great German Art Exhibit in 1937 is significant:

> In reference to the exhibit in the House of German Art, I viewed it with best intentions in order to joyously welcome everything there

that is truly valuable. However, one cannot even really say that a significant exhibit of outstanding German art was assembled here, or that something was presented here which had not been seen for twenty years at every art exhibit and which was accordingly criticized. It seems that one is visiting an exhibit which had been already shown annually in the Glass Palace. Three-quarters of the paintings are industrious and nice, but are of no artistic consequence. They are created by the dime-a-dozen talents who have always existed. One would not need to liberate them.[68]

The attempt to replace the traditional "bourgeois" theater with something distinctive also failed miserably. It was easier to construct the "festival arenas" intended for the new plays than to write the necessary plays to be performed in them. The new operas also proved to be unsuitable, which Goebbels had to admit in 1937 at a cultural-political press conference.[69]

In general, one had to be satisfied with a mixture of traditional works and contemporary emptiness. On January 30, 1937, Germans were legally prohibited from accepting the Nobel Prize, and instead a German National Prize for Art and Science was established. This, in particular, was an expression of a defiant will of self-preservation within an increasingly international isolation. However, the more intelligent men of the regime could not really be satisfied with Martin Bormann's formula for a cultural policy where one would need only an "honest heart" and the "healthy understanding of an old Nazi." However, many honest but also insignificant artists who committed themselves to nationalist ideals identified with such an attitude, which declared their own limited horizon to be a generally acceptable one.

The reactionary, fundamental current against everything new in art, which had already existed since the beginning of the century, and the artists who supported this won out. For several years, they were able to triumph and rule the official exhibition market. This did not change the fact that they were mediocre, and therefore, after 1945, nothing remained of them, when the free forces that were condemned by Hitler were reinstated.

In 1911, the most famous of the reactionary writings, "A Protest from German Artists," appeared. The landscape painter Carl Vinnen created it. Vinnen originally belonged to the artists' colony of Worpswede, and in 1903 he moved to Munich. In the following years, he became increasingly convinced that his lack of success was due to manipulations in the art market. The impetus for his protest was the acquisition of a van Gogh by the Kunsthalle in Bremen. The first sentence in his pamphlet is:

In view of the great invasion of French art which has been taking place for several years in so-called progressive German art circles, it seems to me necessary that German artists voice a warning and that they do not retreat in front of the objection that they are motivated only by jealousy.[70]

Due to the "French flood," millions are lost annually for "national art." It is our goal "to recapture a place in the sun for our art ideally and materially."[71]

One hundred eighteen artists supported Vinnen's protest. By far the largest contingent, with fifty three signatures, came from Munich. The best-known signatories were Th. Th. Heine, Friedrich August von Kaulbach, Carl von Marr, Adolf Oberländer, Leo Samberger, Paul Schultze-Naumburg, Franz von Stuck, and Wilhelm Trüber. Heinrich von Zügel, an insignificant genre painter who painted portraits, especially of housepets, and who was a professor at the Academy was another participant. In the above-cited essay, Oldenbourg regarded him as the leader of a specific Munich movement of Impressionism, which was positively received. In 1937, Zügel was represented with four works at a Great German Art Exhibit (Große Deutsche Kunstausstellung). In 1940, for his ninetieth birthday, he was given the Goethe Medallion for extraordinary service. Today Zügel ranks among the highest-paid painters of the so-called Munich school.

I cannot and I do not want to comment here on the numerous appeals and explanations of reactionary and nationalistic circles, which of course increased particularly after the power grab. Only one still needs to be mentioned, i.e., "The Protest of the Richard Wagner City of Munich" of April 16, 1933. The occasion was Thomas Mann's commemorative speech on Wagner, and the protest was against "Mr. Mann, who, unfortunately, lost his earlier nationalistic ideology during the establishment of the republic and exchanged it for a cosmopolitan-democratic attitude."[72] The entire Academy of the Fine Arts was represented in the list of signatures: its president, German Bestelmeyer, professors Bernhard Bleeker, Max Doerner, Hermann Groeber, Olaf Gulbransson, Hermann Hahn, Julius Heß, Angelo Jank, Franz Klemmer, Carl von Marr, Karl Miller, and Adolf Schinnerer—the same gentlemen whom we will later find in the Great German Art Exhibit. Only one was missing, a fact for which he would dearly pay—the most significant representative of Christian-inspired art, Karl Caspar. In 1922, against bitter opposition from the members of the Academy, he succeeded Heinrich von Zügel. He was the only one who refused to sign the petition. In 1937, he was the only Munich painter whose pictures were exhibited not at the Haus der Deutschen Kunst (House of German Art) but a few hundred meters further north, in the "Degenerate Art" exhibit (Entartete Kunst). In the same year he was also forced to apply for an early retirement. Fearing for his life, he left Munich and retreated to the countryside.[73]

This is the same Academy of Fine Arts that signed the "Protest of the Richard Wagner City of Munich." Included among the signatories were Lord Mayor Fiehler, the general director of the Bavarian State Theater; Clemens Franckenstein, the director of the Musical Academy; the State Opera director Hans Knappertsbusch; Hans Pfitzner, who was appointed to the Academy of Musical Arts in 1930; Richard Strauss; and others. This Academy had nothing better to do in 1933 than to honor Adolf Hitler, who "rectified the situation so that the national ideology would again be the focal point of intellectual life and the guiding light for artists and who redirected anew, with his foresight, art to its own task, to be the language of the people."[74]

I hope it has become clear that Munich, not unjustly, had a special importance in the strategic considerations of the Nazis. Of course, in other places there were also opportunistic and enthusiastic Nazis—who would like to judge which is worse—but Munich was the place where reactionary traditions, National Socialist commitment, bourgeois opportunism, and the mobilization of dull antimodern resentments culminated in a special fashion. Unfortunately, Adolf Dreßler was probably right when he wrote in 1937: "The life of Munich was not determined by mind but by feelings; and, therefore, Munich became the best fertile ground for a movement which, first of all, addressed the feeling and then the belief."[75]

JÖRG WOLLENBERG

The Expropriation of the "Rapacious" Capital by "Productive" Capital

The City of Nuremberg as an Example of Aryanization

FROM DISCRIMINATION THROUGH THE PROFESSIONAL BAN TO THE
DEJUDAIZATION OF THE GERMAN ECONOMY

> When one deals with something so morally low as a collective ha-
> tred, the healing characteristic of a "liberating" murder gets along
> very well with the healing characteristic of a "liberating" robbery. It
> is not simply the case that the money taken away from the Jews
> does not stink, it is also "liberated" money which in the purse of
> the robber—may it be the state or whoever—so to say, is being lib-
> erated from the power of evil.[1]

This description by H. G. Adler explains the process of the National
Socialist "dejudaization" and extermination policies which the former
Jewish concentration camp inmate from Theresienstadt documented
and analyzed in his work.

Next to Raul Hilberg's monumental work on the entire history of
the Holocaust,[2] Adler's indefatigable research remains unsurpassed up
to now. The collective hatred described by H. G. Adler served as the
foundation for and the realization of the largest expropriation campaign in German history, the removal of Jews from all positions in
economic life. In the jargon of the Nazis, this process was called the
"Dejudaization of the German economy." With the Nuremberg Laws
of 1935, the term "Aryanization" became familiar, which, according to
Genschel, at first described in a most specific sense the transfer of
ownership of a Jewish enterprise into "Aryan" hands. However, as
late as 1938 it meant the removal of every Jewish influence in the

118

economy through the Aryanization of all firms, associations, real estate, and whole branches of the economy.[3] According to National Socialist ideology, Jews did not belong to the German "nation." After the passage of the Nuremberg Laws, Jews were therefore formally and "legally" excluded from the "national community." Thus Jews had no right to "national property." Their property and their assets were viewed as fraudulent, "gathered up," and "rapacious" capital that had to be returned to the nation or to "fellow countrymen" as the rightful owners. This process, which was accompanied during the Nazi period by 430 decrees and ordinances for forced transfer of the "rapacious" capital to "productive" capital, i.e., the transfer of Jewish property to the Aryans, occurred in two phases with a total of 170 "special rights" for Jews in questions regarding the economy:[4]

1. The so-called voluntary Aryanizations from January 1933 till November 1938. These were the situations where the Jewish "sellers" turned over, in some cases under great pressure and boycotts, their ownership to German buyers through "voluntary" contracts. The Jews were then forced to emigrate.
2. The so-called forced Aryanization, i.e., those transfers, based on official decrees, which took place after the Jewish pogrom of November 1938 in which the Jews were forced to sell their property. The Decree for the Elimination of the Jews from German Economic Life of November 12, 1938 stipulated, in regard to this:

¶1

As of January 1, 1939, Jews are prohibited from operating stores, delivery businesses, or mail order businesses, as well as from carrying out a trade. Furthermore, effective on the same day, they are prohibited from offering goods or services, from advertising, or from taking orders at markets of any kind, fairs, or exhibits.

Jewish enterprises which, in spite of this ban, continue to operate are to be closed by the police.

From January 1, 1939 on, a Jew is not allowed to work as a manager, according to the Law for the Order of National Labor.

If a Jew is in a managerial position of an enterprise, he can be fired with a six-week notice. With the firing, all claims are terminated.

The process of the exclusion of the Jews and Aryanization resulted in the Aryan portion of the economy absorbing most of the Jewish enterprises. The Aryan sector also profited from the significant number of forced liquidations. Even today, we do not have the sum total of the extent of these profits; it is only certain that the purchaser of a Jewish enterprise had to pay at most 75 percent and often less than 50 percent of its value. As a rule, the German opportunists of Jewish liquidation had to invest little or nothing at all. The gain for the economic sector, therefore, certainly amounted to many million Reichsmarks (RM). The minister responsible for the four-year plan, Hermann Göring, and the Reich's government acquired a large portion of the Jewish property. They brought in cash and other liquid assets which the Jews received for the purchase of the companies during the Aryanization process. The Financial Ministry collected this money through two types of property taxes: the Reich's Escape Tax, which was collected in 1931 for the first time and which was strengthened by the decree of April 26, 1938, whereby all Jews living in Germany were requested to "report" their assets of more than five thousand RM in Germany and abroad. That, at the same time, was one of the most effective measures in preparation for the upcoming Aryanization process. The Jews were hit with a second property tax, a required "atonement," which was announced on November 12, 1938, by Göring as the "atonement" for the murder of the Foreign Ministry consul vom Rath in Paris for which the Jews were blamed. Twenty percent of reported income was payable in four installments between December 15, 1938, and August 15, 1939.

The two taxes amounted to a total sum of 2 billion RM. This was the largest profit which the Third Reich made during the entire European war of annihilation. Hermann Göring's Pogrom Decree which was enacted on November 12, 1938, aimed in toto to eliminate "the Jews from German economic life" once and for all, to burden them with a contribution of 1 million RM to the German Reich, and to fine them through the Decree for Restoration of the Appearance of the Streets for the rectification of all the damage that occurred between November 8 and 10, 1938. In addition, the insurance claims by Jews who were German citizens were acquired by the German Reich.

"The Forced Dejudaization of the Industrial Enterprises and Their Respective Property and Living Spaces," which was combined with the above decrees, turned out to be an expropriation. The "dejudaization profit" made during the forced sale had to be reported to the authorities and was heavily taxed. The proceeds which the Jews received for the Aryanized property after 1938 were in many cases not sufficient to pay for the property taxes. In addition, there was a restriction against taking any money abroad. Since many Jews were now so impoverished that they could not even finance their emigration, they hardly had a chance to avoid the oncoming systematic process of annihilation.

In January 1933, about one hundred thousand enterprises in the

German Reich were owned by Jews: among them, besides the private banks, department stores, and enterprises, were doctors' and lawyers' offices, handicraft shops, and some retail stores. After the enforcement of the boycott, only 39,523 Jewish enterprises remained in April of 1938. Thus almost 60 percent were already Aryanized or liquidated before the Jewish pogrom. This was also true in the city of Nuremberg.[5]

As the boycott activities of April 1, 1933, affected small retail stores, the displacement measures after an "illusion of respite" (Barkai) from 1934 to 1937 targeted larger enterprises. The owners who waited and hesitated too long were robbed after November 1938—during the "final burst" in the race for Jewish enterprises—and were fortunate to escape with their lives, after "protective custody" and the concentration camp. Basically, the distinguished and well-bred Aryan managers of large firms did not act any differently than the lesser middle-class Nazis. When they "gathered up" Jewish property for themselves, they were, in the final analysis, not very prim in the selection of their methods. They simply attempted not to dirty their own hands too much. So, for example, the purchaser Georg Karg began his successful career as the owner of the Hertie department store by acquiring the Jewish property from Hermann Tietz, which had already been Aryanized in 1933 by a consortium of banks. Helmut Horten, who was Leonhard Tietz's apprentice and later became a buyer, "bought" the Alsberg Jewish department store in the city of Duisburg in 1936 with the help of banks. He later expanded his department-store empire with a takeover of Schocken. Josef Neckermann started his career with the Aryanization of the Carl Joel department store in Nuremberg.[6] And Friedrich Flick, who waited too long to purchase the Simson factory, was "compensated" during the Aryanization of the Petschek Enterprises in the Sudetenland with a profit of $9 million.[7]

Many Jewish businessmen, physicians, lawyers, and managers who were affected by the professional ban and the "Aryanization race" had to survive as beggars. Only a few were able to leave Germany in time.[8]

The impoverishment of German Jewry led through the "exclusion of Jews from the economy," to unemployment, forced labor, and deportation to concentration and extermination camps. At the beginning of 1933 about 525,000 Jews lived in Germany; in May 1939, 214,000 remained. Only thirty-four thousand of them had jobs. The largest number of Jews lived in large cities, almost a third of them in Berlin. Before 1933, more than 60 percent of all Jewish employees worked in the trade and transportation industry. The proportion of self-employed Jews, at 46 percent, was also clearly higher than that of the total population (16 percent). The Jewish concentration in particular lines of business always supported anti-Semitic propaganda, which made the small Jewish population appear all-powerful. So, for example, about 11 percent of all practicing physicians were Jews, as were 16 percent of all self-employed lawyers.[9] Other segments with disproportionately high Jewish participation were the cattle trade, the clothing and shoe industry, several branches of the metal trade, and the department stores. As a whole, Jewish influence was restricted to a few noticeable or crisis prone branches of the economy.

The Jews were strongly represented in occupations left open to them by the "holes and cleavages of the medieval order." In his memoirs, the Jewish sociologist Franz Oppenheimer commented on this issue:

> There is no doubt that the Jews, in relation to their number, participated strikingly strongly in the development of German capitalism and its auxiliary trades, namely also the press. But one should also accept the fact that in former times they were pushed into positions as businessmen and bankers almost by force, because they were not only blocked from the offices appointed by the state: the civil service in the army and the administration, the judicial branch, teaching positions in schools and universities, etc., but also from the trades. As Sombart correctly interpreted, they were only able to place themselves in the holes and cleavages of the medieval order; here they learned new methods, and they learned them more quickly and thoroughly than others because they were not hindered by any traditions: the sociologist calls this a "pioneer psychology."[10]

"FRANKS FORWARD": THE DEJUDAIZATION POLICY AND THE ARYANIZATION SCANDAL IN NUREMBERG

> Nuremberg is one of the few cities which served as a model for a radical solution of the Jewish question. Not only was this "Treasure of the Holy Roman Empire within the German Nation" ... able to expel the Jews from its walls in 1499, but it has remained free of Jews for almost four hundred years.

So begins the 539-page publication by Richard Wilhelm Stock, *The Jewish Question through Five Centuries*, which appeared at the beginning of 1939 from the Stürmer Publishing House. Stock continues to describe the process of the persecution and annihilation of the Jews in Nuremberg, which was unique in history:

> And as Nuremberg's solution to the Jewish question served as a model for the whole nation at the beginning of modern times, so may Nuremberg also pride itself today on having carried the storm banner in the final struggle of the German nation against the Jews

according to the old motto "Franks forward." Therefore, the laws of the Führer for the Protection and the Purity of the German Blood justifiably carry the name "Nuremberg Laws."

Indeed, the Franks acted in an exemplary manner. Julius Streicher and his many aides, who had connections to Deputy District Leader Karl Holz, Lord Mayor Liebel, and Police President and Gestapo Chief Benno Martin guaranteed this. In August 1923, Streicher founded the *Stürmer*, which became the embodiment of National Socialist anti-Semitism. The Nuremberg elementary school teacher, who was dismissed from his position in 1924, littered the "National Community" every week with five hundred thousand copies of his paper which called itself "the German weekly in the struggle for truth" with the constantly repeated motto: "The Jews are our Misfortune." Whoever did not want to touch the *Stürmer*, ran across this pornographic anti-Semitism in numerous show cases located in the cities and the countryside from 1933 on. One can also blame the fanatical self-chosen "leader of the Franks" for the fact that even before 1933, there was a massive agitation against the Jews in the city of Nuremberg. Additionally, after 1933, there were numerous boycotts of Jewish stores. The Nurembergers of Jewish faith were exposed early on to the psychological terror of discrimination and occupational bans, so that the central Franconia area was one of the worst districts in Germany for the Jews.[11]

In August of 1938, three months before the organized November pogrom, Streicher instigated the destruction of the main synagogue of the Israelite cultural community, which was constructed in the Moorish style and located on Hans Sachs Square. On August 10, 1938, in front of one hundred thousand Nuremberg citizens, the Nazi district leader (Streicher) gave a "directive speech:"

There will be a time when the Jewish question will be radically solved in the whole world because humanity cannot find any other way. Today we are destroying a synagogue here, and it will never again be rebuilt. In this city we want to vigilantly ensure that German blood and German soul remain pure because, if the Jew gains power once again in Germany, then the German nation is doomed forever. We are living in a great period. The seed which we have sowed is rising. The dice have fallen. The time of the Jews is over forever. You workers of the city of Nuremberg who were once slaves of the Jews and who now are joyfully assisting in the construction of the new Reich of Adolf Hitler, I am now giving you a historical order: Begin![12]

In Nuremberg, the night of the pogrom was especially brutal. Of the 111 Jews in Germany murdered during that night, eleven were from Nuremberg. Ten committed suicide as a result of this event. The Nazi Lord Mayor Liebel "reported" to the city council that there were twenty-six Jewish victims during the pogrom night. The Nurembergers, like many other Germans, did not want to know of the final results of this episode of progressive lawlessness. Those people who especially gained from the Aryanization process concealed the steps which led to the pogrom, namely, the numerous decrees and boycotts which prevented Jews from living ordinary lives in public and professional positions. It becomes clear from this information as to why the expulsion of Jews from cultural life and the economy in Franconia took place so early. Of the 120 Jewish physicians who practiced in 1930, only sixty were left in the city of Nuremberg in 1938. And while on June 16, 1933, 7,506 Jews or 1.8 percent of the 410,300 inhabitants resided in Nuremberg, at the end of 1939 only 2,628 Jews were left. Of the Jews who were still living in Nuremberg in 1941, 1,631 were deported to Theresienstadt and to Auschwitz. Only seventy-two Nuremberg Jews survived the Holocaust. And in spite of this, in 1935, 21 percent of. registered firms were supposedly owned by Jews in Nuremberg.[13] These numbers need to be investigated provided that the exact number of the Jewish enterprises before 1933 can be determined. Schneider and Müller estimated Jewish participation in Nuremberg economic life in 1930 without considering the size of individual firms and their market share.[14] A comparison of those branches where the Jewish composition was a least 10 percent in 1930, netted the following results: 583 of the 2,374 enterprises in Nuremberg were owned by Jews. According to the restitution documents, 230 of the 583 firms were Aryanized. Records concerning the other 350 firms and their "Aryanization profiteers" were missing. Other documents from the local government and the Industrial and Trade Chamber were burned shortly before the end of the war or else were destroyed by bombs. Since the remainder of the existing records were distributed among the numerous offices and archives after 1945 and even today have only been partially analyzed, the complex context of the Aryanization in Nuremberg, as well as in the whole German Reich, cannot be precisely evaluated. One can understand why German companies did not use the fiftieth anniversaries of their founding as a pretense for finally opening up their company archives to allow for the investigation of and reporting on the dejudaization and the Aryanization of Jewish enterprises.[15]

Several industries that Jews once dominated in Nuremberg were later Aryanized and eventually lost their significance. The trade in hops, for example, was almost exclusively in Jewish hands and was concentrated in Nuremberg. The city was the distribution center for overseas export as well as the storage center for German and Bohemian hops. In 1895 there were 364 hops trading companies, but by 1930 only 99 of the total of 141 were in Jewish hands. The most significant and internationally known representatives were Ludwig Gerngros and Berthold Bing. The friend and sponsor of the inventor of the Diesel engine was also a member of the Bing family,[16] which developed modern production facilities for the metallurgical industry (Bing Brothers' Nuremberg Metal Factory) on Blumen Street and in Gleishammer.

One cannot examine the internationally significant bicycle industry in Nuremberg which was co-developed by Jews, without considering Karl Marschütz, a jew who until 1938 owned Hercules Enterprises, or Frankenburger and Ottenstein, who took over Victoria Enterprises in 1895. The numerous retail shops and department stores were also important. We shall list their share and that of other enterprises from Nuremberg's economic life in the following list of twelve branches of business in 1930 as a remembrance of the Aryanization which was later intentionally forgotten, although it was so publicly executed:[17]

The Jewish Share in Nuremberg's Economic Life around 1930

1. *Banks*:
   Of thirty-five banks, twelve were in Jewish hands, among them the Anton Kohn Bank, on Lorenz Square, the largest private bank in Bavaria.

   In addition: Hopf & Co., A. H. Meyer, Max Spaeth, Oskar Marcus, Louis Schwab.

2. *Motorcycle and Bicycle Factories*:
   Of forty-five enterprises, six were in Jewish hands, among them the Mars-plant (Jacobowitz), which also produced machines for making tools
   Hercules-plant (Marschütz)
   Triumph-plant (Adelung-Riegelmann)
   Victoria-plant (Ottenstein)
   Ardi-plant (Bendit)
   Heilo (Heilbrunn)
   Triumph-plant, in addition, began to produce typewriters in 1909.

3. *Iron, Steel, and Metal Goods*:
   Eleven out of ninety-three enterprises; among them: S. Guldmann, Adolf Rosenfelder, successors of Sämann Brothers (the Nuremberg Bolt Factory), Leo Reichsthaler, the Bing Brothers' Nuremberg Metal Goods Factory

4. *Hops Businesses*:
   Ninety-nine of 141 Nuremberg enterprises were owned by Jews, among them L. Gerngros-Frauenfeld, A. Bamberger, Bernhard Bing, J. Dessauer, S. Kohnstamm, Hermann Lust, Hermann Strauss, S. Silbermann, Brothers Tuchmann, A. Ullmann & Co., S. Weil & Sons, Hermann Rosenzweig, Anton Prager

5. *Department Stores*:
   Five of ten department stores were owned by Jews: Hermann Gerson, Moritz Schmuckler, Schocken Department Store, the Strauss House of Goods, Hermann Tietz & Co. (White Tower Department Store, known today as Wöhrl).

6. *Mail Order Stores*:
   Two of eleven were in Jewish possession: Karl Joel (taken over by Neckermann) and Ignatz Meier

7. *Toys*:
   Twenty of 273 Nuremberg stores were owned by Jews, among them: Adolf Aal, C. Abel-Klinger (Thurnauer), Bing-plant, Johann Distler (Braun/Meyer), Kuno & Otto Dressel (Ullmann), J. G. Drossel (Strauss), Josef Falk, J. Fischer & Co. (Adelsberger), Georg Herz, Josef Krauss & Co., Georg Künast (Schwab), Theodor Lebrecht, Georg Levy, Max Moschkowitz, Leo Prager, Tipp & Co. (Ullmann), Eugen Reis, Schuko, Trix Toys

8. *Manufactured Goods*:
   Seventeen of twenty-six stores were Jewish; among them: L. Goldbaum, Max Jacoby, W. B. Schloss, Oppenheimer & Friedmann, Moritz Salomon

9. *Textiles*:
   Eighteen of sixty-two stores were owned by Jews; among them: Isaak Berger, Kalman Berliner, M. Edelstein, J. Gerngross & Co., Kellermann & Co., Joachim Landmann, Adolf Stein, Moses Steinhaus, Samson Wilmersdörfer

10. *Clothing Factories*:
    Seven of thirteen enterprises; among them: J. Abraham, Leopold Rosenfeld & Co., Stein & Co.

11. *Radio Transmitters*:
    Two of thirty-five enterprises: Leo Reichsthaler and the Nuremberg Bolt Factory & Custom Lathes (Saemann)

12. *Ornaments and Trinkets*:
    Thirty-four of 127 stores were in Jewish possession; among them: Adler & Ullmann, Friedmann & Co., J. Gutmann & Co.

Other important Nuremberg enterprises that were owned by Jews were the Camelia works, which belonged to the United Paper Factories of the Rosenfelder family and were "taken over" by Gustav Schickendanz, the Quelle boss after the Rosenfelders' immigration to England. In addition, the Cromwell AG leather works, which were "taken over" on November 3, 1938, for a small fee by Paul Harnishmacher and Dr. Pfähler, who afterwards gave 22,500 RM to Strobl, the district economic consultant.[18] Also, the Noris Wine Distillery, the Medicus-Shoe Factory, and several others.

As previously mentioned, highly esteemed retail stores of the textile industry were also outfitters for ladies and gentlemen including Marmorecke (J. Langstadt), Adolf Stock (today Fischer & Co.), the Manes Brothers (today Sundermann), Aufhäuser & Co., and Heinrich Prager. Even today the following names of firms are well regarded in Nuremberg: Max Goldberg, Robert Guggenheimer, Schloß AG, W. B. Schloß, Jakob Goldberger, D. M. Katzenberger, Weinstock, Paul Baruch, Josef Levinger, Hugo Gutmann, Berliner, Wilmersdörfer, Feuchtwanger and Schloßberger, Walter Lessing, and many others.

Some of these Nuremberg enterprises were Aryanized "voluntarily" before 1938. The large department store owners, such as Hermann Tietz & Co.—known in Nuremberg as the White Tower Department Store (KWT) since 1934—gave up their property rights after the power grab more or less voluntarily. The department stores were Aryanized for the time being, on behalf of a consortium of banks. Salmon Schocken gave up only after the Christmas boycott of 1937 before emigrating with his sons. The national Nazi media kept silent about the Christmas boycott of 1937, which was organized by the Nazi regional command without first communicating with the Reich's leadership. It was announced, however, in the Nuremberg dailies and on advertisement pillars. In contrast, the foreign media reported thoroughly on Streicher's private campaign against Jewish stores and warehouses in Nuremberg. For example, the "Germany Reports" of the Social Democratic party in Exile (SOPADE) commented extensively:

> The largest single local event in Nuremberg in the last month was the Christmas boycott. Two-meter-high red posters were placed in front of all the Jewish stores. The posters reflected the call by Streicher, . . . : "No German purchases in Jewish stores!" At the same time, civilian sentries arrived in front of all the Jewish stores in order to keep a watch at the stores' entrances so that it was impossible to enter them. . . . The next Sunday, "Silver Sunday," the Jewish stores, just like the Aryan ones, had to be open for business. The employees had to enter the stores. Only the customers were not allowed to enter. . . . The police did not get involved. . . . The above-mentioned red posters were also placed in front of the Schocken

department store for the first few days, but were replaced after eight days by others. This replacement took place for the following reason: Schocken, which was previously predominantly a Jewish firm, had been transformed some time ago into a corporation, and it is said that much English capital was invested in this firm. . . . These mitigating circumstances, however, manifested themselves so that instead of the standard red boycott poster, another poster was placed at the Schocken department store, which had approximately the following text: "64 percent of the stocks of the Schocken firm are in English hands, the remainder are in Jewish possession. Therefore we are fighting against this Jewish business!"[19]

The Franconian retail business community greeted the well-prepared boycott with a thank you address to Streicher, the regional administrator, and an appeal for donations for his fifty-third birthday: "We honestly admit that this boycott . . . has brought us small retailers business advantages as well." This was written in a proclamation of the Nuremberg-Fürth Retailers Association which was published in January 1938 and signed by Friedrich Maier of 29 Harmonie Street.[20]

Successfully—and as a rule, without coordination with Berlin—the regional Nazi leadership practiced illegal denunciations of customers, supervision of customers, and blockades of Jewish shops and department stores, time and again after the official boycott of April 1, 1933, from March/April of 1934 on. This policy of "creeping" displacement of Jews from the Nuremberg economy was fully supported by the Fighting Association of the Business Middle Class, which continued to perfect a method recommended by the Jewish Council of the SS in Franconia in order to motivate the Jewish owners to "voluntarily" give up their businesses. The "unrolling of the Jewish question from below" through the mobilization of the "people's anger" organized from above could be skillfully channeled for one's own interests through such anti-Jewish boycott actions. After the early "sale" by the department store owners Hermann Tietz (known today as the Hertie Department Store) and Leonard Tietz (known today as the Kaufhof Stockholding Company), the boycott measures of the years 1933 and 1934 quickly forced numerous Nuremberg firms which were owned by Jews into a "voluntary" retreat before the "official" forced Aryanization; among others were the wholesale suppliers of office machines and office furniture Hugo Gutmann and Josef Levinger. The oldest galvanized coal factory, owned by Dr. Walter Lessing, previously valued by the Berlin Nazi authorities at 1,400,000 RM, was sold for 500,000 RM to Murchi, the police president of Nuremberg at that time.[21] And one of the best-known Nuremberg textile stores, the Marblecorner (Marmorecke) at

Josef Square, was "sold" for about 250,000 RM by owner Julius Langstadt on January 14, 1938, after tremendous pressure and imprisonment by the Gestapo, although the Nazis even valued the store at least at 700,000 RM. The compensation received for the forced sales, furthermore, was placed into a restricted account, and was not, or at most only to a small extent, at the disposal of the "seller."[22]

From the announcements in the Nuremberg dailies, one can see the situation which existed immediately before the Jewish pogrom of November 1938 and before the start of the forced Aryanization in Nuremberg. Nuremberg appeared to be, even before the stricter public decrees of November 12, 1938, "free of Jews." From March until June of 1933 the announcements by Nuremberg firms which assured the public that they had been transferred into Aryan ownership multiplied: "The owner is now Aryan," "Oettinger & Co. is now an Aryan Enterprise," "The supervisory committee, management, and employees now consist of Aryan members," etc.[23]

The "Germany Reports" of the SOPADE of February 1938 give a clear impression of the increasing ghettoization of the Jews in Nuremberg. This ghettoization encompassed all areas of life and business relations and it forecast the completion of the dejudaization of Nuremberg:

> The campaign, "Jews off the main streets," refers to the business streets, especially König Street, the Karolinen Street, and Kaiser Street. It is probable that the Jewish businesses, which were especially disliked, will not be able to obtain a store at all: i.e., no one will give them permission to settle on another street, no home owner will rent them a store, and no craftsman will be willing to remodel their store. In any case, there are enough ways to get rid of the unloved Jews without drawing great attention. The media does not write anything about these things, but this is the atmosphere in which the employees of Jewish stores and the owners of Jewish enterprises live. One has to consider that although one deals with a small number of these stores, they are the largest and the most representative stores in the city. The majority of them are textile stores, i.e., clothing stores of every kind, trinket shops, department stores, etc.
>
> By 1933, the Jews in Nuremberg were prohibited from using bathing facilities, such as those in the river and the indoor baths. They were allowed to use only the municipal showers. In December of 1937, permission to use even these was retracted. Lord Mayor Liebel explained verbatim during a City Hall meeting: "One cannot expect any German to climb into a bathtub which was previously used by a Jew." . . . In January the trade chamber retracted membership cards from Jewish associates. The members of the retail association had until January 31 to sign a declaration in which they agreed not to

buy from Jewish firms and not to receive Jewish trade associates in the future. The owners of larger firms were summoned to the retail agents' association, where they were given corresponding oral instructions. For the time being, Jewish retail and wholesale trade are being boycotted; later Jewish industry will probably also get its turn. Schacht's resignation has accelerated this development; this is the general opinion.[24]

As in other large cities, the "Aryanization campaign" seriously began in Nuremberg with the systematic removal of Jews from the economic infrastructure on November 9–10 of 1938. The Jewish pogrom of 1938 can also be viewed in Nuremberg as a beginning, unparalleled in history, of the expropriation and expulsion of Jewish enterprises. In contrast to the developments in the Reich, however, this act of dejudaization was carried out here in an extremely brutal fashion. The National Socialist German Workers party and its agencies under the leadership of Streicher and Holz did not leave this "business" to the public agencies that were instructed by law to carry this out. Instead, they took the Aryanization process into their own hands so much that only an investigative commission, created by Göring, was able to stop the corrupt Nuremberg Aryanization process with its tremendous enrichment for the local Nazi leadership. The Regional Economic Council member and president of the Industrial Trade Chamber of Nuremberg, AEG [major electronics firm, Am. ed.] director Strobl was included in this Franconian "Aryanization Scandal." Except for the events in Austria, where "the night of the long fingers" and the private robbery campaigns began right after the "Anschluß" to Germany in March of 1938, there was no known Aryanization action carried out with similarly illegal methods and to such an extent as the one in the cities of Nuremberg and Fürth.[25]

What happened? Numerous dignitaries of the National Socialist German Workers party did not agree with the "solution" of the Aryanization problem because so far the "middle class" and "little chauffeurs of the district administrators" had been passed over. In the district of Franconia the party decided to carry out its own economic solution. Assuming that no time should be wasted, the party offices of regional leader Streicher started their work on the eve of the November decrees. One by one, Jews were ordered to the German Workers Front in Essenwein Street, where they were forced to sign a paper transferring their business, home, or property to the district or to some recipient who was held worthy. For a total of 100 RM the City of Fürth obtained from its Jewish community property valued at 100,000 RM. One private person took over a property valued at 200,000 RM for 180 RM. One Jew after another reported to the place, and one document after another was signed. The Nazis kept a written record of this Aryanization campaign, and they later "reconstructed it" so that numerous affected Jews could report on the events one more time under oath to the Göring Commission in January/February of 1939.[26] One of the these Jews, businessman Fritz Friedmann, stated among other things on January 27, 1939:

> Friedmann Fritz, businessman, born on June 11, 1883, married, two children, racial and avowed Jew, residence in Nuremberg, Wodan Street No. 76/II, is making the following statement:
> During the registration of my property in April, I quoted my property, located at No. 15 Luitpold Street, at 200,000 RM. I had bought this property in 1921 for the price of about 1.2 million Papermarks . . . my firm, the Fritz Friedmann South German Laundry Factory, was located in this house. . . . On November 11, 1938, I was picked up from my apartment by car by two SA people. I was brought to the Workers Front building on Essenwein Street and was led immediately to the office of a certain Mr. Schätzler, who told me: "You have the house at No. 15 Luitpold Street, sign now that you are giving it up for 100,000 RM." . . . I refused. . . . I was laid over a chair and another Jew had to beat me. . . . Then I had to beat another Jew in the same fashion. . . . After I refused the sale again, I was led to a dark room. . . . At 9:30 P.M. I was led to Mr. Schätzler one more time. . . . I was so exhausted and broken, I then signed under the weight of the circumstances. . . . Shortly after midnight I was dismissed. . . . According to the note of December 27, 1938, Deputy Regional Administrator Holz took over my house.[27]

During these transactions problems soon cropped up because several court officials refused to register their transactions in the real estate registry, a step necessary for the "legal blessing" of the transaction. One of the judges, District Court Counsel Leis, from Fürth, even wanted to record these details of the questionable transactions. Additionally, several justice officials insisted on recording District Administrator Streicher as the purchaser of the property transferred to the district, because the district did not represent a person in a judicial sense. Party officials, however, decided to keep the name of the district official out of these affairs and instead offered the name of Deputy District Administrator Holz as the "trustee." State Secretary Schlegelberger from the Justice Ministry had no objection to this procedure. On the other hand, Nuremberg's main public prosecutor, Joël, became more and more concerned. On February 15, 1939, he presented a critical report which attempted to justify the district government's actions, in spite of judicial objections, because "the district of Franconia has distinguished itself, particularly in regard to the Jewish question, and, therefore, it should retain special rights as well. The district is also justified in obtaining special assets because of its duties in preparing the city for the Reich's Party Days and due to the fact that it is weaker in comparison to other districts and was especially badly plundered by the Jews."[28]

Such an understanding led, during the forced Aryanization of properties, houses, furniture pieces, pianos, and motor vehicles, to a decree issued immediately by the district government, as it stated, "after the protest action of November 9–10 of 1938" and from which we cite the most important passages:

> Immediately after the protest action a commission was formed under the leadership of Deputy District Administrator Holz, in which SA officer Hutzler of the district administration, SS officer Ritter, and real estate agent Pessler had leadership roles. The purpose of this commission was the *transfer of Jewish property into Aryan hands.* The process of Aryanization is as follows:
> The Jewish home owner or his wife shall be summoned to appear at the German Workers Front Office (DAF). In case of refusal, they shall be brought in by SA men, later by police officers....
> The police officers were instructed to consider their mission complete when they brought the Jews to the offices of the DAF. The Jews who were brought in were placed in a cellar for several hours. To some extent, they also waited in special rooms for their summons. Then, they were presented with a notarized document. As far as anyone knows here, these documents were signed in every case. Accordingly, the Jew committed himself to sell his property to the regional government of Franconia at *10 percent of its unit value.* In some cases, the Jews were given only 5 percent of the unit value as the purchase price.... The same process as that which was employed with the properties is also to be carried out for several days with the *automobiles* that are owned by Jews.[29]

Holz supplemented these organizational measures and instructions for the purchase price of 10 percent of the unit value or the designated value of the Aryanized property with the explanation that Jews usually obtained their properties during the period of inflation at one-tenth of its true value—a claim which was not even accepted by the Göring Commission. In any case, numerous "old fighters" and district government collaborators finally acquired their "property" in this fashion. Fritz Herwerth, the chauffeur of the district administrator, obtained an NS-Fiat car listed at 2,750 RM for 100 RM. Liebscher, the chief editor of the *Franconian Daily,* "bought" a Wanderer car for 80 RM that had a resale value of 2,000 RM. The district official and district spokes-man Fritz Leikhein took possession of a Ford limousine for 150 RM (list price 5,785 RM). The closest collaborator of Chief of Staff König, Hans Roth, acquired a BMW for 200 RM which was listed for 5,548 RM. Harren, the district administration photographer, even acquired a Daimler-Benz for 100 RM when the list price was 9,600 RM. These cars were taken from wealthy Nuremberg Jews such as Louis Saemann, Franz Cohn, Paul Wohl, or Dr. Lessing and Albert Rosenfeld, who were arrested on November 10, 1938, and consequently transported to the Dachau concentration camp.[30]

Without a doubt, Hermann Göring also referred to these unbelieva-ble forced transactions of Jewish property when, at the well-prepared government conference of November 12, 1938, in the presence of top administrators of various departments such as Frick, Gürtner, Goebbels, Funk, Stuckart, Heydrich, Woermann, and Blessing, he urged the leg-islation of legal decrees to better prepare for the transformation from the persecution to the extermination of the Jews in Germany. How-ever, at the same time he wanted to bring about more "legal assur-ance" in light of the events in Franconia. In this connection, Göring stated at this government conference:

> It is humanly understandable that one is actively trying to bring party comrades into Jewish business. . . . I have seen terrible things in the past: that little chauffeurs of district administrators enrich them-selves to such an extent that, at the end, they brought into their possession half a million worth of property. Do these gentlemen know anything? . . . We have to insist that the Aryans who take over the business know something about the industry they are in.[31]

Let us sum up Göring's intervention one more time: once again, the Franks led the way, and in this case they went too far. In Nuremberg a primitive and radical anti-Semitism was propagated. This made the expropriation of the Jews by the district government of the National Socialist German Workers party possible. This should document Nu-remberg's key position during the dejudaization of Germany as part of the Aryanization process. Streicher intensified his "private campaign" against the Jews without the consent of the Reich's government through numerous boycotts from 1933 on and especially with the Christmas boycott of 1937 against Jewish stores. Here, an unbridled addiction for enrichment had been unmasked as the main force behind the anti-Semitism of those who thought of themselves as "the one on the short end of the stick" and who now wanted to be counted among those who made it. So, the chauffeurs, photographers, and other district government collaborators "helped themselves" to the limousines of

formerly wealthy yet now imprisoned Jews. In spite of occasional protests from the administrative apparatus and from segments of the judicial branch, the party authorities under the district administration
of Streicher and Holz had their way long enough that even the supreme party leadership and the Reich's government were fed up with
it. The "investigative commission" appointed by Göring stopped the
plundering activities in Nuremberg and Fürth, without, of course, rec-
tifying the injustice. As a whole, the report of the Göring Commission
for the period from November 9, 1938, to February 8, 1939, which was
to be investigated, concluded "that a confused legal situation exists in
Franconia which had been created by completely unlawful Aryanization
measures."[32] Furthermore, it stated:

> The Aryanization of Jewish enterprises came to a undoubted con-
> clusion in the district of Franconia on November 9, 1938. This is
> especially true for the more important Jewish enterprises. Accord-
> ing to the assessments in the time span from November 9, 1938, to
> February 8, 1939 . . . the government in Ansbach, in the region of
> Franconia, permitted seventy-two Aryanizations in the areas of in-
> dustry and wholesale trade. Of those, sixty-eight were small and
> middle-sized businesses and only four were larger enterprises.
> The three specifically named enterprises were investigated more
> closely because of suspicion of corruption (Magirus, Stern, Kromwell).
> Thirty-three businesses were investigated more closely by the man-
> aging director under the head treasurer of Nuremberg for the possi-
> bility of an Aryanization profit. . . . In the case of the thirty-three
> inspected businesses the Aryanization profit amounts altogether to
> 14,399,077 RM. From this, a reasonable percentage (in individual cases
> between 25 percent and 70 percent) in the best case is the gain of an
> amount of about ten million RM from the Aryanization tax.[33]

While also investigating eight hundred properties and houses which
were Aryanized, the commission calculated, that a profit of 21 million
RM was realized after resale. The investigative commission's dealings
with numerous special cases resulted in interesting information. In the
case of the Hercules Works the report states, among other things:

> The Jew Marschütz is the owner of the stocks of the Hercules Works
> firm in the total amount of 26,000 RM. The total capital of the com-
> pany amounts to 620,000 RM. According to the decree of the Reich's
> economic minister, the firm is to be viewed as non-Jewish. How-
> ever, according to the customary attitude in the district of Franconia,
> the firm, Hercules Works AG, was treated as a Jewish business. The
> district supervisor of the DAF, Emmert, demanded from the Jew
> Marschütz through Kramer that he deposit the stock package im-

mediately at the Bank of German Labor. The Jew Marschütz's objections were energetically rejected. Under pressure, the stock package was deposited on November 19, 1938, in the Bank of German Labor. It was planned that the stocks would be sold by the Bank of German Labor and that the net proceeds were to be credited to the restricted "Aryanizing Industry" account.[34]

An extensively treated "extreme case of Aryanization" from the point of view of the Göring Commission was that of the White Tower Department Store, formerly Hermann Tietz & Co. The owner, Theo Hartner, was considered an Aryan who married into the department store. His wife was a Jewess and part owner of the White Tower Department Store, as well as of the Strauss department store. Although the party leadership had no political concerns against the Aryan Hartner, the White Tower Department Store was constantly exposed to boycotting measures. Hartner believed that he could save his business from ruin by divorcing his wife, which ultimately caused her death. Yet the "Holz-Troop" still did not leave him in peace. In the Göring Commission's report, the case reads:

> The White Tower Department Store (KWT) has been boycotted for years through the instigation of the district government of Franconia. The owner of the KWT, Hartner, is an Aryan, his wife—who died in the meantime—was a Jewess. The boycott measures were explained through the claim that Hartner was a Jewish servant and that there was suspicion that the KWT worked with Jewish capital. The directives of the Reich's Economic Ministry which stated that the KWT should be viewed as an Aryan enterprise were completely irrelevant for the district government and also for Strobl. Hartner states believably that in several cases Strobl threatened him with the concentration camp if Hartner would not submit to all the wishes of the district government. Strobl declared that he participated in all the measures against Hartner because this was the wish of the district government, especially of the deputy district administrator, Holz, and because he himself viewed Hartner as an evil servant of the Jews. . . .
>
> In his efforts to keep his firm recognized as Aryan, Hartner also gave shares to Leissing, the head manager of the German Labor Front.
>
> In June 1938—during an appearance at the Trade Chamber—Hartner found out what the district government's conditions were, which upon fulfillment his business would finally be recognized. Accordingly, the following demands were made:
>
> 1. Proof that all parts of the business were indeed in his ownership.
> 2. Sale of the branch affiliate in Fürth.

3. The appointment of a supervisory council for the management of the business.
4. The summoning of a party member to the management itself.
5. Divorce from his non-Aryan wife.[35]

The Göring Commission worked for several months and its findings led to the irrevocable fall of District Administrator Streicher. Even Streicher's order to SA leader König, as a friend, collaborator, and the main incriminating witness of the district administrator, to commit suicide, which König indeed also carried out, did not save Streicher. The supreme party court sentenced him on February 13, 1940, as one "who is not suited for leadership over human beings."[36]

The police president and Gestapo chief, Benno Martin, allegedly played a role in the fall of Streicher, who had withdrawn to his estate and again edited the *Stürmer*, and of Holz, who volunteered for front-line action and returned only in 1942 as district administrator for Nuremberg. In spite of the documents presented by Grieser, I tend to believe now, as well as before, that Martin's claim was a retroactive justification for his actions, which was supposed to detract from his own responsibility.

THE SWORD OF THE MURDERER UNDER THE CLOAK OF THE JURIST: DEJUDAIZATION OF GERMANY IN THE NUREMBERG JURY HALL

The Nuremberg courthouse on Fürth Street with its Jury Hall No. 600 documents the close connection between the city of Nuremberg and National Socialism in a special way. The city of the Reich's Party Days, which also had to give its name to the racial laws in 1935, is, at the same time, the location of the Nuremberg trials. It is the place where an attempt had been made to clear up the war crimes of the National Socialists in front of a military tribunal and to sentence them in Jury Hall No. 600.

One of the most scandalous Nazi sentences, which led to the murder of Leo Katzenberger, preoccupied the judicial authorities in four additional postwar trials in front of the military tribunal, the regional court of Nuremberg, and the federal court in Karlsruhe.[38] What was it about? In Jury Hall No. 600 on March 13, 1942, at a public hearing of the Nuremberg court, Leo Katzenberger, the head of the Israelite cultural community in Nuremberg, was sentenced to death because of "racial disgrace." The alleged intimate relationship between the sixty-eight-year-old Katzenberger and a young Aryan photographer, Seiler, caused the court to pronounce the death sentence. The regional court director and the head of the special court, Oswald Rothaug, commented:

"It is enough for me that this swine said that a German girl was sitting on his lap." The offense of racial disgrace for which Katzenberger was accused fell under Paragraph 2 of the Law for the Protection of the German Blood and German Honor. The paragraph stated: "Extramarital relation between Jews and citizens of German or related blood is prohibited."

With this application of the Nuremberg Laws of 1935, we see an especially terrible case of solving the "Jewish question" by "legal means." Hans Globke, at that time the ministerial counsel in the Reich's Ministry of the Interior under Frick and later the state secretary in Adenauer's Chancellory, offered in 1935 an official interpretation which, with the judicial introduction of "alternative actions," made the Rothaug-sentences possible: "Relationship outside the marriage is only a sexual relationship. Under sexual relationships, one should not only place intercourse but also actions related to sexual intercourse, e.g., mutual masturbation."[39] With the Nuremberg Laws and their juridical interpretations, a new and decisive stage of discrimination began against Jews. The stages of the removal of civil rights, the boycott, the dejudaization of the German economy, and the persecution ended with extermination in the gas chambers of Auschwitz and Birkenau.

Ten years after the Nuremberg Laws, the city of the Reich's Party Days became the tribunal for the trial against the principle war criminals of the National Socialist system. In the main war-criminal trial from November 20, 1945, until October 1, 1946, in Jury Hall No. 600 of the Nuremberg court, the International Military Tribunal (IMT), composed of representatives from the victorious powers, sentenced the accused due to the conspiracy to spread and carry out war crimes and because of the perpetration of major crimes against humanity. The "leader of the Franks," Julius Streicher, was sentenced to death along with other responsible Nazi leaders such as Hermann Göring, Wilhelm Keitel, Hans Frank, Alfred Rosenberg, Fritz Sauckel, Joachim Ribbentrop, Wilhelm Frick, Arthur Seyß-Inquart, and Alfred Jodl. Streicher, the fanatical anti-Semite, was also incriminated by the documents which the Göring Commission gathered in 1939. Twelve more war-criminal trials against the elite of the German government, military, and industrial apparatus followed from 1946 until April 1949 under the sole responsibility of the United States (Nuremberg succession trials against 199 accused).

On December 3, 1947, the Nuremberg court issued a decision against especially zealous jurists. Among others, it sentenced Nuremberg special judge Rothaug to life in prison. It also characterized as a whole the "prostitution of a legal system which aimed toward the achievement of criminal goals . . . committed in the name of the law under the authority of the Justice Ministry and with the aid of courts," with the classic sentence: "The sword of the murderer was hidden under the cloak of the jurist."[40]

As part of a wave of pardons, Rothaug was released after nine years and applied to the Bavarian state government for a pension. When in 1968, after an eight-year inquiry by the Regional Court of Nuremberg, the co-accused members of the Nuremberg special court, Karl Ferber and Heinz Hugo Hoffmann, were sentenced as participants in the Katzenberger trial to three- and two-year prison sentences respectively. They appealed to Germany's supreme court (Bundesgerichtshof), which for the first time had to deal with the judges of racial disgrace. The supreme court upheld the appeal against the decision of the Nuremberg regional court in July of 1970 and opened the path for the sentencing of the accused from the Nuremberg district court in Jury Hall No. 600. This, of course, never materialized. The trial before the Fifth District of the regional court of Nuremberg was closed on August 20, 1976, because of the physical and psychological frailness of the accused. The expert witness, Professor Dr. Bodnik, determined that Hoffmann, the accused, suffered from an atrophy of the brain.[41]

Another heavily accused war criminal got away even more easily: Friedrich Flick, who, through gains from Aryanization, climbed to become the largest private businessmen in the Third Reich. Although he was sentenced to seven years in prison on December 22, 1947, as one of the principle accused persons in the Flick trial due to the exploitation of slave labor, the plundering of occupied territories, and the promotion of the SS, the profits that Friedrich Flick made from the Aryanization process were not debated, not even the most valuable possession which was ever Aryanized in the National Socialist system: the Ignaz-Petschek Group, which was located in the Sudetenland.[42] Friedrich Flick's highly developed sense of injustice made the repression of that guilt easier. In front of the court he declared: "No one from the large circle of those who know my co-defendants and me believes that we have committed crimes against humanity, and nothing will convince us that we are war criminals."[43]

In the "clemency fever of the fifties" (Robert M. W. Kempner) Flick, Krupp, and other sentenced war criminals and Aryanizers were soon released from the penitentiary—Flick, by the way, a week after German chancellor Adenauer petitioned formally in 1950 in front of the high commissars of the occupation powers for the formation of a West German army. The new armament business needed its old weapons makers and the assistance of conspirators. Should one be surprised then that other war-criminal trials which were prepared by Americans against the major profiteers of Aryanization never took place? For example, the financial department of the American military government, after intensive research into IG-Farben, the German Bank, and the Dresdner Bank, unanimously stated "that they represented an abnormal concentration of economic power and that they participated in carrying out the criminal policies of the Nazi regime in the economic area." It is so stated in the summary of those investigations that was finally published in 1985–86 by the Archives of National Socialist Politics in Hamburg by the Greno Publishing House and that contains a plethora of incriminating accusations and documents about the problems of Aryanization.[44]

After looking at those incriminating documents, American president Roosevelt wrote to Secretary of State Hull on September 8, 1944: "The history of the utilization of IG-Farben by the Nazis can be read like a detective story. After the defeat of the Nazi armies, the total destruction of these weapons of economic warfare must follow."[45] This would not be the case, however. Roosevelt's successor, Truman, soon initiated the Cold War, since its former opponents were well suited as allies. "The Cold Amnesty" made it easier for National Socialist perpetrators such as Krupp, Flick, and company to integrate into the new state. "The community of the wrongdoers dissipated without a trace into postwar society, where it did not act suspiciously, and, at the present time, is passing away peacefully. The National Socialist perpetrators did not hinder the building of democracy and a constitutional state. The greatest crime committed in history was concluded with the greatest resocialization project."[46]

"Himmler's man in Nuremberg," Dr. Benno Martin was also among the resocialized. He was an SS brigade commander, Gestapo chief, and Nuremberg police president, who became newly interpreted as a covert resistance fighter and supporter of the July 20th uprising.[47] Martin, who was among other things responsible for the transportation of Jews to the concentration camps at Flossenbürg and Langenzenn, was summoned several times to court but was set free again & again, the last time being July 1, 1953. After a four-year process, the judges of the district court at Nuremberg in Jury Hall No. 600 pronounced Benno Martin innocent of being responsible for the deportation of 4,754 Jews from the district of Franconia to the extermination camp at Auschwitz. At that time, Martin was known in Nuremberg, among many who should have actually known better, as one of those who participated in order to prevent worse things from happening. He promoted his own exoneration with a defense paper written in 1946, "My Struggle against Streicher," in which he also discussed the Aryanization scandal. The metropolitan chapter of the city of Bamberg supported this "turnaround" with a unanimous decision of June 20, 1951, when it asked the Bavarian president "for a complete pardon" of Martin.[48]

Such pointed integration of the Holocaust employees into the new constitutional state contributed to the repression of memories of the anti-Jewish measures in the National Socialist system. The restitution, which was long fought over and which was enacted by Adenauer against significant resistance from his own party members, gives the impression that the "special Nazi laws for the Jews" could be "reconciled." With this, however, a deeper understanding of the systematic destruction of European Jewry which led from these "special laws" to formally legalized mass murder was also lost. Former Deputy Chief Prosecutor Robert M. W. Kempner appropriately summarized this unique legalized process in the following terms:

> Their jobs were taken away, their possessions were stolen, they were not allowed to inherit or bequeath, they were not allowed to sit on park benches or keep a canary, they were not allowed in restaurants, movie theaters, or at concerts, special racial laws were valid for them, they were deprived of all civil rights, their freedom of movement was taken away, their human rights and their human dignity were trampled into the dust until they were deported to concentration camps and went into the gas chambers. . . . In order to carry out this extermination program, supported by racial madness and greed, a giant apparatus was constructed within the state administration of the National Socialists German Workers party and the various professional groups. . . . This extermination apparatus grew like a cancer little by little through all the parts of the entire state apparatus. Its creators and executive branches were possessed by the thought of legitimization. They believed they were not murderers if they veiled their crimes against Jewish citizens behind "legal" cloaks and if they packaged every misdeed against the Jews in the form of decrees, orders, arrangements, etc.[49]

JÖRG FRIEDRICH

"The Apartment Keys Are to Be Relinquished to the House Manager"

The Cannibalization of Jewish Estates

At Frankfurt's Auschwitz trial a certain Dr. Capesius was accused of murder and robbery. In addition to his service at the railroad ramps, he was incriminated by fifteen suitcases of gold teeth. However, the court was not able to see greed as the motive for the murders. Capesius probably thought that the body, which in a legal sense is not a person but an object, and its valuables, belonged to the German Reich. What he robbed was the German Reich, which he had not killed, and the ones who were killed, the Jews, he did not rob. The Reich's citizens who did the robbing thought in a similar fashion. After all, they believed in vain that those whom they had been plundering since 1933 would not be ruined by this. Capesius, at his railroad ramp in Auschwitz, thought again that the human freight, its wedding rings, spectacle frames, and golden teeth would be returned to the German Reich's bank and would be looked upon only as material objects in their homeland. It was a container of foreign things that belonged to the Reich's citizens. The Nuremberg police, finance, and railroad officials who sent the fourth transport of Franconian Jews on September 10, 1942, from the railroad station in Schweinau probably also saw a characteristic of this. This pandemonium of official criminals, however, did not agree on the legal accuracy with which the property was dealt with.

A court official appeared who delivered to each displaced person an order for the confiscation of property according to the decree on the "confiscation of property which is against the interests of the people or the state." This was combined with the decree of the Interior Ministry of March 2, 1942, stating that all Jews who were designated for deportation were guilty of antistate activities. During the deportations

141

from Cologne in October and December of 1941, Jews who were led to the fairgrounds had to individually confess their Communist activities to the court's executors, in order to receive a certificate signed by the president of the government stating that they were plundered. The plundered goods waited in the meantime, cleaned and catalogued for new owners.

> I have to prepare my apartment in such a fashion [it was written in a Würzburg notice] that it can be sealed by the police after my departure. I have to turn off the gas, electricity, and water. I have to remove anything that can spoil. The fire in the ovens has to be extinguished. I have to leave my apartment in clean condition. The gas and electric bills have to be paid at the municipal plant ahead of time. I have to notify the house manager of my evacuation.

Finally, one was also to turn in the apartment keys to the house managers, while the keys for the rooms and the closets should be left in the locks. The police first issued an eight-page, then a sixteen-page questionnaire, which asked about all kinds of possessions imaginable. "Do you have a safe and what is in it? Which claims are you entitled to from your licensing contracts, patents, authorships, trademarks and design rights? Do you own paintings, stamp or coin collections? Where are they located? The deposit slip is to be enclosed." The apartment inventory was divided according to rooms: bedrooms with the number of carpets, curtains, pillowcases, and bedspreads, etc. The kitchen with the number of cooking pots and irons, the living room including the globe, lexicon, and wastebasket. Also the napkins, towels, and pajamas had to be Aryanized, as well as the shawls, neckties, and underwear. Even when the Jews were loaded up like excrement, one was able, at the same time, to slip comfortably into their underwear. The authority which was in charge of the distribution was at the same time knowledgeable and sensible. It was the Revenue Office.

The head of the Supreme Revenue Office in Berlin was appointed as the Supreme Liquidator of the Booty, and he delegated this task to local Revenue Offices. In order to free the apartments quickly, professional representatives of moving companies were used for the deployment of the liquidation assignments, while the mortgage loan companies and official auctioneers determined the estimated values. The Revenue Office in Schwäbisch-Gmünd recorded a list "of confiscated items from the Jewess Ella Sara Fuchs": seventy-six items altogether for 445.80 RM, which were acquired by Ost, the high-ranking SS officer and police chief for the southwestern district of Stuttgart, with the exception of thirteen towels, which were taken by the Revenue Office itself. Among them were three pairs of slacks for two Marks, a corkscrew for thirty pfennigs, and an umbrella for one mark.

Prices were always appropriate, the state did not waste anything, and the SS customers hardly ever received any financial gains. There was nothing strange in this. Personal advancements from Aryanization were made only as long as the Jews existed as forced sellers. After their deportation, a Revenue Office acted as the auctioneer, and the large number of customers who were interested in Jewish estates made sure that the sales prices were correct. For example, Popp from Würzburg, the "fellow German in the party," petitioned the Gestapo in writing during the evacuation to obtain a knapsack from the Jews at estimated value. He had an urgency slip for such a knapsack. The Gestapo informed him "to check on the purchase of a knapsack with the Revenue Office in Würzburg." The Gestapo officers did not deal with such things under the counter, so the SS-Oberscharführer from the staff of the 81st SS unit who was interested in five Torah scrolls had to certify with his signature that these were "given to him on loan for his studies" because their proper place was in the State Archives.

The Revenue Office did allow itself *one* privilege, the processing fee. The public administration skimmed off all kinds of junk from the Jewish property for its own use. It began with the typewriters, which were fought over enviously because they were always in short supply, and continued with the bedroom sets, tablecloths, and harmonicas for the state convalescent homes. The revenue officials were the first ones to rummage through the heap which needed to be dissolved. This annoyed Himmler, who in his position as Reich's commissioner, wanted to adequately establish settlers from the East who could be made into Germans in order to strengthen the nation. This also upset the Reich's postal service and railroad. Even the police, the executive authority of the deportation, felt slighted by the arrangements for the settlement of estates. A pertinent decree, the Eleventh Decree to the Reich's Citizen Law, coolly booted the Gestapo out of this business. The Gestapo took the Jewish contents from the apartments but did not gain ownership of it. It was too late for this. Retroactively since November 15, 1941, everything belonged to the Reich, personified by the Revenue Office, with Himmler's henchmen as the bearers. One had to pay the police only one sum: the fare to Auschwitz and the cost of extermination. This was not stated in this manner, but it was charged; 25 percent of the Jewish cash had to be paid as a donation by the victims to "Special Account W" of the Reich's Association of Jews in Germany, a subdivision of the Gestapo. The amount was much too high to cover the cost of transportation, and it was much too low to cover the pretended resettlement costs, but it was sufficient for killing. This much could be recognized from this half-crazy-sounding exactitude of the settlement of accounts.

There is a significant behavior differential between the wasteful extermination of several millions of people and the precise documentation of even the last alarm clock. What is the sense of the addendum to the records of the Künzelsau Revenue Office which recorded the quantities of fruit left behind by Jews or the jam and canned vegetables which were delivered "to our soldiers in the field hospitals" and were also given to the victims of winter crop damage? Why has that been recorded? The path of our fellow human beings leads soundlessly into nothing; only the path of the apples on the kitchen shelves is being carefully recorded. There has to be a reason for this.

The ownerless furniture helped to cover, without a doubt, the shortages which occurred when the workers in the wood industry were transferred to the armament industry. Living space was destroyed during the bombardments, and replacements for space and furniture needed to be found. In the middle of 1943, the National Socialist Welfare asked for one hundred beds, one hundred wardrobes, one hundred night tables, and one hundred sinks "from the supply of Jewish furniture" for nursery schools because the mothers stood "totally in the service of the Reich's defense." The army in Russia needed furs and wool materials. The administrators of the Lebensborn project [a secret project aimed at creating the master race; "Aryan" mothers were inseminated by "Aryan"-looking officers to produce superior "Aryan" children; Am. ed.] hoped, due to the overcrowding of its breeding places, to acquire other facilities such as the emptied Jewish spa Nordrach/Baden "for around fifty mothers and fifty children" and mistakenly asked the Reich's Main Security Office "for an urgent occupation, at least by an advance squad." The Finance Ministry reserved Jewish property for sale to "the wounded of the present-day war." The ministry directed watches and jewelry to the pawnshops with instructions to sell the better pieces abroad for foreign currency and the remainder "to melt down and make available as basic material for the armament industry." With the same aim, the Württemberg economic minister on December 24, 1942, ordered all scrap-iron dealers, as was the case throughout the Reich, to take apart the metal letters, gates, monuments, and fences from the old Jewish cemetery and to scrap them, with the profits going to the Main State Bank in Stuttgart.

The municipal pawn brokerage informed the Reich's bank in September of 1942 that it should not count on obtaining significant profits from the delivered ornaments because they were mostly damaged, old-fashioned, and used, and the customers did not want to pay much money for them. And indeed, at the time of the deportations, most of the German Jews were very poor. Little by little they were pushed out of their careers, and, since they were cut off from their assets, which were frozen in restricted accounts, they lived off of their belongings for years. They could hardly cause anyone to become envious. Their apartments had nothing that was attractive. Measured by the proud living standard of the average population in 1941–42, the Jews had the appearance of wretchedness. They were also supposed to look as shabby as possible; therefore, according to the decree of June 26, 1941, the men could no longer obtain any shaving soap. Nevertheless, the revenue authorities suspected that these people, who were threatened by deportation, could privately sell, loan, or give away their remaining property and thus get around the legal confiscation. Therefore, retroactively from October 15, 1941 on, such activities were prohibited and annulled. Jewish property should not waste away anonymously as junk. No, it had be brought back home into the Reich, freed from the sin of Jewish occupation. It was supposed to be incorporated seamlessly, justly, and properly—even the bones. No bed linen was allowed to be lost in this ritual of tidy administration and questionable practices. The miserable beggar booty was counted, taxed, and distributed as during the miraculous bread multiplication, not only for the sake of advantage and gain. No, there was also an element of bigoted self-gratification in finally seeing the racial unity decompose for better or worse.

The fetish of repatriating Jewish property sometimes also cost money, rather than bringing it in. In the harbor of Genoa since the beginning of the war, there were eighty-five tons of ship luggage from German-Jewish refugees which was confiscated by the Italian government as enemy property. The Berlin Revenue Ministry, which made its claim with the Italians as the new owner of the suitcases, based on the Eleventh Decree of the Reich's Citizen Law, was not taken seriously. Italy dealt with the bounty exactly the same way as Germany. It offered to sell it for 1.50 RM per kilogram. So, the Reich's Treasury paid 130,000 marks in foreign currency for the three-year-old rotting Jewish household goods, furniture, and laundry, which were to be used for helping the victims of bombardment.

After the German Jews each turned in a declaration of personal property (even the property of patients in psychiatric hospitals had to be declared) and after they had cleaned up their apartments ("binoculars and cameras placed well inside the room"), they arrived at the gathering points, which were located, depending on the whim of the police chiefs, in places like the slaughterhouse in Düsseldorf or a dance hall in Würzburg. They were met there by the deep distrust of the police and revenue officers who suspected that illegal property had been smuggled out in hand luggage or body cavities. The officers were especially looking for weapons and ammunition, poison, explosives, knives, forks, scissors, matches, razor blades, and nail files. To be proper, the police used midwives or their cleaning women for body searches of the undressed women. They were professionally consulted by the specialist of the customs agency which, as in Würzburg, recommended checking belt buckles and sanitary napkins in which money was occasionally smuggled. "Offenses against Paragraph 16 of the Foreign Currency Law" was written in a customs agent's official letter of March 30, 1942, are "punishable according to Paragraph 69, Line 1, No. 4. I recommend, if necessary, to have one of my officials participate as a spot checker."

Because there was no foreign currency trade or special punitive action for foreign currency offenses in Auschwitz, such steps were proof of the delirium which entered the heads of German officials while they were dispatching the Jews. The urge to deprive the victims of human dignity and to nullify one's own sympathy for the misery of these creatures was simply overwhelming. The simple carrying out of the deportation was not sufficient. In order to get rid of excess fighting spirit, one still had to defeat the last Jewish trap. There were the Würzburg criminal investigators who confiscated five jars of facial powder, one pair of sugar tongs, three fever thermometers, one silver chain, seven lighters, one ear protector, 356 six pfennig postcards, thirty-seven twelve pfennig reply postcards, etc. from hand luggage. It was an assortment of small items that these people, who were condemned to death, hoped to find useful in some way. Or they may have found comfort in their memorabilia and good-luck charms.

The policemen celebrated their success with a lottery and as always gave the profits with a delivery slip to the Revenue Office. The Revenue Office channeled the confiscated items on to the needy and the National Socialist Welfare; among them were such things as three boxes of buttons for slacks, three pairs of shoelaces, a dice game, and similar objects. The Gestapo appropriated for itself a mixed load in which there were two toothbrushes, one sponge, a jar of Nivea cream, six Maggi bouillon cubes, three sunglasses, forty-five packages of laundry soap powder, and three suspenders. A handful of coins in five different foreign currencies was sent by a delivery boy to a bank for exchange: value 1.40 marks minus 1.40 marks charged as exchange fee, thus the value of the coins was annulled.

When this list of bounty was made up at the end of March 1942, it was certain that the Gestapo did not suffer from a lack of toothbrushes. Even the People's Welfare Agency was not dependent upon the four notarized boxes of sardines and one bag of hulled barley. What made it want to absorb these leftovers? What motivated the fuming super race to distribute coats, clothes, and suits that came back from the extermination places with the directive to carefully tear away the Stars of David and to mend possible bullet holes?

The Jewish writer H. G. Adler dealt, in one passage, with the double connotation of the word *to liquidate*. First, it designates a business process. An ownership is being dissolved, liquified, made liquid, set in circulation. Second, it can also mean the killing of persons. The liquidation of Jews included both processes, the dissolution of the body and its property, its housing, its environment, and its world. The process was separated into covert and overt halves. There is a difference between killing a human being and wearing his shirt. One did not kill because of the shirts. The liquidation of the deported and the liquidation of their utensils were similar but not only in words. There are essential similarities. Both use a tabula rasa principle, the dissolution of the previous condition to dust. The earthly trace of those chased away was extinguished at home. No final solution can be more final then when one has emptied the rooms.

The type and quality of the German awareness of the extermination process are dubious. There are also more nuances than the key question "Did you or didn't you know" can decode. In any case, the liquidation fever for the leftover Jewish property was just as strong as the extermination fever.

The deported people left behind them a character type which, four years later, claimed not to have known anything—or, as Hans Mommsen calls them, the repressers. That which was later repressed was not something which was previously secretly desired, known, or suspected. Rather, it was a reality that was easily recognizable but was ignored while it was happening, partially due to disinterest, partially due to uneasiness. This is true for the majority of the perpetrators themselves and, therefore, also for their subordinates, families, and fellow Germans. There was a lot to be done. When the deputy director of the Reich's railroad, Ganzenmüller, reported to Wolff, Himmler's chief of staff, that "from July 22, 1942 on there has been a daily train with five thousand Jews from Warsaw to Treblinka," he, as well as the train personnel had to ignore the fact that the camp area was only six hundred meters long and four hundred meters wide. How could 329,000 Jews from the Warsaw ghetto fit there all together? What work could they do?

Let us examine more closely the attainment of repression in the head of a German administrative official. After all, the six extermination factories in Poland functioned in the middle of an area which was controlled by a pedantic German civilian administrator. For more than a year at the beginning of the extermination process, the financial and business officials calculated the supply and profit situation of the ghetto with its 2.5 million inhabitants. They calculated statistically the monthly ghetto consumption of, for example, synthetic honey or the number of eggs. In the Lodz ghetto, between January 30 and August 31 of 1941, the consumption amounted to 307 metric tons of synthetic honey and 397,348 eggs. The reduction of food supply soon caused epidemics and mass deaths, just as in the Warsaw ghetto, where the city commander of the German army became nervous and reported this fact through the official channels. Yet Poland was supposed to supply the Reich with its surplus food, and indeed during the extermination of the Jews the deliveries of meat doubled, those of potatoes tripled, and those of wheat grew tenfold. This happened at the same time the Jews from western and southeastern Europe arrived by the hundreds of thousands in freight trains in order to work there, according to the displacement scheme of the war economic administration in Berlin and Poland. How were they supposed to be fed? Where did one calculate the consumption of 4 million people who were housed in the camps after they were evacuated from the ghettos and transported to the camps? Where did one calculate the consumption of food, the raw materials, tools, and, furthermore, the need for overseers, engineers, and bookkeepers?

As one knows, some of the work was done in Auschwitz. During the construction of the IG-Farben Buna plant more than one hundred firms participated and in the process wore out twenty-five thousand of the thirty-five thousand inmates who were used. The armament inspections of the army, the SS-owned enterprises, the Death Organization, and numerous private industrial managers constantly argued over the Jews who were able to work; they demanded again and again to search for workers among those in the camps and ghettos. While they were doing this, did they drive out the thought of the destiny of those who were not able to work? At no time did they find more than four hundred thousand people who were able to work. Therefore, those who were repressing their memory had to assume that millions of Jews who were unable to work had to be provided for by the German Reich at the camps and that this would lead to idleness. The fiction of the accomplishment of work by those who were not able to work again suggests that one was using invisible tools to build invisible streets which led nowhere, that one was manufacturing invisible goods from invisible materials which would invisibly take care of the supply needs in invisible ways.

What did the obedient war economy bureaucrats create through their fantasy? Which necessary factors for calculating were omitted by the clever administrations of armament, raw materials, work force, transportation, food supply, and security? Did those who knocked on every living bone for possible work energy, who made inventories of every bag of cement, and who were used to count every egg eaten by Jews, did they ignore the millions of "useless eaters" on purpose? What kind of officials were they? Ignoramuses, sleepyheads, speculators? No, they were those ingenious economic strategists who armed "Fortress Europe" for four years against a world of enemies. They did this so creatively, stubbornly, and precisely that the Americans, English, and Russians, after their victory, had a hard time hiding their high esteem for these officials. The civilian army of the war economic leadership which literally squeezed out every resource in the occupied continent, which channeled every Jewish urn from a cemetery for recycling, which feverishly consulted with the commanders of the armies on how many million Soviet city dwellers and prisoners would have to starve to death in order to squeeze out sufficient amounts of meat and grain, were these bureaucrats supposed to have miscalculated the cost utility factor of 4 million Jews who were concentrated in Poland? Regarding this hole in the head, it appears to me that Hans Mommsen's diagnosis of repression is too mild.

It may be that one has to invent a new term for the mental attitude of this administrative hierarchy. The uniqueness of the Jewish experience of suffering may be contrasted by a not less singular experience of liquidation. A final solution per se cannot be articulated. Notwithstanding the "secrecy due to the war," any discussion inhibits the execution and burdens the executioners with a responsibility that they are unable to cope with. Since they are state officials, they strictly carry out their functions and do not want to know more than is necessary in their job. A thirst for knowledge and understanding of the subject in broader terms, which was not necessary for the more narrow accomplishment of the job, is classified as not being job-related and, therefore, stands outside the job as a private matter, which is not acceptable. Such is the attitude of the civilized official toward genocide. When he acts he knows nothing, and when he knows he does not act. Even supplying Zyklon B gas does not have to be understood as an action leading to murder, but again the understanding of murder itself does not commit a murder. The railroad employee was transporting, the statistician was calculating. Their excessive knowledge, necessary as qualified experience for the avoiding of accidents and permanent misunderstandings, is hidden in private malicious speculations and reappears anonymously in the destructive feelings of the people. Such is the attitude of the executive class which personifies the general rapacity, rancor, hunger for revenge, and profitable killings of the war years. The excess human beings hindered chances for a victory. The little party member, who is well trained in national hygiene, covers up the similar behavior of his governing bodies in the same fashion. The more the one understands the others, the fewer the words that are necessary. And since everything is succeeding without words and based on falsehood, there must exist a deeper agreement. Otherwise one would initiate pure chaos. The follower of the Führer does not disrupt by loud talk and questions what the Führer can accomplish without much noise. The ban on speaking in the nation apparently continues since the chorus of "have not known anything" can hardly be all of the oral history. However, it is strange that historians who well up with criticism like they do with the belief in witches during Inquisition, are investigating a state of consciousness which still exists vividly in the memories of millions of fellow citizens. Why is there an evasion of the handing down of this information?

Characteristically, any events that deal with the "final solution" in particular, such as the liquidation of Jewish property are avoided. All the commemoration accumulates at those sites of suffering which in those days were hidden from public view, such as the Zyklon pits. In contrast, the close proximity of the fellow citizens to the extermination, characterized by the acquisition of a cooled-down bedsheet, disappears in the horizon. That which was formerly close by moves far away, and the mysterious distance of Treblinka becomes familiar. Every television viewer is aware of the nakedness of the gas chamber, but he is less familiar with the ten-year-long plunder which the gas chamber put to an end. People turned to ashes, their property did not. It became public and private property, however, and, according to today's sensitivity, an embarrassing corpus delicti. Although robbery was not the motive for murder, there exists a transition in taking all the life's property from a group of people and finally also taking life itself away from them. A human being from whom everything is taken becomes too expensive in the end; he consumes food instead of producing it. As a consequence of this, killing is recommended as necessary during the war, with or without racial hatred. Now the human being is disposable. Absorbed through the years with material advantage, he is ultimately absorbed by it. One feared hurting oneself if one would have had to subsidize the ill-treated lives of Jews.

The mixture of racial hatred and profit was divided only afterward. A pure anti-Semitism is easier to tolerate. One can distance oneself more easily from it than from the Aryanization gains. There were many who profited from it. There were certainly some anti-Semites, such as Hitler, Himmler, and various criminals who participated in the Reich's Crystal Night. The Reich's Crystal Night, consequently, became stylized as a medieval pogrom, a case of dark excess of a racial mob. But television screens do not show the roots of the fire which lie in the forced Aryanization of property at the beginning of the war, which is well researched in scholarship. One is horrified rather by a burning synagogue than by the Dresden Bank.

However, in retrospect, it is difficult to pinpoint racial hatred beside the hunger for Aryanization. The German National Socialist trials, which are not known for having sentenced the perpetrators but for having cleanly clarified the state of events, did pursue the events in connection with the deportations in a few cases. Indeed, it was a period of poisonous racial hatred that saturated the bizarre dispossession of Jewish property. In July 1954, the circuit court in Cologne tried the two former Gestapo chiefs of the city, Sprinz and Schäfer, as well as the counsel for Jewish matters, Matschke. The sentence at first emphasized that the extermination of the Jews was more than unlawful: "a bitter injustice which was screaming toward heaven." On earth very few heard this scream because injustice was "strictly secret." "Plans and orders were passed on under code names to the next lower authorities." Therefore, the murderers were those who gave orders and who defrauded: Hitler, Heydrich, and Eichmann.

The Gestapo acted differently. The policemen chimed in with the oath of all of the land: "did not know anything." One had "assumed at that time that the Jews would be brought to a reservation similar to those of the Indians in the United States." By recording the evidence in this regard, something interesting was produced. The secretaries of the police testified that in the middle of 1942 soldiers on leave from the Eastern Front told them that masses of Jews were killed there. A colleague of theirs who participated in these executions was supposed to have fallen into mental derangement. The stories of the soldiers were vividly discussed, and unanimously the conclusion was drawn "that Jews were sent to death."

Personal conclusions were not of importance when one judged the officials. The court made the judgment that legally the only thing that mattered was "that the accused were not informed through official channels on the fate of the Jews." Because Hitler did not follow the official channels, the court characterized the deportation to extermination as "deprivation of liberty in office." According to Paragraph 239, Section 2, this involved a detainment for more than a week, "and all three accused were clearly aware of this." According to the sentence, Sprinz, the accused, "who was an honest and clean official, as well as the Gestapo chief," could hardly tolerate the deprivation of liberty. He became "disgusted" and confessed to his landlady "that he was sick and tired of everything" that was happening in his Gestapo headquarters. However, "inhibited by nature," he swallowed all of his anger, and cleaned all the Jews out of Cologne in fourteen transports of 8,500 people. Consequently: three years' imprisonment. His predecessor in the office, Schäfer, deported only one third as many Jews, three thousand, resulting in one year of imprisonment. The counsel for Jewish matters, Matschke, was, according to the court's judgment, a racial idealist who "honestly believed in the state at that time" so that "during the collapse, his world also collapsed." Not earlier. Thus he was sufficiently punished, and he was sentenced to two years of imprisonment.

The previously described dejudaization of the Franconian area with its 4,754 victims from Nuremberg, Würzburg, Regensburg, and Bamberg was judiciously checked by the Nuremberg district court though four-years of proceedings from 1949 to 1953. Seven high officials of the Gestapo, including its head, Dr. Martin, were accused. In their defense, they gave the court logical problems: the Gestapo supposedly participated in deportations out of fear for their own lives. If they had refused, Hitler would have incarcerated the Gestapo into a concentration camp. Additionally, they supposedly acted with complete justification: Chaim Weizmann, who later became the president of Israel, declared war on Hitler on behalf of world Jewry (Professor Ernst Nolte from Berlin just recently confirmed this), "so that their expulsion from Central Europe and their extermination were necessary for the security of the state."

What was the court supposed to believe of this? It decided "that if somebody thinks that he is acting in a lawful manner, he cannot be acting under coercion." Only one thing was correct, and that was, according to the court's argument, the coercion. Hitler only partially succeeded in conquering the Gestapo, because the policemen obeyed their natural instincts wherever they could. They deported in such a subdued and careful fashion in order to express more protest than anything else. In the sentences, the behavior of the accused was described "as always decent and humane toward the Jews and the politically persecuted, as it was witnessed by all sides, which proved that they did not carry out their task of persecuting the Jews with a joyful heart." On the contrary. Their boss, the Nuremberg Gestapo chief Dr. Martin, made sure "by the authority of his position that the process of the evacuation of the Jews in Franconia would be free of humiliation, abuse, and mistreatments and that the victims would be treated in a correct, humane fashion." Dr. Martin, who represented "the interest of the Jews, did not need to have a sense of guilt here because his desire to help and to alleviate cannot be viewed as injustice."

The kindness and helpfulness of the Gestapo people was rewarded with an acquittal. According to the court's judgment, the Gestapo members did not know that they were helping to send the displaced persons at the railroad station to their extermination, but they had to witness "that the Jews in Germany were continuously exposed to suppression and chicanery." The Gestapo regretted this, but this made its job easier, because "the accused could tell themselves that the Jews would at least essentially not experience anything worse in their new settlements in the East." One could certainly not encounter anything worse than the Gestapo. Thus the Gestapo people saved the Jewry from their own chicanery. If one would believe the judges, the Jews in Germany were never treated so well as during their deportation to Auschwitz.

It is not enough that they had to prepare for their robbers a list of the goods to be robbed.

It is not enough that they had to pay their deporters and executioners in advance for the cost of their deportation and extermination.

It is not enough that they had to undress at the railroad station which was used for the loading of cattle, and that they had to allow themselves to be touched and robbed of their last postage stamp.

The judicial system of the Federal Republic of Germany even reserved for itself the privilege of ridiculing them in their graves.

Punctually on the Ramp

The Horizon of a German Railroad Worker

On September 26, 1939, at the end of the war against Poland, the commander in chief of the army thanked the Reich's transportation minister for help received from the Reich's railroad system. The railroad had "significantly contributed by cooperating with the armed forces so that the campaigns could be carried out in the desired fashion and with the necessary speed." The thank-you notes were delivered to the Reich's Transportation Ministry as well as to all offices which had been located in the East during the entire war. On February 29, 1944, the supreme commander of North Army Group, Colonel General Walter von Model, thanked Field Railroad Detachment No. Four: "In particular, during the retreat of the front the railroad has returned almost all transportable material with over three thousand supply trains and in spite of complications caused by bombings and air attacks." In the spring of 1944, the town of Kowel, at least one hundred kilometers to the east of Lublin, was surrounded for three weeks. In addition to the military and Weapons-SS units, there were also five hundred members of the German Reich's railroad in the pocket. Once the pocket was opened up, the commander of Kowel thanked the railroaders:

> While surrounded and up until today, the railroaders defended, with weapons in their hands, the railroad station area, which later became the front line, and thus proved to their comrades in the army and the Weapons-SS that they know how to fight until the end. In the hour of departure, I extend, in the name of the SS commander and the lieutenant general of the Weapons-SS, Gille, a cordial farewell to all the members of the Reich's railroad stationed in Kowel, and I thank them at the same time for their self-sacrificing effort.

This quote is taken from the book *The German Reich's Railroad in the Eastern Campaign 1939–1944* by Hans Pottgießer, published by the Kurt Vowinkel Publishing House in Neckargemünd in 1960. The author entitled the fourteenth chapter "The Appreciation for the German

154

Railroaders in the East." The last paragraph reads:

> The few comments by higher officers, in addition to the descriptions and data in the particular chapters of this study, are a clear proof that the German Reich's railroad managed to fulfill its designated transportation tasks extremely well within the framework of the war events on the Eastern Front. Moreover, the German railroaders of all units distinguished themselves in every phase of their activity through diligence and their readiness for action, their courage and selflessness, their comradeship and bravery.

Pottgießer supplements his study with an "Alphabetical Directory of Places, Rivers, and Geographic Regions," in addition to a "Railroad Surveying Map." The directory as well as the map is not quite complete. Although the author did not forget too many places, he did leave out several important ones, because from 1941 on many thousands of trains went to these places; to Auschwitz, to Majdanek, to Sobibor, to Treblinka, to Belzec, to Chelmno, only to name a few.

Pottgießer is not an exception. Fifteen years after him, the respected publishing house Musterschmidt in Göttingen published the volume entitled *The Railroads in the Administrative Area of the Axis Powers during the Second World War*. The subtitle read: *The Deployment and Performance for the Sake of the Army and the War Economy*. The author, Eugen Kreidler, was able to publish his 440-page-long work in the series "Studies and Documents of the History of the Second World War," edited by the Circle for Military Studies in Stuttgart. The table of contents itself is revealing. The individual chapters are entitled "The War with Poland," "The War with France, Belgium, and Holland," with Denmark, with Norway, as if one was not dealing with attacks on those countries. In his conclusion, Kreidler states:

> Since the Second World War took place thirty years ago and the number of the railroaders who participated in the war activities is constantly shrinking, one forgets their accomplishments more and more. In the presented work they should finally find a portrayal and appreciation because, in spite of the lost war, they will always remain interesting and exemplary.

Thus Kreidler had the intention to set up some kind of monument for the railroad employees, because he uses the auxiliary "should." The author has accomplished his intention, however, through improper means. When Pottgießer's book appeared, the public probably did not have to think about the role of the German Reich's railroad during the Holocaust. When Kreidler's book was available for sale, there was a trial in which that question was the focal point. It was a trial against the former state secretary of the Reich's Transportation Ministry, Dr. Albert Ganzenmüller. The trial began at the Düsseldorf district court on April 10, 1973, and it ended after only six days on May 3. Ganzenmüller, who was sixty-eight years old at the time, suffered a stroke—so said the physician.

The German as well as the international press reported extensively about the first days of the trial, especially in regard to the Reich's railroad's participation in the deportation to the extermination camps. After every session one could read headlines such as: "The Devil's Railroads," *Aufbau*, New York, April 27, 1973; "The Switchmen for Mass Murder—The trial deals with the role of the Reich's railroad deputy chief during the 'final solution of the Jewish question,'" *Süddeutsche Zeitung*, April 13, 1973; "Ganzenmüller Adjusted the Switches and the Trains Rolled to Treblinka," *Hannoversche Allgemeine*, April 12, 1973; "The Trial Train Departs with Delay—Is former state secretary Ganzenmüller responsible for the death trains to the extermination camps in the East?" *Stuttgarter Zeitung*, April 9, 1973; "Billionfold Murder of Jews in the Court—He put together the trains to the concentration camps," *Aachener Volkszeitung*, April 12, 1973; "Final Solution and the Reich's Railroad," *Aufbau*, New York, July 16, 1973; "State Secretary in the Reich's Transportation Ministry under Accusation," *Mannheimer Morgen*, April 12, 1973; "Ganzenmüller Let the Wheels Roll for the Mass Murder," *Die Tat*, Frankfurt, April 15, 1973; "Millions of Jews Transported to Their Death," *Frankfurter Allgemeine*, April 3, 1973; etc., etc.

Eugen Kreidler, as the author of a book about the Reich's railroad during the Second World War, should have known about this trial, and he should have written differently. He did not do this. This was dishonest.

This complaint should not be made against Ron Ziel, the author of the volume *The Wheels Must Roll: The Railroads of the Second World War*, published by the Frank'sche Verlagshandlung, Stuttgart, in 1973. He could not consider the Ganzenmüller trial, and besides, as far as I can see, he was the first German author who at least did not exclude the Reich's railroad's connection with the mass murders. Ziel writes:

> The concentration camps were set up at various remote places in Germany and the occupied territories. Then the Jews, Gypsies, and others were mercilessly assembled, squeezed into closed freight cars, and brought to the concentration camps where they were systematically exterminated. Unfortunately, the Reich's railroad was used for carrying out these pitiful transports.

Certainly, the Reich's railroad was used, but in no way against its own will and not at least to its financial disadvantage. The first publicist to prove this was the American historian and political scientist Raul Hilberg. The title of his American edition is *The Role of the German Rail-Roads in the Destruction of the Jews*, published in 1976 as a manuscript. In 1981 the Dumjahn editorial house in Mainz published the German translation.

However, Hilberg's study also is incomplete in one essential point. He does not mention the man who even before the end of the Nazi period, had decided to accuse, after the Allied victory, both Reich's Transportation Minister Julius Dorpmüller and his state secretary, Albert Ganzenmüller at the first Nuremberg trial. This man was professor Dr. Robert M. W. Kempner, the prosecutor in numerous Nuremberg trials, who later, in his function as the representative for the families of murdered victims, became a secondary prosecutor also at the Ganzenmüller trial in Düsseldorf. In a conversation which Kempner and I had in May of 1982, he told me that Ganzenmüller was at that time nowhere to be found. After he reappeared again, Kempner immediately set everything in action to bring Ganzenmüller to trial.

What Kempner, who had to flee Berlin because of Nazis, could not know upon his return to Germany in the summer of 1945 was that Ganzenmüller was not far from Nuremberg. He was imprisoned by the Americans. On May 20, 1945, he was brought in to the detention and work camp in Moosburg. In 1947, he was transferred to another camp close to Berchtesgaden. On December 9, 1947, he was supposed to be taken back to Moosburg. The night before, he successfully escaped. He went to Argentina, and in 1949 he was classified in absentia by a denazification chamber into group two, as "burdened." In 1952, he married in Argentina; he returned briefly to Bavaria at the end of 1953 or beginning of 1954 in order to apply for his pension as a former state secretary. He was turned down, but he appealed against the decision. In November of 1955, he ultimately returned from Buenos Aires, took over the transportation department of the Hoesch firm in Dortmund, and in 1968 he retired.

Thus both the American occupation authorities and the German police are to blame for the fact that Ganzenmüller was brought to trial only in 1973. If the American investigators had only been a little bit more careful in 1945, they would have quickly thrust Ganzenmüller into their camp in Moosburg. If the German justice system had placed Ganzenmüller on their wanted list, he would have already been arrested in the winter of 1953.

However, Ganzenmüller was placed into pretrial confinement as late as November 13, 1969. But in January 1970 he was already allowed to leave the penitentiary in Düsseldorf. The Fifth Chamber of the district court in Düsseldorf, with district court director Dr. Hedding, district court counsel Polenz, and court official Berghoff, decided on December 17, 1970, not to allow a trial against Ganzenmüller as accessory to murder and for deprivation of liberty in office, an offense which carries the death penalty. The rejection decision contains forty pages and reads grotesquely.

Ganzenmüller was heavily implicated by both witness depositions and documents while he was in pretrial detention. He must have known very well why the SS needed more and more freight cars and what the people who were deported in the trains were to expect. Two examples should suffice in order to prove this.

The witness McKee, Ganzenmüller's former receptionist and lover, testified that when she once asked what was happening with the Jews in the East, he avoided answering her. Ganzenmüller also mentioned that he would rather schedule the trains used for the transportation of Jews "as vacation trains." According to the Düsseldorf judges, this statement "can be interpreted in various ways."

Still more incriminating was a document: a letter by Ganzenmüller to Himmler's chief adjutant, Karl Wolff.

Dear Party Comrade Wolf!
In reference to our phone conversation of July 16, I am sending to you for your information the following report of my head administrative office for the eastern railroads (Gedob) in Cracow:
"Since July 22, a train with five thousand Jews has travelled daily from Warsaw through Malkinia to Treblinka. Additionally, twice a week there is a train with five thousand Jews from Przemysl to Belzek. Gedob (administrative office) is constantly in touch with the security office in Cracow. They are in agreement that the transports from Warsaw through Lublin to Sobibor (next to Lublin) should be interrupted because the reconstruction work on this line makes the continuation of these transports impossible (approximately October 1942)."
These trains were arranged for by the commander of the security police in the regional government for Poland. The SS and police chief of the Lublin district, SS Brigade Commander Globotschnigg, has been notified. Heil Hitler! Yours faithfully, Ganzenmüller.

Week after week three thousand five hundred Jews were sent from Warsaw to Treblinka—and Ganzenmüller should not have known that they were murdered there? That he did not know how to spell the names of Karl Wolff, Odilo Globocnik, and the extermination camp Belzec is a trifle.

Himmler's chief adjutant, SS-Obergruppenführer Karl Wolff, was so happy about the news from Ganzenmüller that he answered only fifteen days later, on August 13, 1942.

Dear Party Colleague Ganzenmüller!
In the name of the Reich's Führer of the SS, I would like to thank you very much for your letter of July 18, 1942. I am especially happy to acknowledge your report that for fourteen days already there has been daily a train with five thousand members of the chosen people to Treblinka, and that it continues to roll. . . . I took the initiative to get in touch with the participating authorities to assure execution of the whole project without problems.

Robert Kempner published both letters in excerpts at least in his book *Eichmann and Accomplices* in 1961. Eugen Kreidler should have also known them and considered them.

His omissions apparently seemed to be in agreement with the interests of the West German Railroad and the West German Transportation Ministry. Neither the Ministry nor the main administration of the Federal Railroad in Frankfurt keep documentation concerning the role of the Reich's railroad during the Holocaust. I was at least assured of this in May of 1982. Not even Raul Hilberg's study is known there. The archives of the Federal Railroad also do not include the study published in 1977 by Serge Klarsfeld, *The Final Solution of the Jewish Question in France*, in which one can also find numerous documents on the role of the Reich's railroad during the "final solution." Apparently, there are also no relations with the district court in Düsseldorf. Otherwise, the Federal Railroad Archives would possess the accusation documents against Ganzenmüller which were composed at the time by Chief District Attorney Alfred Spieß. At the beginning of the 1970s, Spieß was the chief administrator of Cologne's Central Documentation Office for the Solving of the National Socialist Crimes in the Camps and probably the most knowledgeable prosecutor in the National Socialist trials. He interviewed all accessible witnesses in laborious detail and composed an accusatory document which was valid and without repudiation. Of course, Ganzenmüller knew this as well, and this could be why, out of fear, he started having heart trouble.

Today, Spieß and Kempner are the experts in matters concerning the Reich's railroad and the Holocaust. Unfortunately complete publications on this subject were not published by them—an omission which, it is to be hoped, can be still rectified. In Robert Kempner's memoirs, which were published in 1983 under the title *The Accuser of an Era* by the Ullstein Publishing House, the Ganzenmüller case is treated only summarily (pp. 417–418). Spieß already proved to be the expert at the opening of the trial against Albert Ganzenmüller when he asserted:

During the extermination process, about three million Jews, men, women, and children, were brought by railroad to concentration and extermination camps and there, primarily due to racial hatred, were killed by gas. The victims were made to believe that they would be resettled or they would be sent to work. Based on this deception, most Jews had no concerns when they entered the railroad cars and, at the destination, where the gas chambers were camouflaged as shower rooms. There, they died an excruciating death. The deportation to the camps took place primarily by freight trains. The Jews were so tightly squeezed together in the trains that, along with the carry-on luggage, each only had a few square decimeters of room at his disposal.

The cars, often filled with more than one hundred people, were regularly sealed. Their small windows were secured with iron bars or with barbed wire. . . . During the train ride, they received neither drink nor food. Therefore, they suffered from hunger and thirst, and in summer they were exposed to heat and in winter to cold. Normally they had no access to a toilet, so that they had to take care of their personal needs in the railroad cars. Due to these circumstances, an undetermined number of Jews, especially the sick, the frail, and the children, died during transport. . . .

This happened in the second half of 1942, during the deportation of more than five hundred thousand Jews from the Warsaw Ghetto and the rest of occupied Poland to the extermination camps of Treblinka, Belzec, and Sobibor.

This also happened at the end of January 1943, during the deportation of at least 120,000 Jews from the occupied Russian territories, occupied Poland, and greater Germany to the concentration and extermination camps of Auschwitz and the camps in the district of Lublin.

There is enough suspicion that the accused was aiding the murder of at least one million Jews during the time period from July 1942 until the spring of 1943 by knowing the purpose of the transports.

Ganzenmüller, describing his life in his Bavarian dialect, did not forget to point out his membership in Rheno-Palatia, the Münich "fencing fraternity," which of course was superfluous. A large scar on the left side of his face could not be overlooked.

When one came to the point, i.e., Ganzenmüller's role during the Holocaust, the accused fell silent, in the same way as the railroad employees who were questioned in 1964 in the Düsseldorf Treblinka trial did. When the former Reich's railroad councillor and schedule coordinator in Cracow, Erich Richter, was asked his opinion on where the tens of thousands of Jews were transported to by railroad, he answered: "I always thought that the Jews were supposed to build an eastern wall in Treblinka similar to the one in the West." Richter's postwar career was not affected by this: He became a Federal Railroad head councillor in Nuremberg.

Hans Pitsch was a railroad station director in Bialystok, a station through which many death trains rolled. If the Jews attempted to flee the railroad cars, they were shot by the accompanying guards. This was true in Bialystok as well. "I have, in accordance with the rules, kept records of the dead bodies which were found in the vicinity of my railroad station. The records were then sent to the headquarters. I have thereby fulfilled my duty." Egon Weber was an engineer on several death trains to Treblinka. "I did not see the shootings by the guard units along the side of the train, because I never turned around. I only looked ahead." Weber took over the Federal Railroad directorship in Hamburg after the war.

Walter Stier put together the schedules for the trains in the East, as well as for the death trains. "I did these things at my desk only, thus I took care of the trains only in the schedule-technical sense." After the war Stier became the administrative councillor with the Federal Railroad in Frankfurt.

Albrecht Zahn was a railroad official with the eastern railroad; thus he was responsible for keeping the tracks free for the death trains. "It is possible that I have signed destination order no. 565, but it certainly came upon my desk by accident, and I signed it without suspecting anything." Zahn obtained a high administrative position with the Federal Railroad headquarters in Stuttgart.

Martin Zabel was a schedule coordinator for freight trains in Cracow. "Although I have given my signature, I was not responsible. The gentleman responsible at that time was a Mr. Schulze, but I do not know which Mr. Schulze." Indeed, the Reich's railroad had an interest in participating in the Holocaust. In doing this, it was able to alleviate its deficit. Although the Jews themselves had to pay for the trip to the gas chamber, this was not always possible, e.g., as in the case of the mass deportations from Warsaw. Then someone else had to pay the expense. An agreement was reached that stated that the one who ordered the trains would be responsible for the expense. The transportation expense was based on the fare of a third-class ticket. However, only freight cars were made available, and if possible those which were old and run down. They were good enough for the Jews. Thus, for every deported person one had to pay four pfennigs per kilometer of track. Children under four years had to pay half the price; infants rode for free. The transportation to the death camps was thus twice as expensive as the transportation of soldiers. The Reich's railroad charged them 1.5 pfennigs per kilometer.

The contact office for the Reich's railroad was the Reich's security headquarters of the SS. As Hilberg discovered, Adolf Eichmann agreed on February 20, 1941 to assume the expenses there. That was almost a year before the Wannsee Conference.

It has not been determined who initiated those special arrangements. But it is certain that in July of 1941 the SS had to pay only half of the agreed price if at least four hundred people were deported. At the beginning, the German Reich's railroad charged for the deportation trains from abroad, e.g., Slovakia, if its rail system was being used. At the beginning of 1942, the Reich's railroad offered a rebate of 25 percent for such trips. They argued about every mark. If one dealt with trains from Western European countries, thus, e.g., from the Netherlands, France, or Belgium, then the Reich's railroad also received usage fees.

On June 11, 1942, a conference convened in the Reich's head security office in Berlin, in which among other things the cost for the deportation of the French Jews to Auschwitz was discussed. The SS-Hauptsturmführer Theoder Dannecker summarized the results in his office in Paris on June 15. Serge Klarsfeld found the document. Under item 2 is the statement: "The transportation costs, such as the money per capita (around 700 RM per Jew), has to be paid by the French government." In addition to the cost, the transportation room became more and more of a factor the further the front moved to the East. In the middle of 1942, the Reich's railroad possessed about 850,000 freight cars. Most of them were needed by the army. The SS asked for special trains for the deportations to the death camps. In the railroad schedules they were given a special code. In general, the transport of the Jews were designated with a "Da," an abbreviation for "David." The transports of Polish Jews were coded with a "Pj." Meetings for setting up the schedules convened normally every two months, in various places. They lasted five to six days. Occasionally, Eichmann or his deputy, SS-Hauptsturmführer Hans Günther, participated.

When it became more and more difficult for Eichmann to obtain sufficient transportation room, he accepted the offer to take trains that were bringing forced laborers from the East to the West. Trains with essential war material always had the right of way. Thus it happened that the deportation trains often had to wait for a long time until the tracks were clear. In addition, more and more human freight was squeezed into the cars, and the trains were lengthened.

Originally, the Reich's railroad transported one thousand people, in each train, but at the end of 1942 there were already two thousand, and on shorter routes, such as within Poland, there were five thousand. That amounted to one quarter of a square meter of space per person. Longer trains with more people meant lower speeds and, thus, longer travel time. Raul Hilberg calculated in one case that the deportation train took twenty-three hours for a distance of four hundred kilometers. When the death trains had to wait, and this happened frequently, at railroad stations, the occupants screamed for water. Of course, the traveling civilians heard this, which was uncomfortable for the SS and also bothered the Reich's railroad. However, one accepted all this as something that could not be changed.

Once the trains left the territory of the German Reich, little effort was made to conceal anything. Hilberg published the note of a German sergeant's observations in August 1942.

> We drove past the camp at Belzec. Before that we drove for a lengthier period through high pine forests. When a woman yelled "It's coming now," we saw a high wall of pine trees. One could clearly notice a strong, sweet smell. "They already stink," said the woman. "Oh nonsense, that is the gas," laughed the railroad policeman. In the meantime, we had passed about two hundred meters, the sweet smell turned into a sharp burning smell. "That comes from the crematorium," said the policeman. A short time later the fence ended. One could see a watchtower with an SS sentry in front of it. A dual track led into the camp. The one track was a branch off of the main track; the other led across a turn plate from the camp to a row of sheds which were located approximately 250 meters further away. On the turn plate, just at that time, stood a freight car. Several Jews were preoccupied with turning the plate. SS sentries with their guns under their arms stood next to them. One of the sheds was open, and one could clearly see that it was filled to the roof with bundles of clothing.

Thus even the policemen of the Reich's railroad knew about the mass murders. The trains did not always return to the West with empty freight cars. After all, they were commissioned to bring the clothing and all the property of the murdered people back into the German Reich. When the air attacks on German cities increased and many people became homeless, they received the murdered people's clothing. The clothing was previously sorted out in the death camps and packed in bundles.

The SS and the camp administrations negotiated with the Reich's railroad over where the track should be laid in the death zones, to the ramp in Auschwitz, to the gas chambers in Sobibor, Belzec, and Treblinka. Everything was ordered, and nothing was for free. It happened that the Reich's railroad was not able to meet the demands of the SS due to the lack of transportation room, e.g., during a transportation ban from December 15, 1942, to January 15, 1943. SS-Obergruppenführer Friedrich Wilhelm Krüger, who was at the same time a high-ranking SS officer and a high-ranking police officer in occupied Poland, complained about it on December 5, 1942, when he found out about the projected ban of the Reich's railroads. He wrote to Heinrich Himmler: "These measures critically endanger the entire plan of Jewish resettlement. I obediently request negotiations with the Reich's head offices of the army headquarters transportation ministry so that at least three sets of two trains each become available for the urgent task." Himmler turned to Albert Ganzenmüller, and the trains rolled again. And that happened immediately before the capitulation of the Sixth Army at Stalingrad, when every car was urgently needed for the army units and their supplies.

Himmler knew in July of 1942 at the latest that thanks to Ganzenmüller the Reich's railroad participated in the Holocaust without any significant limitations. During that summer of 1942, the German advance into the USSR went on at high speed. Without the Reich's railroad the army units could not be supplied, and the distances became longer and longer. In spite of an unlimited ban on nonmilitary transports, the SS continued to receive trains with the designations "Da" and "Pj." Himmler's closest associate, the SS general Karl Wolff, took care of this, indeed with Albert Ganzenmüller. This has already been thoroughly discussed.

After the above-mentioned conference on scheduling, the head administrative office of the German Reich eastern railroad informed all the participating directorates that they would have to make trains and locomotives available. Several of these express letters have survived. The telegram of August 8, 1942, stated in the introduction: "In reference to special trains for resettlers, helpers for the harvest, and Jews in the time period from August 8 to October 30, 1942."

Of the fifty announced trains, only five did not have the designation code "Da," but the destination for all fifty trains was the concentration camps or extermination places in the East. On January 16, 1943, the directorates were informed about the special trains for the time period between January 20 and February 28, 1943. There were seventeen trains in this case—ten with Auschwitz as their destination; the remaining seven went to Treblinka. On January 27, the Reich's railroad assembled four special trains for "Pj" "as commissioned by the security police at Bialystok." Under the total number of deportees listed in the section "Remarks concerning the Occupants," in no case was the additional comment "among them children under ten years of age" missing. In all, there were 9,161 people, 2,720 of them children under ten years of age. And the Reich's railroaders believed that one was dealing with work details here!

The telegrams were not classified as secret. They were delivered like all other telegrams. This was also true for the messages sent by tele-printers in which deportations of "Da" or "Pj" were discussed. The attorney general, Alfred Spieß, found out that the notation "for office use only " merely meant that one was not dealing with public trains here.

There were documents which stated that when the trains arrived in the camps, one would occasionally find more dead than living people. In the summer of 1943 a train arrived in Sobibor in which the bodies were already in a state of decay. That also explained the order by the Reich's railroad: "After every completed trip the cars have to be well-cleaned; if necessary, the bodies need to be removed."

The Berlin historian Wolfgang Scheffler is an expert on the number of trains which were made available by the German Reich's railroad. After making thorough investigations in Belgium, France, Holland, Slovakia, Croatia, Bulgaria, Greece, Italy, Hungary, Theresienstadt, Lodz, and the districts of Warsaw, Lublin, Galicia, Radom, Cracow, Warthegau, and Bialystok in occupied Poland, as well as in the German Reich and Austria, the scholar reached the following conclusion: "One has to assume that altogether there were at least three million people who were transported on the Reich's railroad system to the extermination camps." This is, and the scholar, for good reason, stresses the point here, "*not a calculation of the total number of the murdered people during the 'final solution,'*" but this is only the number of people who were transported by the German Reich's railroad to their death.

Although details were not yet known when the first major National Socialist trial began in the winter of 1945 in front of the International Military Tribunal in Nuremberg, Robert Kempner and his associates already knew at the opening of the main trial that there was a seperate department for these special trains within the Reich's Transportation Ministry. He told me in a conversation in May 1982 that according to his recollection the Reich's transportation minister, Julius Dorpmüller, could not be located at that time. In the meantime this has changed. A bust of the man, who was seventy-six years old at the end of the war, decorates the Transportation Museum in Nuremberg today. There is still no bust of his state secretary.

The Federal Railroad likes to brag today about the achievements of its predecessor, the German Reich's railroad. It provided well for the German population up until the end of the war. That is correct, but at whose expense? When, after the victory over Poland and later from the depths of the Soviet Union, train after train rode westward into the German Reich with grain, potatoes, sugar, meat, eggs, lard, etc., they were indeed robbery trains, because they were transporting what was stolen from the inhabitants. No one will ever be able to calculate how many Poles, Ukranians, Estonians, Latvians, and other Eastern Europeans starved to death because their food was taken by the Reich's railroad to the West: Wolfgang Scheffler calculated that the same out-fit was also to blame for at least 3 million deaths during the Holocaust. Except for the attempt to ascertain Albert Ganzenmüller's responsibility, the role of the Reich's railroad never became a subject of public discussion. That should change. Robert Kempner also shares this view when he states:

> Without the participation of the Reich's railroad, this mass murder would have probably not been possible at all, because one did not want to carry out such murderous activities like these in any city or in just any camp that was somewhat more harmless. Even techni-cally, it would have been impossible. Without the generous help of the Reich's railroad, the whole occurrence would have had to be tremendously delayed.

One must agree with this without question. During his preparations for the main trial against Ganzenmüller, attorney general Spieß took depositions from a large number of witnesses, among them many former Reich's railroad employees. They were, at that time, employed by the German Federal Railroad, which should have known something about these depositions. However, it is not known whether the Federal Railroad, which is one of the largest employers in the Federal Republic, has at any time attempted to present this chapter of its history. Whoever travels through the Federal Republic today, perhaps in a comfortable Intercity train, may occasionally take a look at the Railroad Travel Guide, a well-made journal with travel suggestions and promotional pictures of the Federal Railroad. In principle one cannot object to this. Only—if the railroad has the means to produce such an expensive journal in spite of its high deficit, it should also contribute a sum of money to help the long-overdue research into the role of the Reich's railroad during the Holocaust. For this task, the project could use those documents already which have already been found. The attorney general, Dr. Adelbert Rückerl, the former head of the Central

Documentation Office for the Solving of National Socialist Crimes located in Ludwigsburg which is next to Stuttgart, wrote a preface to Raul Hilberg's study entitled *Special Trains to Auschwitz*. He began with a statement by a Reich's railroad official:

> It was on a Sunday around 1:30 p.m. We received word from Sawada that a transport of Jews would be arriving. At our station in Zwierzynieg the locomotives were always filled with water. This was also the case with the above-mentioned train. A small Jewish girl squeezed out from the train which had stopped; I estimate that she was ten to twelve years old. She came up to me and offered me a five-mark bill to pay for water. She spoke about a spoon full of water. I ordered my Polish station supervisor to give the girl water in my water glass. I told the girl to put her money away. While the girl was still drinking, the SS transportation coordinator suddenly appeared behind me. . . . With a horsewhip, he first knocked the water glass out of the girl's hand, and then he continued to beat the girl. The girl's father squeezed out of the train, and on his knees he begged the SS official to be merciful to his child. The SS coordinator pulled out his pistol and killed the father with a shot to his neck. The girl was thrown into the car and so was the dead man's body. The SS officer screamed at me, calling me a servant of the Jews and that I was not worthy to be a German civil servant.

Hilberg has quoted a confidential report by the captain of the Security Police, Salitter. Salitter was in charge of the escort for a transport of Jews which left Düsseldorf on December 11, 1941, and reached Riga after sixty-one hours. The report began in this manner:

> In the transport of Jews of December 11, 1941, there were 1,007 Jews from the cities of Duisburg, Krefeld, and several small cities and villages of the Rheinland Westfalian industrial area. There were only nineteen Jews from the city of Düsseldorf. There were Jews of both sexes and of various ages in the transport, from infants to people up to sixty-five years old. . . . The unloading of the Jews was finished by 10:15 A.M. After switching the tracks several times the train left the railroad freight station of Düsseldorf-Derendorf around 10:15 A.M. in the direction of Wuppertal.

This introduction is followed by a detailed description of the route through Wuppertal, Hagen, Schwerte, Hamm, and through all of the German Reich. Salitter complained that the second-class car which was reserved for the escort was placed at the end of the train and remained cold during the whole trip because the pressure from the heating pipes was insufficient. On December 14, the train reached Riga.

Here we found out that the Jews were not destined for the Riga ghetto but for the Skirotawa ghetto, eight kilometers northeast of Riga. . . . The outside temperature was already minus 12° C. . . . Because it was already past midnight and it was dark and the ramp was heavily covered with ice, the unloading and the transferring of the Jews to the ghetto which was two kilometers away was only supposed to occur on Sunday morning when it became light . . . I found shelter in the guest house of a higher-ranking SS and political officer.

Salitter summarized his "experiences" in section 4:

(f) It was definitely necessary, in order to distribute the drinking water to the Jews, that on each day of the transport, the Gestapo agreed with the Reich's railroad on a one-hour break at a suitable railroad station within the area of the Reich. It turned out that the Reich's railroad agreed to meet the desires of the transportation leaders only with great resentment because of the fixed schedule. The Jews usually had already been on the road for fourteen hours or longer before the departure of the transport and had already consumed the drinks which they took with them before their departure. If they were not supplied with water then they tried, in spite of the prohibition, to get out of the train whenever it was possible in order to fetch some water or have someone get the water for them.

(g) Furthermore, it is urgently necessary that the Reich's railroad prepare the trains at least three to four hours before the designated departure so that the loading of Jews and their luggage can proceed in an orderly fashion.

In case the German Federal Railroad would decide to devote its attention to this topic some day, one could recommend *A Biographical Dictionary to German History*, 1973, volume 1, column 565. There, one can read under "Dorpmüller, Julius Heinrich" that he died on July 5, 1945, and that he was the Reich's transportation minister.

Thus he was responsible for all of the railroad and highway operations in peace as well as under the various difficulties of the war. After the collapse of the Reich, the Allies intended, through several negotiations near Paris, to entrust the seventy-six-year-old with the building of the German railroad. However, this was prevented by his death.

Collaboration and Deportation in Holland

On the Behavior of the Non-Jewish Population during the Persecution of the Jews in the Netherlands

On the eve of the German invasion on May 10, 1940, there were approximately 140,000 Jews in the Netherlands. Among them there were about fifteen thousand German and Austrian refugees and additionally ten thousand Jews from other European countries, especially from Poland.[1] One cannot give details here of the measures which were taken by the Germans against the Jews. Essentially, they were no different than in other European countries which were also occupied by Germans.[2]

In the Netherlands, Jews were also deprived economically and socially by decrees and ordinances. Little by little they became isolated from the rest of the Dutch population. They were concentrated in the so-called Amsterdam Jewish Quarters, placed under the supervision of a Jewish council, which was created on the order of the Germans; they were carefully registered and marked with the Star of David. All this was done in preparation for their deportation from Holland.

The mass deportation of Jews began on July 15, 1942, and continued up until September 13, 1944. During these two years 107,000 Jews were deported from the Netherlands, especially to the Auschwitz and Sobibor extermination camps. Sixty-eight trains with more than sixty thousand Jews were sent to Auschwitz. Of those, only 1,052 Jews ever returned. Within five months nineteen trains with 34,313 people were sent to Sobibor; of those only two survived. Altogether, of the 107,000 deported people, 5,500 (thus, about 5 percent) returned. Altogether, 75 percent or 145,000 Dutch Jews were murdered.[3]

These numbers may perhaps reveal the tremendous extermination campaign against the Dutch Jewry. If one looks at these figures within a European framework, then they can only be compared to the events in the occupied areas of Eastern Europe. In the West there was no country which had such a high extermination quota as the Netherlands.[4] Based on this statement a number of questions arise, especially in regard to the behavior of non-Jewish citizens during the persecution of the Jews.

The problem could best be illuminated by an example: Anne Frank was murdered by a German, she was arrested by an Austrian, and she was betrayed by a Dutchman. How exemplary is the case of Anne Frank for the persecution of the Jews in the Netherlands? In other words: what was the extent of the collaboration of the non-Jewish Dutch citizens with the German occupational force during the persecution of the Jews?

These persecutions were initiated and carried out by Germans under the leadership of Austrians, such as the Reich's commissioner Seyss-Inquart, the higher-ranking SS officer and police chief Rauter, and a number of top officials who almost exclusively belonged to the so-called Austrian Connection.

However, it is also a fact that after Queen Wilhelmina and her ministers left for England, the Dutch civilian administration continued to work quite loyally and also executed the Anti-Jewish measures under this German-Austrian leadership without hesitation.

In regard to this, I would like to quote the Dutch historian Ben Sijes:

> The decision of the general secretaries (they were the highest officials in the administrative bureaucracy) to collaborate loyally with the Germans had far-reaching consequences. The general secretaries not only passively provided an example, but they also incited the entire officialdom, the economic life, even the Dutch society as a whole, to follow their example. The general secretaries did not offer a convincing resistance, and therefore their protest also could not impress the Germans. Without a doubt this must have led to the consequence that the Germans seized the opportunity all the more to carry out unweariedly and as quickly as possible their task which was already fulfilled in Germany and in other occupied territories. Instead of shielding the Jews, who, after all, were also citizens of the Netherlands, the general secretaries let them down. Practically, this meant that the Jews could not count on any protection from the Dutch state institutions. This situation contributed to the fact that the Jews could later be declared free as birds—and the general secretaries acted as accomplices to this.[5]

Surely, this is a tough but, unfortunately, a generally fair assessment. The objections by the general secretaries *against* the anti-Jewish measures of the occupational power had just as little credibility as their collaboration in *carrying out* these measures. However, the result was quite satisfactory, if one viewed it from the point of view of the persecutor.

One example: on November 1, 1941, a conversation transpired between the higher-ranking SS officer and police chief Rauter and Fredericks, the Dutch general secretary of the Interior Ministry. Frederiks was responsible for carrying out most of the anti-Jewish decrees. During this conversation, Rauter asked Frederiks how he felt about a possible deportation of Dutch Jews to Poland. Frederiks answered that he would strongly protest against such a decision and that he and his colleagues in the office as well as the majority of the Dutch officials would resign in a moment. According to Frederiks, the Germans should then see how they could handle things by themselves. Upon hearing this, Rauter asked whether Frederiks would also react in the same way if the deportation would be limited only to the *German* Jews in the Netherlands. I would like to quote Frederik's answer from the transcript: "No, they are your subjects, who have been under your jurisdiction since the occupation. As a Dutch official, I cannot do anything against that."[6] With this statement, the Dutch official opened the door, with one stroke, for the deportation of more than fifteen thousand people who had received political asylum in the Netherlands before the war.

And when the deportations, indeed, *also* of the *Dutch Jews*, began in summer of 1942, Frederiks had apparently already forgotten his clear position in regard to his Jewish compatriots; neither he nor his colleagues resigned. And the administrative apparatus which was under their leadership also continued to function efficiently during the execution of the anti-Jewish measures, certainly not due to a fundamental acquiescence to the measures or a complete recognition of their consequences, but nevertheless to the complete satisfaction of the German leadership.

A completely different category of Dutch collaborators during the persecution of the Jews were the so-called Jew grabbers. They were specifically recruited from the Dutch National Socialist movement and from the police. They specialized in hunting down Jews who were hiding and Jews who managed to avoid their deportation in some other ways. In this task they were strongly incited by the Germans, who offered a reward for every arrested Jew. At the beginning of April 1943, this so-called head-hunter reward system was announced to the whole police apparatus and, already a few weeks later, the security service reported the "positive" results: with the aid of this system, within six weeks the arrest of several thousand Jews, some of whom were in hiding, was enabled.

It makes no sense to classify these groups of "Jew grabbers" and to describe their activities. Let us limit our comments here to a general observation that they were not numerous but very fanatical and, unfortunately, also very successful. One can quote here as an example the so-called Kolonne Henneicke [Henneicke Column; Am. ed.]. It consisted of approximately thirty-five men and had its own office in Amsterdam, from where it also operated. From the beginning of April until the end of September 1943, in almost six months, this group arrested more than three thousand four hundred Jews.[7]

In addition to this organized hunt for Jews, there were also individual betrayals, i.e., informers motivated by various reasons who reported hidden Jews and their helpers, often anonymously, to the police or the security service. The disgusting examples of this do not have to be listed separately. The extent of this phenomenon cannot even be closely determined.[8]

At the end of this outline of the collaboration in the persecution of Jews, those who stood "at the end of the chain of command" and contributed to the deportation of Jews should also be mentioned. These were the policemen who picked up the victims from their homes, and the streetcar and railroad workers who transported them. Only very few of them protested and refused to work, although one can assume that they acted against their will or perhaps thoughtlessly. They were under pressure from official directives or orders. Nevertheless, they also contributed to the history of the persecution of Jews.[9]

Let us now turn to the question of the behavior of the Dutch population as a whole during the persecution of the Jews. The answer to this question is of course difficult, because we are dealing here, as in other occupied territories, with an amorphous mass of people who generally did not offer active resistance against the Jewish policies in their own country. However, by saying that, the behavior of this anonymous mass is not sufficiently outlined. There are, also in regard to the behavior of the Dutch population, certain indications which allow us to make a more specific judgment.

At first, let us go back a little bit into prewar history.[10]

Most Jews who lived in the Netherlands had already been living there for several generations. For the most part, they moved during the seventeenth and eighteenth centuries from other European countries to the Dutch Republic where they built a new livelihood in a tolerant social atmosphere. Of course, anti-Semitism existed in the Netherlands too. However, it was not comparable by far in its inten-

sity or its propagation to the patterns of the hatred for Jews in many
other European countries.[11]

The Dutch historian de Jong wrote in this regard:

> The Jews held a position in our country which was envied by Jews
> in many other countries because excesses against them were unknown,
> their social opportunities were almost the same as those of the non-
> Jews, their assimilation had progressed much further, and most non-
> Jewish Netherlanders made no distinction in their behavior between
> the Jews and the non-Jews.[12]

Perhaps we can best characterize the anti-Semitism in the Netherlands with the statement that there were relatively innocent and mild
patterns of anti-Jewish attitudes which did not fit into the social tradition and therefore were generally rejected.

This is also illustrated by the fluctuating and in no way clear attitude of the Dutch National Socialist movement toward the Jewish
question in the prewar period. At the beginning, it clearly rejected
German anti-Semitism; even in 1935 there were about 150 Jewish members of this movement. The last thirteen Jewish members were excluded
from the party only in the fall of 1940 under heavy pressure from the
Germans, thus about six months *after* the beginning of the German
occupation.[13]

However, little by little this attitude changed to a fundamental
agreement with the anti-Semitic viewpoint of the National Socialist
German Workers party. This was certainly one of the main reasons
why the movement was overwhelmingly rejected by the Dutch population.[14] For example, there were large protests in the Netherlands
against the Nuremberg Laws, especially toward the Anti-Jewish excesses in November 1938. After the Reich's Crystal Night, the parliament animatedly debated, and the government was urged by all parties,
except for the small National Socialist party, to open the borders for
Jewish refugees. The churches, trade unions, various local administrations, and many private citizens also urged immediate help. A
collection of money for the Jewish refugee committee in the Netherlands brought in 3.5 million guilders.[15]

These examples make the fact clear that the radically anti-Jewish
policy of the National Socialists was essentially rejected by the Dutch
population before the German occupation. Little changed in regard
to this after May 1940, although the inconsiderate behavior of the
German occupational power of course made many, not unjustifiably,
afraid to clearly show their opposition.

Nevertheless, there were people who *in spite of this*, protested vehemently and tried to sabotage the anti-Jewish policy thus, endangering their own lives. But these efforts were often successful. I would like to mention here only a few of the most important examples:

Right at the beginning, in November 1940, there were student strikes at the Universities of Delft and Leiden because of the dismissal of Jewish employees. At the Leiden University, Cleveringa, the professor of jurisprudence, made a powerful protest speech in front of his students. He was arrested for this; the Universities of Leiden and Delft were closed for the duration of the war.[16]

A second example:

In February of 1941, there were heavy clashes in the Amsterdam Jewish district between Jewish and non-Jewish workers on one side and the Dutch National Socialists and German police on the other side, whereby one National Socialist got killed. In reprisal, Himmler, who was notified about this event by the above-mentioned higher-ranking SS officer and police chief, ordered the arrest of 425 young male Jews who were supposed to be taken to concentration camps. On February 22 and 23 the first large police raids took place in the Jewish district as a result of this. The German police proceeded with a brutality until then unknown in the occupied Netherlands: about four hundred Jews were arrested on the street and deported.

The reaction of Amsterdam's population followed two days later: a general strike broke out, which quickly spread to other surrounding cities. After two days the strike was violently broken up by SS and police troops, and as a consequence twenty-four people were injured, nine were killed, and a number were imprisoned. The Communist organizers were later executed.[17]

The general strike of February 1941 was the only large and spontaneous protest strike against the persecution of the Jews in the occupied European countries, and it was of major significance for the Dutch situation. On the one hand, this public demonstration symbolized the general indignation within large circles of Dutch society over the radically anti-Jewish policy of the occupational power; on the other hand, it also showed unambiguously the ruthless attitude with which the occupational power carried out this policy.

The third example concerns the aid for the hidden Jews, whose number is estimated at twenty to twenty-five thousand. Of those, as already mentioned, many were eventually captured and deported. One cannot estimate the number of addresses available for hiding or the number of helpers. However, it is a fact that at the beginning individual illegal groups and later an organized resistance movement, *especially* the so-called National Organization for Aiding the Hidden, played a significant and admirable role. Many persecuted Jews, in the city as well as in the countryside, were hidden by all classes of the Dutch population. Finally, it is also a fact that providing help brought great risks with it: the helpers often ended up in the concentration camps as well, after the people whom they were hiding had been arrested.[18]

In conclusion, one should also mention the churches here. In July 1942, the Roman Catholic and the Lutheran churches (with the exception of parts of the so-called Reformed Church) protested publicly against the deportation of Jews. It was, as expected, a futile protest, and, in retaliation, Seyss-Inquart, the Reich's commissioner, ordered 110 Jews who were baptized by the Catholic Church to be arrested and deported to Auschwitz. This also demonstrated that the German occupational power was unrelenting in these questions. One may, however, assume that the churches' protest reflected the feelings and thoughts of many of their members concerning the persecution of Jews.[19]

I would like to make a few conclusions now. During the persecution of Jews in the Netherlands, collaboration and betrayal took place, but also sabotage, willingness to help, and protest demonstrations. One can and may not deny this ambivalence throughout the history of the occupation of the Netherlands. To return to my introductory example once more: Anne Frank was betrayed by a Dutchman, but she was also hidden by Dutch people.

Dutch Jews were terrorized and persecuted by the Germans and Austrians. However, the Germans and Austrians were aided by the Dutch passively and sometimes actively. This usually occurred in response to an order or under heavy pressure; in some cases, however, it also took place due to indifference, greed, or envy, or due to some other base motivational factors.

In contrast to this, a great variety of signs of solidarity with the persecuted existed. Surely, there were also various motives which played a role in this—e.g., religious or political—but they were united, nevertheless, in the absolute rejection of the anti-Jewish measures imposed by the occupiers.

And with this I come to a careful and indeed personal assessment of the behavior of the Dutch population. The German policy of persecution against the Jews was strictly rejected by a majority of the Dutch population. Moreover, it led, because of its harshness, which was completely foreign to the traditions of the Dutch society, to a final break between the occupational power and the population and to an escalation of the contrasts between the two. In regard to the situation of the Jews in the occupied Netherlands, Raul Hilberg wrote:

"Holland was the only territory in the occupied West where the Jews had no (in comparison to the other occupied territories) comparable chances of survival."[20] Unfortunately, one can only agree with this. The chances of survival in the Netherlands *were* unusually poor for Jews. The main reason for this was not the behavior of the Dutch population, because the majority of the Dutch population rejected the National Socialist Jewish policy. However, only a minority actively resisted this policy. This is regrettable, but should it surprise us? After all, the history of the European resistance against the persecution of Jews is unfortunately a history of minorities. In this regard, the Netherlands fits into the European tradition.

APPENDIX

ERNST PIPER

A List of Visual Artists Who Were Exhibited and Honored during The Nazi Period

The basis for the following list is the catalogues of the Great German Art Exhibits from 1937 to 1943. The list includes the names of those artists who were exhibited at least three times during these years. The years of exhibition are listed after the names. The symbols signify the following criteria:

E	Honors during the Third Reich (based on R. Merker. *Die bildenden Künste im Nationalsozialismus.* Cologne, 1983, p. 305ff.) [The Visual Arts in National Socialism]
DtM	Discussed by B. Kroll in *Deutsche Maler der Gegenwant. Die Entwicklung der Deutschen Malerei seit 1900.* Berlin, 1937. [German Contemporary Painters. The Development of German Painting since 1900]
D&B	Discussed by A. Hentzen in *Deutsche Bildhauer der Gegenwart.* Berlin, no year. [German Contemporary Sculptors]
DK	Signatories to the Declaration of the German Artists Association "German Art Is in Danger!" (*Völkischer Beobachter,* June 12, 1933)
M	Exhibited in the Munich Art Exhibit 1941
MG	Exhibited in the Exhibit of Munich's Contemporary Art 1937
A	Listed in the (very small) "List A" of the "Immortals." These artists were exempt from serving in the war; their work was not to be interfered with in any way (based on V. Reimann, *Dr. Joseph Goebbels* [Vienna, 1971]).

I would have liked to compare this list with "List B" of the seventy-three painters, thirty-four sculptors, fifty architects, and twenty-three commercial artists who were also exempt from serving in the war as "divinely blessed." Unfortunately this list was not published and could not be obtained from the Berlin Document Center.

Adolf **Abel** 37, 38, 40, 41, 42, 43; Curt **Agthe** 37, 40, 41, 42; Gottfried **Albert** 40, 41, 43; Richard **Albitz** 38, 39, 40, 42, 43; Erhard **Amadeus-Dier** 38, 40, 41, 42, 43; Adam **Amend** 38, 39, 40; Heinrich **Amerdorffer** 37, 38, 39, 41, 42; Hermann **Amrhein** 39, 40, 41, 42, 43; Ludwig **Angerer** 40, 42, 43; Otto **Antoine** 38, 42, 43; Cirillo **dell'Antonio** 39, 40, 42, 43.

Alfred **Bachmann** 39, 41, 42, 43, MG; Rudolf Christian **Baisch** 39, 40, 42, 43; Hanns **Bastainer** 37, 38, 39, 40, 41; Georg **Bauch** 40, 41, 43; Karl **Bauer** 37, 38, 39, 40, 41, M; Hans **Baumann** 39, 40, 41; Thomas **Baumgartner** 37, 38, 39, 40, 42, 43, E, M; Fritz **Bayerlein** 37, 38, 39, 40, 41, 42, 43, M; Hugo **Becher** 40, 41, 42; Hans **Beckers** 38, 40, 41, 42; Fritz **Behn** 37, 38, 39, 40; Gustav **Behre** 41, 42, 43; Ottohans **Beier** 37, 38, 39, M; Franz **Belting** 39, 40, 41, 42, 43; Wilhelm **Belz** 38, 39, 40; Claus **Bergen** 37, 38, 39, 40, 41, 42, 43; Max **Bergmann** 37, 38, 39, 40, 41, 42, 43; Josef **Bernhart** 37, 38, 41; Otto **Bertl** 37, 39, 42; Hans **Bertle** 40, 41, 43; Hans **Best** 37, 38, 39, 40, 41, 42, MG; Fritz **Best-Cronberg** 38, 39, 40, 41, 42, 43; Max **Bezner** 37, 38, 39; Richard **Biringer** 37, 39, 40, 41; Albert **Birkle** 38, 41, 42; August **Bischoff** 39, 40, 41, 43; Walter **Bischoff** 38, 39, 40; Bernhard **Bleeker** 37, 40, 41, E, DtB, DK, MG; Wolf **Bloem** 38, 39, 41, 42, M; Carl **Blos** 38, 39, 40, 41, M, MG; Hans **Blum** 38, 39, 40, M; Karl **Boehme** 37, 38, 39; Herbert **Böttger** 39, 41, 42; Rudolf **Böttger** 38, 40, 41, 42, 43; Theodor **Bohnenberger** 37, 38, 39, 40, 41; Hans **Bohrdt** 38, 39, 41, 42; Ludwig **Bolgiano** 37, 38, 40, M; Arnulf **de Bouché** 38, 41, 42; Ernst **Brand** 40, 41, 42, 43; Wilhelm **Brandenberg** 38, 39, 40, 41, 42, 43; Gustav-Adolf **Bredow** 39, 40, 41, 42, 43; Rudolf **Breidenbach** 38, 41, 43; Arno **Breker** 37, 38, 39, 40, 41, 42, 43, E, DtB, A; Hans **Breker-Rekerb** 37, 41, 42; Hermann Wilhelm **Brellochs** 37, 38, 39, 41; Hans **Bremer** 39, 40, 41, 42, 43; Carl Alexander **Brendel** 37, 38, 39; Friedrich Franz **Brockmüller** 37, 38, 39, 40; Georg **Broel** 37, 38, 39; Paul **Bronisch** 39, 40, 41, 42, E; Max Alfred **Brumme** 37, 38, 39, 40, 41, 42, 43; Artur **Brusenbauch** 37, 38, 39, 40; Lothar-Günther **Buchheim** 41, 42, 43; Robert Wilhelm **Büchtger** 38, 39, 41, M; Hans Adolf **Bühler** 40, 41, 42, 43; Hans **Bullinger** 37, 39, 40, 41, 42, 43; Josef **Burger** 37, 38, 39, 40, 41, 42, 43; Arnold **Busch** 37, 38, 39, 40, 41, 42, 43; Marcella **Busching-Isler** 40, 41, 43, M; Bernhard **Butzke** 39, 40, 41, 42, 43.

Eduard **Cauer** 38, 40, 41, 42, 43, M; Hanna **Cauer** 37, 38, 39, 40, 42, 43; Stanislaus **Cauer** 38, 41, 42; Hellmuth **Chemnitz** 39, 40, 41; Hermann **Christlieb** 37, 38, 39, 40, 41, 42, 43; Max **Clarenbach** 37, 38, 39, 40, 41, 42, 43; Otto **Coester** 37, 38, 39, 43; Edward Harrison **Compton** 37, 38, 39, 40, 41, 42, 43; Fritz **Coubillier** 39, 40, 41; Robert **Curry** 39, 40, 41, 43.

Joachim **Daerr** 38, 40, 41, 42; Karl Heinz **Dallinger** 37, 38, 40, 41, 42, DtM; Johannes **Darsow** 37, 38, 39, 40; Max **Dellefant** 41, 42, 43; Johanna von **Destouches** 38, 40, 41; Fridel **Dethleffs-Edelmann** 40, 41, 42, 43; Erich **Dichtl** 38, 40, 41, 42; Trude **Diener** 40, 42, 43; Elmar **Dietz** 37, 39, 41, 42, 43; Lothar **Dietz** 39, 40, 42, 43, M; Hermann **Dietze** 37, 38, 39, 40, 41, 42, 43; Otto **Diez** 37, 40, 41, M; Felix **Dittmar** 38, 39, 40, 41, 43, M; Sepp **Döbrich** 41, 42, 43; Willi **Döhler** 37, 38, 39, 40, 43, M; Otto **Dörfel** 37, 40, 41, M; Bernhard **Dörries** 37, 38, 39, 40, 41, 43, DtM; Ernst **Dombrowski** 38, 39, 40, 42, 43, E; Karl von **Dombrowski** 38, 39, 40, 43; Günther **Dommerich** 39, 40, 41, 43; Siegfried **Dorschel** 40, 41, 42; Michael **Drobil** 37, 38, 39, 43.

Elk **Eber** 37, 38, 39, 40, 41, E, DtM, MG; Lissy **Eckart** 37, 38, 39, 40, 41, 42, 43; Paul **Ecke** 37, 38, 39, 40, 41; Carl **Ederer** 37, 39, 40, 41; Georg **Ehmig** 37, 38, 39, 40, 41, 42, 43, DtM; Paul **Ehrhardt** 37, 39, 40, 41, 42, 43, M; Franz **Eichhorst** 37, 38, 39, 40, 41, 42, 43, E, DtM; Walter **Einbeck** 39, 40, 42; Gerd **Eisenblätter** 40, 41, 42; Rudolf **Eisenmenger** 37, 38, 40, 41, 42, 43, E, DtM; Richard **Enders** 38, 39, 40, 42; Julius **Engelhard** 41, 42, 43; Otto **Engelhardt-Kyffhäuser** 38, 39, 40, 41, 42, E; Max **Esser** 37, 39, 40, 42, E; Erich **Erler** 38, 39, 40, 41, 42, 43, M; Bruno **Eyermann** 37, 39, 41, 43.

David **Fahrner** 38, 39, 40, 41, 42, 43; Heinrich **Faltermaier** 38, 39, 40, 42, 43, M; Luise **Federn-Staudinger** 37, 39, 41; Toni **Fehr** 38, 39, 40; Jakob **Fehrle** 39, 40, 41, 42, 43; Roman **Feldmeyer** 38, 39, 40, 41, 42, 43, M; Irmtrud **Ferdin** 40, 41, 42, 43; Albert **Feßler** 39, 40, 41; Alfons **Feuerle** 37, 40, 41, 42; Erich **Feyerabend** 37, 38, 39, 40, 41, 42, 43; Alfred **Finsterer** 37, 39, 40, 41, 42; Jakob **Fischer-Rhein** 41, 42, 43; Bruno **Flashar** 38, 39, 40, 41, 42, 43, M; Philipp **Flettner** 38, 39, 40, 41, 42, 43; Ferdinand **Flosdorf** 39, 41, 42; Karl Alexander **Flügel** 38, 40, 41, 42, 43, DtM, M; Erica **Flügel-Steppes** 40, 41, 42; Peter **Foerster** 40, 41, 42; Richard **Förster** 38, 39, 41; Joseph **Frank** 38, 39, 41; Leo **Frank** 37, 38, 39, 40, 41, 43; Robart **Frank-Krauß** 38, 39, 40, 41, 43; Wilhelm **Fraß** 37, 38, 39, 40, 43; Eugen **Frey** 40, 41, 42, 43; Oscar **Frey** 37, 39, 40; Roland **Friederichsen** 37, 39, 43; Lore **Friedrich-Gronau** 39, 40, 41, 42, 43; Ludwig **Fuchs** 38, 39, 41; Max **Fuhrmann** 40, 41, 42, 43.

Franz **Gebhardt-Westerbuchberg** 40, 42, 43, M; Hermann **Geibel** 37, 38, 39, DK; Kurt **Geibel-Hellmeck** 39, 40, 41, 42, 43; Otto **Geigenberger** 40, 41, 42, DtM, M; Kurt **Geipel** 41, 42, 43; Hugo **Geissler** 38, 39, 40, 41; Ludwig **Geistreiter** 40, 42, 43; Constantin **Gerhardinger** 37, 38, 39, 40, 41, 42, E, DtM, M; Franz **Gerwin** 37, 38, 39, 40, 41, 42, 43, E; Richard **Gessner** 38, 39, 40, 41, 42, 43, DtM; Fritz **Geyer** 37, 40, 43; Hildegard **Glade** 39, 40, 41, 43; August Wilhelm **Goebel** 38, 39, 40, 41, 42, 43; Otto **Goebel** 37, 38, 39, 40, 41, 42, 43; Hanns **Goebl** 38, 39, 41, 42; Hermann **Göhler** 37, 38, 41; Karl **Goetz** 37, 39, 41, 42; Ernst **Gorsemann** 37, 38, 39, 40, 41, 42; Hermann **Gradl** 37, 38, 39, 40, 41, 42, 43, DtM, A; Franz **Gräßel** 38, 39, 40; Theodor **Grätz** 37, 38, 39, 40, 41; Fritz **von Graevenitz** 37, 40, 41, 42, 43, E; Oscar **Graf** 37, 38, 39, 40, 41, 42, 43, E, M; Wolfgang **Grau** 38, 39, 40, 41, 42, 43; Anton **Grauel** 37, 38, 39, 40, 41, 42, 43; Ernst **Greiner** 39, 40, 42, 43; Arthur **Griehl** 37, 39, 41, M; Hans **Grieß-mayer** 38, 39, 40; Oswald **Grill** 38, 39, 43; Paul **Groß** 39, 40, 42; Ludwig **Gschoßman** 39, 40, 41, 42, 43; Theo **Guillery** 38, 39, 42; Olaf **Gulbransson** 37, 38, 41, 42, 43, E, M; Wilhelm **Gut** 41, 42, 43.

Kurt **Haase-Jastrow** 37, 38, 39; Hans **Haffenrichter** 39, 41, 43; Fritz **Hafner** 38, 39, 40, 41, 42; Oscar **Hagemann** 37, 39, 40, 41, 42, 43; Karl **Hageni** 40, 41, 42; Hermann **Hahn** 37, 38, 39, 42, 43, DtB; Fritz **Halberg-Krauß** 37, 38, 39, 40, 43; Otto **Hamel** 37, 39, 40, 41; Willy **Hanebal** 38, 39, 41, 43; Willy **Hanft** 38, 40, 42; Walter **Hannemann** 39, 40, 43, M; Hanns **Hanner** 37, 38, 40; Hans **Happ** 37, 38, 39, 40, 41, 42, 43, DtM; Bernhard **Hartmann** 37, 38, 39, 40; Hugo **Hartmann** 40, 41, 43; K. W. Heinrich **Hartmann** 41, 42, 43; Bernd **Hartmann-Wiedenbrück** 41, 42, 43; Max **Hartung** 37, 40, 42; Max **Hartwig** 37, 38, 39; Daniel **Hauenstein** 40, 42, 43; Leopold **Hauer** 41, 42, 43; Christian **Haug** 38, 39, 40; Paul **Hauptmann** 39, 40, 41, 42, 43; Walter **Huaschild** 38, 39, 42; G. Adh **Hedblom** 37, 39, 40, 41, 43; Fritz **Heidenreich** 39, 40, 41, 42, 43; Fritz **Heidingsfeld** 40, 41, 42; Otto **Heinrich** 38, 39, 40, 41, 42; Emil Ernst **Heinsdorff** 37, 38, 39, 40, 41, M; Willi **ter Hell** 37, 38, 39, 40, 41, 42, 43, E, DtM; Hans **Hemmesdorfer** 39, 41, 43; Walter **Hemming** 38, 39, 40, 41, 42; Wilhelm **Hempfing** 37, 38, 39, 40, 42, 43; Josef **Hengge** 41, 42, 43; Eugen **Henke** 37, 38, 40, M, MG; Karl **Hennemann** 37, 38, 39, 41, 42; Albert **Hennig** 39, 40, 41; Albert **Henrich** 37, 38, 39, 40, 41, 42, 43; Ernst **Henseler** 37, 39, 40; Maria **Henseler** 38, 40, 41, 42, 43; Paul **Herrmann** 39, 40, 41, 42, 43, E; Friedrich **Heubner** 37, 38, 40, 41, 42, 43, DK, M; Richard **Heymann** 39, 40, 41, 42, 43; Alfred **Hierl** 39, 41, 42, 43; Anton **Hiller** 38, 40, 41, DtB, DK; Sepp **Hilz** 38, 39, 40, 41, 42, 43, E, M; Christian Gotthard **Hirsch** 38,

39, 40, 41; Otto **Hirth** 39, 40, 41, 42, 43, E, M; Hugo **Hodiener** 37, 38, 39, 40, 41, 42, 43, M; Walther **Hoeck** 37, 38, 39, 40; Erich **Hoffmann** 38, 39, 40; Maria Theresia **Hofmann** 38, 39, 40, 41, 42; Oswald **Hofmann** 37, 38, 39, 40, 41, 42, 43; Ludwig **Hohlwein** 37, 38, 39, 40, 41, 42; Richard **Holst** 38, 39, 40, 41, 42, 43; Conrad **Hommel** 37, 38, 39, 40, 41, 42, 43, DtM; Franz **Homoet** 37, 38, 39, 40, 41, 42, 43; Emil **Hub** 37, 38, 39, 40, 42, 43; Richard **Huber** 39, 41, 42, M; Paula **von der Hude** 37, 38, 39, 40, 41, 42, 43; Richard **Hüfer** 41, 42, 43; Arthur **von Hüls** 37, 38, 39, 42, 43; Rudolf **Hünerkopf** 38, 39, 41, M; Albert Hinrich **Hußmann** 40, 42, 43.

Arthur **Illies** 41, 42, 43.

Adolf **Jäger** 38, 39, 40, 41, 42, 43; Albert **Janesch** 37, 38, 40, 41, 42, 43; Angelo **Jank** 37, 38, 39, 40, DK; Chrysille **Janssen** 39, 40, 43; Ulfert **Janssen** 37, 38, 39, 40, 41, 42, 43; Carl Paul **Jennewein** 37, 38, 39; Ewald **Jorzig** 37, 38, 40, 41, 43; Julius Paul **Junghanns** 37, 38, 39, 40, 41, 42, 43; Reinhard Paul **Junghanns** 37, 38, 39; Hermann **Junker** 37, 38, 39, 40, 41, 42; Josef **Jurutka** 37, 41, 43.

Robert **Kämmerer-Rohrig** 37, 38, 39, 40, 41, 42; Theodor **Kärner** 37, 38, 40, 41; Rudolf **Kaesbach** 39, 40, 41, 43; Hermann **Kätelhön** 38, 39, 40; Fritz **Kaiser** 39, 40, 42; Richard **Kaiser** 37, 38, 39, 40, 41; Friedrich Wilhelm **Kalb** 37, 38, 39, 42, 43; Barbara **v. Kalckreuth** 38, 40, 41, 42, 43; Alex **Kalderach** 38, 39, 40, 41, 42; Peter **Kálmán** 37, 38, 39, 40, 41, 42; Marcel **Kammerer** 38, 39, 40, 41, 42, 43; Herbert **Kampf** 37, 39, 40, 41, 42, 43, A; Adolf **Kapfhammer** 38, 39, 40; Luigi **Kasimir** 37, 41, 42, 43; Hermann **Kaspar** 37, 38, 40, E, DtM, M; Paul **Keck** 39, 40, 41, 42; Woldemar **Keller-Kühne** 38, 39, 40, 41, 43; Georg **Kemper** 38, 40, 41, 42, M; Gottlieb Theodor **Kempf-Hartenkampf** 38, 39, 41, 42; Lilli **Kerzinger-Werth** 37, 38, 40, 43; Erwin **Kettemann** 38, 39, 40, 42, 43; Albrecht **Kettler** 38, 40, 43; Franz **Kiederich** 38, 39, 40; Michael **Kiefer** 38, 39, 40, 41, 42, 43, M; Emil **Kiemlen** 38, 39, 41; Dorothea **Kirchner-Moldenhauer** 37, 38, 39, 40, 41, 42, 43, M; Alfred **Kitzig** 37, 38, 40, 41, 42; Johannes **Kiunka** 37, 38, 41; Richard **Klein** 37, 38, 39, 40, 41, 42, 43, DtM, DK, M, MG; Marcel **Kleine** 37, 42, 43; Walther **Klemm** 37, 38, 39, 40, 41, 42, 43, DtM; Heinrich **Kley** 37, 38, 39, 40, 41; Fritz **Klimsch** 37, 38, 39, 40, 41, 42, 43, E, DtB, A; Walter **Klinkert** 37, 38, 39, 40, 41; Wolfram **Kloß** 39, 41, 43; Robert **Knaus** 39, 40, 41, 42, 43; Richard **Knecht** 37, 39, 40, DK; Frieda **Kniep** 39, 40, 41, 42; Erwin **Knirr** 37, 38, 39, 40, 41, 42, 43: Johannes **Knubel** 38, 39, 41; Hella **Koch-Zeuthen** 39, 41, 42; Reinhold **Koch-Zeuthen** 37, 38, 39, 40, 41, 42, 43;

Fred **Kocks** 41, 42, 43; Fritz **Köhler** 38, 41, 42; Fritz **Koelle** 37, 38, 39, 40, 41, 42, 43, DtB; Wilhelm **Körber** 37, 38, 49, 40, 41, 42, 43; Wilhelm **Kohlhoff** 38, 41, 43; Friedrich Hans **Koken** 37, 38, 39, 40, 41, 42; Georg **Kolbe** 37, 38, 39, 40, 41, 42, 43, E, DtB, A; Gerhardt **Kraaz** 40, 42, 43; Albert **Kraemer** 37, 38, 39, 40, 42, 43; Georg **Krämer** 38, 39, 40, 41, 42, 43; Heinrich **Kralik** v. **Meyrswalden** 37, 38, 39; Hans Otto **Kraus** 39, 40, 42; Hermann **Kricheldorf** 37, 38, 39, 40, M; Willy **Kriegel** 37, 39, 40, 41, 42, 43, A; Emil **Krieger** 40, 41, 42; Wilhelm **Krieger** 38, 39, 40, 41, 42, 43; Hans **Krückeberg** 37, 38, 43; Anton **Kürmaier** 37, 38, 39, 40, 41, 42, 43, M; Heinrich **Kugler** 38, 40, 43; Ernst **Kunst** 40, 41, 42, 43, DtB; Hermann **Kupferschmid** 37, 38, 39, 42, 43; Flex **Kupsch** 37, 38, 39, 40, 41, 43.

Adolf **Lamprecht** 40, 41, 43, DtM; Heinz **Langrebe** 37, 38, 42, M; Andreas **Lang** 38, 39, 41, 42, 43, M; Hubert **Lang** 38, 39, 40, 41, 42, 43, M; Carl **Lange** 37, 39, 40; Alois **Langenberger** 40, 41, 42; Hubert **Lanzinger** 37, 38, 43; Friedrich Carl **Lattke** 38, 39, 40, 41; Ernst **Laurenty** 40, 41, 42, 43; Hias **Lautenbacher** 39, 41, 42, 43; Georg **Lebrecht** 37, 38, 39, 40, 41, 42, 43; Wilhem **Legler** 39, 40, 42; Otto **Leiber** 38, 39, 43; Karl **Leipold** 37, 38, 39, 42; Karl **Lenz** 37, 38, 39, 40, 42; Maximilian **Leo** 39, 40 41, 42; Harm **Lichte** 38, 39, 40, 43: Adolf **Libermann** 42, 42, 43: Ernst **Liebermann** 37, 38, 39, 40, 41, 42, M, MG; Ferdinand **Liebermann** 37, 38, 39, 40, 41, M; Helmut **Liebermann** 37, 38, 40, 41, 42, 43; Erich **Lindenau** 38, 39, 40, 42, 43; Theodor **Linz** 39, 41, 42, 43; Berhard **Lippsmeier** 39, 41, 42; Rudolf **Lipus** 41, 42, 43; Hans **List** 37, 39 42, 43; Switbert **Lobisser** 37, 38, 39, 40, 41, 42, 43, E; Friedrich **Lommel** 37, 38, 39, 40, 41, 42, 43, M; Heinrich **Lotter** 38, 39, 40, 41; Heinrich **Loy** 39, 40, 41; Anton **Lutz** 38, 39, 41, 42, 43.

Wilhelm **Maaß** 40, 42, 42; Max **Märtens** 39, 40, 41; Julius **Mahainz** 40, 41, 42, 43; Alfred **Mailick** 39, 40, 41; Erik **Mailick** 38, 39, 40 41, 42, 43; Hans Jakob **Mann** 37, 38, 39, 40, 41, 42, 43; Konrad **Mannert** 39, 41, 42, 43; Emil **Manz** 37, 38, 39, 40, 41, 42, 43; Konrad **Mannert** 39, 41, 42, 43; Emil **Manz** 37, 38, 39, 40, 41, 42, 43; Oskar **Martin-Amorbach** 37, 38, 39, 40, 41, 42, 43, E, DtM; Hanns **Maurus** 38, 39, 40, 41; Karl **May** 38, 39, 40, 41, 42, 43, M; Ernst **v. Maydell** 39, 40, 41, 42, 43; Eugen **Maye-Fasßold** 37, 38, 39, 40, 41, 42, 43, M; Hermann **Mayrhofer-Passau** 37, 38, 39, 40, 41, 42, 43; Sepp **Meindl** 37, 38, 39, 40, 41, 42, 43; Hugo **Meisel** 38, 39, 40, 41, 42, 43; Enrich **Mercker** 37, 38, 39, 40, 41, 42, 43, E; Elsa **Merkel** 38, 39, 40, 41, 42, 43; Paul **Merling** 39, 40, 42, 43; Julius **Mermagen** 38, 39, 40, 41, 42; Christian **Metzer** 37, 38, 39, 40, 41, M; Hans **Metzger** 37, 38, 39, 40, M; Bodo

Meyner 40, 41, 42; Franz Josef **Mikorey** 37, 38, 40, 41, 42, 43; Alfred **Milan** 38, 39, 40, 41, 42, 43; Paul **Mildner** 39, 40, 42; Richard **Miller** 39, 42, 43; Otto **Miller-Fiflo** 37, 38, 41, 42, 43, M; Hugo **Möhl** 40, 41, 42, 43; Arnold **Moeller** 37, 38, 39, 42, 43; Herbert **Molwitz** 37, 38, 39, 40, 41, 42, 43; Erica **Moufang** 38, 39, 40; Erich Martin **Müller** 37, 38, 40, 41, 42, 43; Georg **Müller** 38, 39, 40, 41, 43, DK; Hans **Müller** 38, 39, 40, 41; Richard **Müller** 37, 38, 39, 41, 42; Hans **Müller-Schnuttenbach** 37, 38, 39, 40, 41, 42, 43, M; Anton **Müller-Wischin** 37, 38, 39, 40, 41, 42, 43, E, DtM, M; Oskar **Mulley** 37, 38, 39, 40, 41, 42, 43.

Oskar **Nerlinger** 39, 40, 41, 43; Heinz Bruno **Nern** 41, 42, 43; Hanns **Neudecker** 38, 39, 40, 41, 42, 43; Rolf **Nida** 37, 38, 40; Rudolf **Nißl** 39, 40, 41, 42, M; Fritz **Nuß** 37, 38, 39, 40, 41, 42, 43.

Ottmar **Obermaier** 37, 38, 39, 40, 41, 42, 43; Oska **Oestreicher** 37, 38, 39, 40, 41, 42, 43; Georg **Ohst** 39, 40, 43; Karl Ewald **Olszewski** 37, 38, 39, 40, 41, 42, 43; Rudolf **Ostermaier** 39, 40, 41, 42, 43, M; August **Ostermann** 39, 40, 41, M; Albert **Otto** 37, 38, 39, 40, 41, 42; Rudolf **Otto** 38, 39, 40, 41, 42, 43; Edmund **Otto-Eichwald** 38, 49, 40.

Paul M. **Padua** 38, 39, 40, 41, 42, 43, E, M; Hermann Joachim **Pagels** 38, 39, 40, 41, 42, 43, E; Josef **Pallenberg** 38, 39, 40, 41, 42, 43; Gisbert **Palmié** 39, 40, 41, 42, 43; Margarethe **Pantanius-Hoffman** 39, 40, 41; Andreas **Patzelt** 39, 41, 42, 43, DtM; Rudolf **Pauschinger** 37, 40, 41, 42, 43; Werner **Peiner** 37, 38, 39, 40, 42, DtM, A; Erich v. **Perfall** 38, 39, 40, 41, 42, 43; Walter **Petersen** 38, 39, 42, E; August **Peukert** 37, 38, 39, 40, 42, 43; Conrad **Pfau** 38, 39, 40, 41, 43, MG; Rudolf **Pfefferer** 37, 40, 41, 42, 43, M; Max **Pfeiffer** 37, 38, 39, 40, 41; Flex **Pfeifer** 39, 40, 41, 42: Alfred **Pfitzner** 37, 38, 39, 40, 41, 42; Peter **Philippi** 37, 38, 39, 41, 42, 43; Dorothea v. **Philipsborn** 38, 40, 42, 43; Ria **Picco-Rückert** 41, 42, 43; Josef **Pieper** 39, 40, 41, 42, 43, DtM; Wilhelm Otto **Pitthan** 38, 39, 40; Otto **Placzek** 39, 40, 41, 43; Hans **Plangger** 37, 40, 41, 42, 43; Ludwig **Platzöder** 37, 38, 39, 40, 41, 42, 43; Bernhard v. **Plettenberg** 38, 39, 40; Franz **Plischke** 40, 42, 43; Johann Peter **Pöppelmann** 38, 39, 42; Karl **Pohle** 38, 39, 41; Otto **Polus** 39, 40, 42; Max v. **Poosch-Gablenz** 39, 40, 41, 42; Georg **Poppe** 40, 41, 43; Wilhelm **Posoreck** 37, 38, 39; Otto **Priebe** 38, 40, 43; Robert **Propf** 39, 40, 43; Carl Theodor **Protzen** 37, 38, 39, 40, 41, 43, M; Henny **Protzen-Kundmüller** 37, 41, 43, M; Erwin **Puchinger** 38, 39, 40, 41, 42, 43; Viktor **Pucinski** 39, 40, 41, 42, 43.

Ernst Andreas **Rauch** 37, 38, 40, 41, 42, DK; Luis **Rauschhuber** 37, 38,

39, 40, 41, 43; Richard W. **Rehn** 40, 42, 43; Adolf **Reich** 39, 40, 41, 42, 43; Albert **Reich** 38, 39, 42, M, MG; Friedrich **Reimann** 38, 39, 40; Ernst **Reiß-Schmidt** 39, 41, 42, 43; Lore **Rendlen-Schneider** 37, 38, 40, 41, 42, 43; Willi **Repke** 40, 41, 42, 43; Fritz **Rehein** 37, 38, 39, 40, 41, 42, 43, E, DtM; Erik **Richter** 38, 39, 40, 41; Klaus **Richter** 38, 39, 40; Heinrich v. **Richthofen** 37, 38, 39, 40, 41, 42, 43; Paul **Ricken** 41, 42, 43; Hannes **Rischert** 37, 38, 39, 40, 41, 43; August **Rixen** 37, 41, 42, 43; Wilhelm **Roegge** 37, 38, 40, 41, 42; Han **Röhm** 38, 39, 40, M; Fritz **Röll** 37, 38, 39, 40, 41; Joss **Röwer** 38, 39, 40, 41, 43; Alfred **Roloff** 40, 41, 42, 43; Paul **Roloff** 37, 38, 43, M, MG; Walter **Rose** 37, 38, 39, 40, 41, 42, 43, M; Otto **Rost** 39, 40, 41, 42, 43; Karl **Roth** 37, 38, 39, 40, 41, 42, 43; Toni **Roth** 37, 38, 39, 40, 41, 42, 43; Leopold **Rothaug** 38, 39, 42, 43; Franz **Rotter** 40, 41, 43; Heinrich **Rudolph** 40, 41, 42; Jakob **Rudolph** 39, 40, 41; Anne-Elisabet **Rühl** 38, 39, 40, 41, 43, M.

Alfred **Sachs** 37, 38, 39, 41, 42; Ivo **Saliger** 38, 39, 40, 41, 42, 43, DtM; Leo **Samberger** 37, 38, 39, 40, 41, 42, 43, E, DtM, M, MG; Leonhard **Sandrock** 38, 39, 40, 41, 42, 43; Liese-Lotte **Sangerhausen** 37, 38, 39, 40, 41; Wilhelm **Sauter** 38, 39, 40, 41, 42, 43; Hans **Schachinger** 37, 38, 39, 40, 41, 42, 43; Rudolf **Schacht** 39, 42, 43; Hans **Schaefer** 40, 41, 42; Edmund **Schaefer-Osterhold** 41, 42, 43, M; Richard **Scheibe** 37, 38, 39, 40, 42, 43, E, DtB; Otto **Scheinhammer** 37, 38, 39, 40, 41, 42, 43, DtM, M; Rudolf **Scheller** 37, 38, 39, 40, 41, 42, 43; Herman **Scheuernstuhl** 37, 38, 40, 41; Anton **Scheuritzel** 38, 39, 41; Paul **Scheurle** 38, 39, 40, 41, 42, 43; Edgar **Schilke** 37, 38, 39, 40, 42; Johann Georg **Schlech** 38, 39, 40; Hans **Schlerth** 37, 38, 39, 41, 42, 43, M; Carl **Schleinkofer** 39, 40, 41, 42; Otto **Schließler** 40, 41, 42, 43; Eduard **Schloemann** 37, 38, 39, 40, 41; Margarethe **Schmedes** 37, 39, 40, 41; Rudolf **Schmid** 41, 42, 43; Kurt **Schmid-Ehmen** 37, 38, 39, 40, 41, 42, 43, E; Josef **Schmid-Fichelberg** 37, 38, 39, 40, 41, 42; Nicholas **Schmidt** 37, 38, 41; Wilhelm **Schmidthild** 40, 41, 43; Erich **Schmidt-Kabul** 37, 38, 41, 42; Else **Schmidt–van der Velde** 37, 39, 40, 41, 42, 43; Hans **Schmitz-Wiedenbrück** 38, 39, 40, 41, 42, E; Wilhelm **Schmurr** 37, 39, 41; Leopold **Schmutzler** 38, 39, 40; Alfons **Schneider** 39, 40, 41, 42, 43; Herbert **Schnürpl** 39, 40, 41, 42, 43; Hans **Scholter** 41, 42, 43; Adolf **Schorling** 39, 40, 41, 42, 43; Heinrich **Schott** 39, 40, 41, 42, 43; Rudolf **Schramm-Zittau** 37, 38, 39, 40, 42, 43 DtM; Richard **Schreiber** 40, 42, 43; Carl Moritz **Schreiner** 39, 41, 42, 43; Paul **Schroeter** 37, 38, 39, 40; Heinrich **Schütz** 38, 39, 41; Friedrich **Schüz** 37, 38, 39, 40, 41, 42, 43; Johann **Schult** 39, 40, 41, 42, 43; Wilhelm **Schulz** 37, 38, 40, 42, MG; Mathias **Schumacher** 39, 42, 43; Josef **Schuster** 39, 40, 43; Raffael **Schuster-Woldan** 37, 38, 39, 40, 41, 42, 43, E; Carl

Schwalbach 37, 38, 39, 40, 41, 42, DtM; Hans **Schwarte-Hellweg** 41, 42, 43; Robert **Schwarz** 39, 40, 43; Hans **Schwegerle** 37, 38, 39, 40, 41, 43; Alois **Seidl** 37, 42, 43, DtM; Hermann **Seidl** 40, 41, 42, 43; Georg **Siebert** 37, 38, 39, 40, 41, 42, 43, DtM; Rudolf **Sieck** 37, 38, 39, 40, 41; Theo **Siegle** 38, 39, 40, 41, 42, 43; Ludwig **Siekmeyer** 37, 38, 40, 41, 43, M; Thomas **Sigl** 38, 39, 41, 42, 43; Hans Albert **Simon-Schaefer** 37, 39, 40, 41, 42, 43; Georg **Sluyterman v.** **Langeweyde** 37, 38, 39, 40, 42, 43; Heinrich **Söller** 40, 41, 42; Josef **Sommer** 41, 42, 43; Otto **Sonnleitner** 37, 38, 39, 43; Anni **Spetzler-Proschwitz** 37, 38, 39; Ferdinand **Spiegel** 37, 38, 40, 41, 43, E, DtM; Axel **Sponholz** 38, 39, 40, 41; Hans **Sponnier** 38, 39, 40; Siegward **Sprotte** 39, 41, 42; Emil **Stadelhofer** 39, 41, 42; Hans **Stadlberger** 40, 41, 42; Ferdinand **Staeger** 37, 38, 40, 41, 42, 43, E, M; Albert **Stagura** 38, 39, 40, 41, 42, 43; Franz Xaver **Stahl** 37, 38, 39, 40, 41, 42, 43, E; Friedrich **Stahl** 37, 38, 40, E; Peter **Stammen** 39, 40, 41; Albert **Stangl** 37, 38, 39, M; Gertrud **Starck** 37, 38, 39, 41; Julius **Starcke** 37, 38, 39, 40, 42, 43; Rudolf **Staudenmaier** 37, 38, 40, 41, 42, 43; Elisabeth **Stechele-Maurer** 37, 38, 39, 40, 41; Josef **Steib** 41, 42, 43; Alfred **Steidle** 37, 38, 39, 40, 41; Arthur **Steiner** 38, 40, 42; Daniel **Stocker** 38, 39, 41, 42; Rudolf **Stocker** 39, 40, 43; Josef **Stoitzner** 37, 38, 39, 40, 41, 42, 43; Hanns **Stoll** 37, 39, 40; Karl **Storch** 37, 38, 39, 41, 42; Robert **Streit** 37, 38, 41, 42, 43; Walter **Strich-Chapell** 40, 41, 42, 43.

Willy **Tag** 40, 41, 42, 43; Wilhelm **Tank** 38, 39, 42; Luise **Terletzki-Scherf** 37, 38, 39, 40; Wolf **Thaler** 39, 40, 41, 42, 43, M; Heinz **Theis** 38, 42, 43; Oskar **Thiede** 37, 38, 39, 41, 42; Johannes **Thiel** 38, 39, 40, 41; Alfred **Thiele** 38, 40, 42, 43; Eduard **Thöny** 37, 38, 49, 40, 41, 42, 43, E, DtM, MG; Josef **Thorak** 37, 38, 39, 40, 41, 42, 43, E, A; Ferdinand **Thurnherr** 39, 40, 41, 42, 43; Hermann **Tiebert** 37, 38, 39, 40, 41, 42; Gustav **Traub** 37, 38, 39, 40, 41, 42, 43; Franz **Triebsch** 37, 39, 40, 41, 42; Karl **Truppe** 39, 40, 41, 42, 43, E; Will **Tschech** 39, 40, 42, 43; Georg **Türke** 37, 38, 39, 40, 41, 42, 43; Karl **Tüttelmann** 38, 41, 42.

Robert **Ullmann** 38, 40, 43; Helmut **Ullrich** 40, 42, 43, M; Reinhold **Unger** 41, 42, 43; Hermann **Urban** 38, 39, 40, 41.

Otto **Vaeltl** 40, 41, 42, 43; Fritz **Vahle** 38, 39, 40, 42, 43; Ingeborg **Vahle-Giesler** 41, 42, 43; Johann **Vierthaler** 37, 38, 39, 40, 42, 43, M; Josef **Vietze** 37, 39, 40, 41, 42; Georg **Vogt** 38, 41, 42, 43; Elisabeth **Voigt** 37, 41, 43, DtM; Walter **Volland** 37, 40, 41, 42; Herbert **Volwahsen** 40, 41, 43; Gerda **Voß** 40, 41, 42, 43.

Josef **Wackerle** 37, 38, 39, 40, 41, 43, E, DtB, DK, M; Carl **Wagner** 38, 39, 42; Emil **Wagner** 37, 39, 41; Josef **Wahl** 37, 38, 40, 41, 42; Willy **Waldapfel** 38, 40, 43; Paul **Waldow** 39, 40, 41, 42; Markus **Walleitner** 37, 38, 39, 40; Renz **Waller** 39, 40, 41; Karl **Walther** 37, 38, 39, 40, 41, 42, 43; Adolf **Wamper** 37, 38, 40, 41; August **Waterbeck** 37, 38, 41, 42; Walter **von Wecus** 37, 39, 40, 41, 42, 43; Alfred **Weczerzick** 38, 39, 40, 42; Alexander **Weise** 38, 39, 40, 41, M; Carl **Weisgerber** 38, 39, 40, 41, 42, 43; Franz **Weiß** 39, 40, 42, 43; Heinrich **Weißer** 37, 38, 39, 40, 41, 42, 43; Otto **Weißmüller** 37, 38, 39, 40, 41, 42, 43; Karl **Wendel** 38, 40, 41; Udo **Wendel** 37, 39, 40, 41; Wenzel Hermann **Wendelberger** 38, 39, 40, 42; Kurt **Wendlandt** 40, 41, 42, 43; Adolf **Wendt** 39, 40, 42, 43; Else **Wenz-Vietor** 37, 38, 39, 40, 41; Carl **Werner** 40, 42, 43; Richard Martin **Werner** 37, 38, 39, 40, 41, 42, 43; Rudolf **Werner** 37, 38, 39, 40, 41, 42; Hans **Werthner** 38, 40, 43; Paul **Westerfrölke** 37, 38, 39, 40, 41, 42, 43; Johann Fritz **Westermann** 38, 39, 40, 41, 42, 43; Wilhelm **Wilcke** 39, 40, 42, 43; Wolfgang **Willrich** 37, 38, 39, 40, 41, 42, M; Otto **Winkelsträter** 39, 40, 41, 42; Curt **Winkler** 37, 38, 40, 41, 42, 43; Friedrich **Wirnhier** 39, 41, 43; Adolf **Wissel** 37, 38, 39, 40, 41, 42, 43; Maximilian **Wittmann** 40, 41, 42; Louis **Wöhner** 39, 40, 43; Franz Xaver **Wölfle** 39, 40, 41, 42, 43; Georg **Wolf** 38, 39, 41; Jörg **Wolf** 40, 42, 43; Walther **Wolff** 37, 39, 42, 43.

Max **Zaeper** 37, 38, 39, 40, 41, 42, DtM; Hermann **Zettlitzer** 39, 40, 41, 42, 43; Adolf **Ziegler** 37, 38, 39, 40, 42, 43, DtM; Otto **Zieske** 38, 39, 40; Rudolf **Zill** 41, 42, 43; Hans **Zimbal** 39, 40, 41; Bodo **Zimmermann** 37, 38, 39, 40, 42, 43; Ernst **Zoberbier** 39, 40, 41, 43; Alfred **Zschorsch** 38, 39, 40, 41, 42; Walter **Zschorsch** 38, 40, 41, 43; Heinrich v. **Zügel** 37, 38, 39, E, DtM; Willy **Zügel** 37, 38, 39, 40, 41, M.

Jörg Wollenberg

Register of Enterprises Aryanized in Nuremberg*

Siegfried **Aal**, Toy Manufacturing; Isidor **Abraham**, Clothing Factory; **Adler und Ullmann**, Toy Wholesale; Wilhelm **Aufochs**, Toy Wholesale; Leon **Aussenberg**.

J. **Bach**, Mirror Factory; **R. Bach und Co.**; **Bachmann und Ullmann**; **Bauer und Hecht oHG**, Ladies' Hats Wholesale; A. H. **Beyer und Co.**, Textiles Store; **Bayerischer Futterstoff- und Schneiderartikel-großhandel**; **Bayerische Werkzeug- und Stahlindustrie**, Götz & Co.; Karl **Bechhöfer**, Textiles Wholesale; **Beckmann und Ullmann**, Georg **Herz**, Georg **Kynast**, Exports; **Benedikt und Dannheiser**, Gold- and Silver-Spinning and Weaving Mill; Willi **Berlin**, Packing Materials Wholesale; Eduard und Charles **Bernhard**, Exports; **Besenbeck und Walter**, Cardboard Factory; Michael **Betz**, Pressing, Stamping, and Drawing Plant; **Bieringer und Co.**, Shoe Factory; Jakob **Blumenfeld**, Carpets; Arthur **Braun**, Travel Agency; Bernhard **Breitenbach**, Chess Wholesale; Adolf **Brenner**, Watch Store.

F. **Danzer Nachfolger**, Furniture Store; **Gebr. Dessauer KG**, Margarine Plant; L. **Dormitzer**, Bristle Wholesale; Kuno und Otto **Dressel**, Toy Exports; Johann Georg **Drossel**, Exports.

Ebert und Landecker, Metal Paper Factory; **Ecco Eckstein und Co. GmbH**; Ludwig **Ehrlich**, Leather Store; Sigmund **Ehrlich**; Josef **Eismann**, Glue Store; **Elektro-Noris oHG**, E. und F. **Jondorf**; **Enn-Werke**, Justin **Neu**; Siegbert **Erlanger und Co.**, Hop Sales; **Ernede GmbH**, Ladies' Coats and Clothing Factory; **Etam**, Textiles.

Siegfried **Federlein**, Tool Store; **Gebr. Feuchtwanger und Co.**, Celluloid and Metal Hardware Factory; H. **Fischer und Co. oHG**; **Fleischmann, Moosbacher, Goldmann, Quast und Wolf**, Hardware

Store; **Fleischmann und Weilheimer,** Hop Sales; Hermann **Fleischmann,** Hardware Wholesale; S. und E. **Fleischmann,** Paints and Lacquers; **Frank,** Wine Distillery; Julius J. **Frank,** Paper Wholesale; **Frankenburger und Oberndorfer GmbH,** Writing Materials Wholesale; Eugen und Sally **Frankenthal,** Machine Factory; Arnold **Friedlein,** Hat Factory Storehouse; **Friedmann und Co.,** Wholesale Woolen and Woven Goods, Toys, and Haberdashery; **Gebr. Friedmann;** Julius **Friedmann,** Butcher.

Ludwig **Gärtner,** Brush Factory; N. **Gast und Co.; Gely GmbH;** Isaak Jakob **Goldberger,** Manufacturing; Benno **Goldschmidt,** Hardware Wholesale; **Gebr. Goldschmidt,** Metal Hardware Factory; M. **Goldschmidt,** Textiles Wholesale; **Graf und Co.,** South German Catgut Factory; Arthur **Grau,** Travel Agency; **Gebr. Greiner,** Light Bulb Factory; **Grünstein, Klein und Co. oHG; Güttermann und Lichtenstätter,** Wholesale Lining and Tailor Supplies; Ella Asarah **Gundelfinger;** Max, Ludwig, und David **Gundelfinger,** Bag Wholesale; **Guttmann und Lämmle; Gutmann und Schmidt,** Textiles Wholesale; Hugo **Gutmann GmBH,** Office Machines; Max **Gutmann und Co.,** Hardware.

Hammelbacher und Co., Lacquer Factory; **Hammerer und Kühlwein,** Toys; **Hasselbacher und Co.,** Lacquer Factory; Martin **Hauers;** Emil **Hausmann,** Exports; Simon **Hedinger,** Amusement Items Factory; Simon **Heid,** Brush Factory, **Heim und Co.;** H. L. **Heimann,** Textiles Wholesale; Ludwig **Heimann und Co.,** Shoe Factory; F. M. **Herberger und Co.,** Files and Tools Wholesale; **Herkuleswerke AG,** Bicycle Factory; **Gebr. Herzfelder,** Horn Plate Factory; Abraham **Hess,** Leather Goods Wholesale; **Hessdörfer und Kolb oHG.,** Clothing Factory; **Gebr. Hesselberger,** Hop Sales; S. A. **Hesslein und Co.,** Furniture Wholesale; G. **Hirsch und Sohn GmbH;** Salli **Hirschen,** Coffee Heater Manufacturing; Fritz S. **Hirschmann,** Hop Sales; **Hopf und Söhne,** Hop Sales; **Holzinger und Kaiser,** Underwear Factory and Knitted Goods Mail Order; **Huck GmbH,** Metal Trimming Factory; David **Hutzler,** Leather Goods Factory.

Alexander, Martin, und Johann **Ichenhäuser;** J. **Ittmann,** Furniture Store.

Louis **Jeelsohn,** Paint Store; **Johannes GmbH,** Hairdresser Supply; Hermann **Johenhäuser,** Brush Factory; G. **Jondorf,** Burner Factory.

J. G. **Kaiser,** Machine Factory; Hermann **Katz;** Cilli **Kenner;** Nathan **Kirschbaum,** Hop Sales; L. **Klein,** Brush Factory; Alfred **Klugmann,** Brushes and Bristle Wholesale; Max **Kohlmann,** Textiles; Simon **Kohn,**

Wine Store; **Kohnstamm und Co.,** Toy Factory; Wilhelm **Krailsheimer,** Haberdashery; S. **Krakenberger,** Hop Sales; Hans **Kraus Nachfolger;** Josef **Kraus und Co.**

Bluma und Gusta **Langer,** Needlework Store; **Lederwerke Cromwell AG; Leiter und Ullmann,** Metal Hardware Factory; Silk House **Lehmann; Lehmann und Co.,** Toy Exports; Hugo **Lehmann,** Bicycle Parts Wholesale; **Lessinger und Heymann,** Metal Etching Plant; Georg **Levy,** Toy and Hardware Factory; **Luma,** Shaving Brush Factory; Josef **Luwitsch,** Wedding and Dowry Store.

Mahag, Machine Sales Company; **Maienthau und Wolff,** Toy Exports; **Marswerke AG;** Friedrich **Mayer,** Spelt and Hop Sales; Ignatz **Mayer,** Knitted Goods; F. **Meinhardt,** Haberdashery and Toys; **Metallbesatz GmbH; Metzger und Böhm,** Wine Distillery; Ludwig **Meyer,** Shoemaker; **Michael und Grünebaum,** Embroidery Sales; Willy, Walter, und Max **Mayer und Co. GmbH;** Bernhard **Münz,** Writing Materials and Fashion Articles Wholesale; Hans **Moos,** Roof Repairs; Hugo **Mossbacher,** Hardware Wholesale; M. **Murr,** Shipping; Moritz **Murr** und Emma **Fliegner,** Redistribution Center and Stamp Factory.

Nathan und Co., Banking; **Neuburger und Co.,** Hop Sales; Jakob **Neumann,** Toy Export; **Neustädter, Oppenheimer und Friedmann,** Textile Sales; J. **Neustädter und Co.,** Shoes Wholesale; Josef **Neustädter,** Textile Wholesale; **Noris Versandhaus,** Woolen and Woven Goods, Toys, and Haberdashery; **Nürnberger Nährmittelwerke GmbH; Nürnberger Sackgroßhandel GmbH; Nürnberger Spielwarenfabrik; Nürnberger Spielefabrik, L. Kleefeld und Co.; Nürnberger Stempelfabrik.**

Oettinger und Co., Linoleum and Wallpaper; Martin Bauers Witwe Rosalie **Öttinger, Oppenheimer und Friedmann; Oppenheimer und Söhne,** Wine Wholesale; **Oppenheimer und Sulzbacher,** Export of Building Materials and Fashion Articles.

Pensel, Machine Factory.

Carl **Quehl,** Amusement Items Export.

Norbert **Rau,** Kitchen Appliances Wholesale; Albert **Raum und Bernet und Sohn,** Hop Sales; Fritz **Reichmann,** Leather Waste Wholesale; **Ricardo und Co.,** Toy Factory; Adolf **Riegelmann** und S. B. **Bing Söhne,** Hop Sales; Max Rosenbaum und E. **Ollendorf und Co.,** Wine Sales;

Rosenfeld und Co., Hop Wholesale; Albert **Rosenfeld**, Iron Wholesale; Moritz **Rosenwald**, Hop Sales.

Jakob **Saemann**; J. S. **Schatt**, Instrument Factory and Foundry; Louis **Schild**, Leather Sales; Julius **Schlachter**, Celluloid Goods; Kaufhaus **Schocken KG**; Georg **Schönner**, Drawing Instrument Factory; **Schumann**, Metallic Toys Factory; M. **Schwarz und Söhne**, Virgin Wool and Textile Wholesale; Richard **Schwarz und Co.**, Groceries Wholesale; **Sero GmbH**, Brush Factory; **Sills-Baby-Bazar**; Heidi **Simon**, Brush Factory; **Spear Söhne KG.**, Games Factory; Sigmund **Spear**, Lithographic Art Studio; J. **Speier**, Shoe Store; N. **Stark und Co.**, Textile Store; **Staudenmeyer und Co.**, Chromium Plating; Adolf **Stein und Co.**, Textiles Mail Order; Arthur **Stern**, Car Repairs; Ernst **Stern**, Toy Export; M. **Stern und Co.**, Steam Factory; David **Stiefel**, Tailoring; **Stollenwerk und Spier**, Lithographic Art Studio; Herrmann **Strauss**, Hop Sales; Paul J. **Strauß**, Hop Sales; S. M. **Strauss Nachfolger**, Lining Wholesale; Wolf **Strauss oHG**; Leon **Sturm**, Polishing Paper Wholesale.

Greta **Tannhauser**, Textile Wholesale; **Transformatoren- und Apparatebau Magnus**; Phillip **Tuchmann**, Hop Sales.

Ullmann und Zenk, Dental Supplies; Cilly **Ullmann**, Fashions; Jacques **Ullmann**; Paul J. **Ullmann**, Bronze Pigment Factory.

Vereinigte Margarinewerke KG; J. M. **Viertel**, Pen Factory; Betty **Vogel**, Corset Store.

Max **Walter und Co. GmbH**, Advertising Supplies; **Wertheimer**; Department Store; **Weisser Turm**; Gebr. **Wolff GmbH**, Celluloid Factory; Theodor **Wolf GmbH**; Leonore **Wuga**, Writing Materials Wholesale.

Zenner und Co., Artificial Horn Factory; **Zentner und Kissinger**, Leather Goods Factory.

*Compiled from the unpublished thesis by W. Kr. Schneider, *Der Arisierungsskandal in Nürnberg und Fürth* (1969), Appendix 4, pp. 59–65. Schneider has analyzed the records of the Restitution Chamber of the Circuit Court in Nuremberg (Volumes I/66–XII/66).

Notes

JÖRG WOLLENBERG, No One Participated, No One Knew

1. Y. Michal Bodeman, "Was hat der Gedenktag überhaupt mit den Juden zu tun? Nachbetrachtung zu der Reichspogromnacht und dem Umgang der Deutschen mit ihrer Geschichte," *Frankfurter Rundschau*, November 29, 1988, 10.
2. I shall mention here several of the most important publications that were republished in connection with the fiftieth anniversary of the pogrom:

    Adler, H. G. *Die Juden in Deutschland. Von der Aufklärung bis zum Nationalsozialismus*. Munich, 1987.

    Adler, H. G. *Der verwaltete Mensch. Studien zur Deportation der Juden aus Deutschland*. Tübingen, 1974.

    Pehle, Walter H., ed. *Der Judenpogrom 1938. Von der "Reichskristallnacht" zum Völkermord*. Frankfurt, 1988.

    Graml, Hermann. *Reichskristallnacht. Antisemitismus und Judenverfolgung im Dritten Reich*. Munich, 1988.

    Döscher, Hans Jürgen. *"Reichskristallnacht." Die November-Pogrome 1938*. Berlin, 1988.

    Barkai, Avraham. *Vom Boykott zur "Entjudung." Der wirtschaftliche Existenzkampf der Juden im Dritten Reich 1933–1943*. Frankfurt, 1988.

    Benz, Wolfgang, ed. *Die Juden in Deutschland 1933–45*. Munich, 1988.

    Büttner, Ursula. *Das Unrechtregime. Internationale Forschungen über den Nationalsozialismus*. Festschrift für Werner Jochmann, vol. 2, 1986.

    Gerlach, Wolfgang. *Als die Zeugen schwiegen. Bekennende Kirche und die Juden*. Institute of Church and Judaism, vol 10. Berlin, 1987.

    Diner, Dan, ed. *Zivilisationsbruch. Denken nach Auschwitz*. Frankfurt, 1988.

    Rüter, Christian Frederic, ed. *Justiz und NS-Verbrechen*, vols. 1–22. Amsterdam, 1968–81.

    Hilberg, Raul. *Die Vernichtung der europäischen Juden. Die Gesamtgeschichte des Holocaust*. Frankfurt, 1982.

    Paucker, Arnold, ed. *Die Juden im nationalsozialistischen Deutschland*. Tübingen, 1986.

    Thalmann, Rita, and Emmanuel Feinermann. *Die Kristallnacht*. Frankfurt a.M., 1987.
3. Important preliminary work to this can be found in the "account" of the latest edition of Bernt Engelman, *Deutschland ohne Juden* (Cologne, 1988).
4. Dr. Richard Wilhelm Stock, *Die Judenfrage durch fünf Jahrhunderte. Stadt der Reichsparteitage* (Nuremberg, 1939), 9.

5. See also Döscher, *"Reichskristallnacht,"* 174.
6. On the decision of July 1, 1953, by the state court in Nuremberg (Az ks 1/ 51) see Rüter, *Justiz und NS-Verbrechen*, 11:184ff. See also the contribution by Jörg Friedrich in this volume.
7. Unfortunately, one of the most important lectures at the symposium, Hans Mommsen's "Repression and Delusion: Reactions of the German Population to the Persecution and Extermination of Jews," could not be included in this volume. His lecture was based on his essay which was published by Walter H. Pehle in the above-mentioned book; thus the interested reader can refer to *Der Judenpogrom 1938.*
8. See also Jörg Friedrich and Jörg Wollenberg, *Licht in den Schatten der Vergangenheit. Zur Enttabuisierung der Nürnberger Kriegsverbrecherprozesse* (Frankfurt and Berlin, 1987).

ERNST WALTHEMATHE, The Race between Life and Death: The Mixed Breeds

1. Klaus Drobisch et al., *Juden unterm Hakenkreuz* (Frankfurt a.M., 1973), 358.
2. *Plenarprotokoll des Deutschen Bundestages vom 29. März 1979.*

ULRICH KLUG, Permission for Murder

1. See also Carl Schmitt, "Der Führer schützt das Recht," *Deutsche Juristen-Zeitung*, 1934, columns 945–950.
2. See also Heribert Ostendorf and Heino ter Veen, *Das "Nürnberger Juristenurteil"* (Frankfurt and New York, 1985), 12, 140.
3. See also Heinz Lauber, *Judenpogrom "Reichskristallnacht"* (Gerlingen, 1981), 232, 233.
4. Lauber, 222–223.
5. Lauber, 224. On the subject of the difficulties in the post–world war Justice Department's search for Nazi criminals see also:

   Friedrich, Jörg. *Die kalte Amnestie.* Frankfurt, 1984.

   Just-Dahlmann, Barbara, and Helmut Just. *Die Gehilfen.* Frankfurt, 1988.

   Müller, Ingo. *Furchtbare Juristen.* Munich, 1987.

   Rückerl, Adalbert. *Die Strafverfolgung von NS-Verbrechen.* Karlsruhe, 1979.

   Spendel, Günter. *Rechtsbeugung durch Rechtsprechung.* Berlin and New York, 1984.

WOLFGANG GERLACH, When the Witnesses Were Silent

1. W. Niemöller, *Kampf und Zeugnis* (1948), 454.
2. Karl Kupisch, *Die deutschen Landeskirchen im 19. und 20. Jh.*, 173, reference 14.
3. Adolf Köberle, "Die Judenfrage im Lichte der Christusfrage," *Christlicher Volksdienst* 39 (Sept. 30, 1933).
4. Quoted from *The Strange Case of Bishop Dibelius*, 66, in the Wiener Library, London.
4a. Both confessions are printed in K. D. Schmidt, ed., *Die Bekenntnisse und grundsätzlichen Äußerungen zur Kirchenfrage des Jahres 1933* (Göttingen, 1934).
5. W. Niemöller, *Die Ev. Kirche im Dritten Reich. Handbuch des Kirchenkampfes* (Bielefeld, 1956), 79–81.

6. Eberhard Bethge, *Dietrich Bonhoeffer* (Munich, 1967), 379.
7. Karl Barth, *Evangelische Theologie* 28 (1986): 555ff.
8. Reitlinger, *Die Endlösung* (1964), 12.
9. See also *Deutsche Informationen* (Paris) 437 (Dec. 24, 1938); *Als die Zeugen schwiegen. Bekennende Kirche und die Juden* (Berlin, 1987).
10. Gerlach, 243ff.
11. Gerlach, 245.
12. Gerlach, 239.
13. Leonore Siegele-Wenschkewitz, *Neutestamentliche Wissenschaft vor der Judenfrage* (Munich, 1980), 26, 29.
14. See also A. Schmidt-Biesalki, *Lust, Liebe und Verstand* (Gelnhausen and Berlin, 1981), 89.
15. *Kirchliches Jahrbuch 1933–44* (Gütersloh, 1948), 481.
16. *Kirchliches Jahrbuch 1933–44*, 482.
17. Rosemary Ruether, *Nächstenliebe und Brudermord* (Munich, 1978), 35.
18. Gregory Baum in introduction to Ruether, 24.
19. Ruether, 79.
20. Rudolf Pfisterer, *Von A bis Z. Quellen zu Fragen um Juden und Christen* (Gladbeck, 1971), 106.
21. Pfisterer, 107.
22. Friedrich Heer, *Gottes erste Liebe* (Munich, 1967), 54.
23. Wolfgang Huber, *Folgen christlicher Freiheit* (Neukirchen, 1983), 87.
24. Siegele-Wenschkewitz, 85.
25. D. Bonhoeffer, *Ethik* (Munich, 1949), 49ff.
26. H.-U. Thamer, *Der Holocaust und die Protestanten* (Zürich, 1988), 225.
27. Thamer, reference 4.
28. Gerlach, 398.
29. Gerlach, 399.
30. Gerlach, 398.
31. Michael Wyschogrod, *Gottes Augapfel* (Neukirchen, 1986), 177.
32. Sigo Lehming, *Kirche für Israel* (Stuttgart, 1978), 24ff.
33. Ako Haarback, *Solange die Erde steht. Der Gemeinde zur Bibelwoche 1985–86* (Stuttgart, 1985), 30ff.
34. Huber, 93.
35. Johann Baptist Metz, *Concilium* 20, no. 4 (Oct. 1984): 382.
36. Bonhoeffer, 31.
37. Gerlach, 121.
38. Ernst Lohmeyer, quotation from *Kirche und Israel*, 1:86, 7ff.

MANFRED MESSERSCHMIDT, The Difficult Atonement Toward Judaism

1. H. Filbinger, *Die geschmähte Generation* (Munich, 1987), 252.
2. Filbinger, 252.
3. Th. Nipperdey, "Jede Epoche ist doch gleich nah zu Gott. Wider die politische Überforderung der Geschichtswissenschaft," *Die Welt* 50 (Feb. 28, 1987).
4. Filbinger, 252.
5. E. Schwinge, *Bilanz der Kriegsgeneration. Ein Beitrag zur Geschichte unserer Zeit* (Marburg, 1978; 4th ed., 1988).
6. Schwinge, 4, 41ff., 50ff.

7. Order by the Supreme Military Command of April 2, 1941 (OKH, GenSt d H/Gen Qu., Abt. Kriegsverwaltung Nr. III O 3 08/41g). See also H. Krausnick and M.-H. Wilhelm, *Die Truppe des Weltanschauungskrieges. Die Einsatzgruppen der Sicherheitspolizei und des SD 1938–1942* (Stuttgart, 1981), 137.

8. This order on the "Regulation of the Use of Security Police and Security Services within the Army Operations" (Federal Archives-MA, RH 22/155a) can be found in G. R. Ueberschär and W. Wette, eds., *"Unternehmen Barbarossa." Der Deutsche Überfall auf die Sowjetunion 1941* (Paderborn, 1984), 303ff.

9. Ueberschär, 306ff.

10. Franz Halder, *Kriegstagebuch, Tägliche Aufzeichnungen des Chefs des Generalstabs des Heeres 1939–1942* (Stuttgart, 1962–64), 2:335ff.

11. Order of May 24, 1941, Ueberschär, 307ff. (Federal Archives-MA, RH 22/155).

12. Federal Archives-MA, RH 19 3/722; see also M. Messerschmidt, "Völkerrecht und 'Kriegsnotwendigkeit' in der deutschen militärischen Tradition seit den Einigungskriegen," *German Studies Review* 6, no. 2 (1983): 237–269 (265).

13. Federal Archives-MA, RW 4/577.

14. *International Military Tribunal*, 26, 53ff.

15. Federal Archives-MA, RW 4/524, App. 3: "Besondere Anordnungen Nr. 1 zur Weisung Nr. 21 ('Fall Barbarossa')," Ueberschär, 312.

16. Federal Archives-MA, L VI AK, 17956/7a.

17. Federal Archives-MA, RH 20-6/493.

18. Federal Archives-MA, RH 20-17/44.

19. *International Military Tribunal*, 34, 129–132.

20. Nuremberg Trial, Document No. 3414; Ueberschär, 346ff., Krausnick, 251ff.

21. See also Chr. Streit, *Keine Kameraden. Die Wehrmacht und die sowjetischen Kriegsgefangenen 1941–1945* (Stuttgart, 1978), 99, 341ff.

22. See more in Streit, 100ff., and in Krausnick, 252ff.

23. Federal Archives in Koblenz, R 58/214–220.

24. "Ereignismeldung UdSSR," No. 28 (July 20, 1941).

25. See also Krausnick, 249ff.

26. Krausnick, 226.

27. Krausnick, 249ff.

28. Military Supreme Command Order of Sept. 12, 1941: WFSt/Abt. L (IV/Qu) No. 0204/41, DOK PS 878.

29. See also Messerschmidt, *Die Wehrmacht im NS-Staat. Zeit der Indoktrination* (Hamburg, 1969), 306ff., 326ff.

30. S. Alfred Streim, "Zum Beispiel: Die Verbrechen der Einsatzgruppen in der Sowjetunion," in A. Rückerl, ed., *NS-Prozesse* (Karlsruhe, 1971), 73f.

31. Krausnick, 237.

32. J. Förster, "Die Sicherung des Lebensraumes," in *Das Deutsche Reich und der Zweite Weltkrieg*, vol. 4, *Der Angriff auf die Sowjetunion* (Stuttgart, 1983), 1030–1078.

33. NOKW 2594; M. Messerschmidt and F. Wüllner, *Die Wehrmachtjustiz im Dienste des Nationalsozialismus. Zerstörung einer Legende* (Baden-Baden, 1987), 217.

34. Messerschmidt, 224.

35. Chr. Browning, "Wehrmacht Reprisal Policy and the Mass Murder of Jews in Serbia," in *MGM*, 1/83, 31–47.
36. For details see "Der Bericht der internationalen Historikerkommission," *PROFIL* 7 (1988): 20–22.
37. Report of the Section IC to HGr. E Ic/AO (April 28, 1944).
38. Federal Archives-MA, RW 40/31, Bl. 11.
39. Federal Archives-MA, RW 51/44.
40. Federal Archives-MA 17729/4, App. 31.
41. Federal Archives-MA 15365/16.
42. Order by the Supreme Military Command of Sept. 16, 1941 (Federal Archives-MA 17729/9, App. 48); Messerschmidt, *Völkerrecht und Kriegsnotwendigkeit*, 258.
43. Keitel to List (Sept. 28, 1941), Federal Archives-MA 17729/8, App. 28; NOKW 458.
44. Federal Archives-MA 17729/9, Anl. 48; NOKW 891 + 557.
45. Rudolph Chr. Freiherr v. Gersdorff, *Soldat im Untergang* (Frankfurt, 1979), 145ff.; "Himmlers Randnotizen," *Archiv Institut für Zeitgeschichte München*, microfilm MA.
46. Federal Archives-MA, RW 51/44.
47. *Information for the Officer Corps*, ed. by the Supreme Military Command–WFSt/WPr since Jan. 1942; here May 1942, 5.
48. Federal Archives-MA, N 63/118, Bl. 62.

Ernest Piper, National Socialist Cultural Policy and Its Beneficiaries

I would like to thank Wolfgang Eitel, Monika Peschel, Martina Petrik, Christian Röthlingshöfer, Ferdinand Sieger, and Ulrich Wank for all the inspiration and helpful comments.

1. J. Wulf, *Die bildenden Künste im Dritten Reich* (Berlin, 1983), 355.
2. E. Kochanowski, "Die kulturelle Auswirkung der Judengesetzgebung im nationalsozialistischen Deutschland," in W. F. Könitzer and H. Trurnit, eds., *Weltentscheidung in der Judenfrage* (Dresden, 1939), 45.
3. Kochanowski, 48.
4. V. Reimann, *Dr. Joseph Goebbels* (Wien, 1971), 179.
5. Memorandum by the Reich's president of the Cultural Chamber to the Subchambers on January 17, 1937. Quoted from V. Dahm, *Das jüdische Buch im Dritten Reich*, Part 1, "Die Ausschaltung der jüdischen Autoren, Verleger und Buchhändler" (Frankfurt, 1979), 64.
6. Kochanowski, 52.
7. Kochanowski, 47.
8. Dahm, 65.
9. See also E. Piper, *Nationalsozilistische Kunstpolitik* (Frankfurt, 1987), 164.
10. E. Fröhlich, "Die Kulturpolitische Pressekonferenz des Reichspropagandaministeriums," *Vierteljahreshefte für Zeitgeschichte* 4 (1974): 347–381.
11. Fröhlich, 363ff.
12. *Münchner Neueste Nachrichten*, Nov. 30, 1936.
13. Kochanowski, 48ff.
14. *Völkischer Beobachter*, Sept. 3, 1933.
15. A. Hitler, *Mein Kampf. Zwei Bände in einem Band* (1936), 318, 322ff, 329ff.

16. *Völkischer Beobachter*, Sept. 3, 1933.
17. *Völkischer Beobachter*, Sept. 10, 1933.
18. *Völkischer Beobachter*, Sept. 10, 1933.
19. *Völkischer Beobachter*, Sept. 10, 1933.
20. Hitler, 138.
21. *Völkischer Beobachter*, July 14, 1937.
22. Both exhibits are substantially described in P.-K. Schuster, *Die "Kunststadt" München 1937. Nationalsozialismus und "Entartete Kunst"* (München, 1987).
23. A. Hentzen, *Die Berliner National-Galerie im Bildersturm* (Cologne and Berlin, 1971), 19.
24. F. Roh, *"Entartete" Kunst* (Hannover, 1962), 230.
25. Speech on the occasion of the inauguration of the Haus der Deutschen Kunst, *Münchner Neueste Nachrichten*, July 19, 1937.
26. *Exhibition Guide for the Degenerate "Art"* (Berlin, n.y.), 2ff.
27. Supplementary page to the exhibition guide.
28. K. H. Meißner, "München ist ein heißer Boden. Aber wir gewinnen ihn allmählich doch," in *Die "Kunststadt" München 1937*, 51.
29. A. Schwarz, "Die Zeit von 1918 bis 1933," in *Handbuch der Bayerischen Geschichte*, vol. 4, ed. M. Spindler, *Das Neue Bayern von 1800–1970* (Munich, 1979), 484ff.
30. H. Kiener, *Kunstbetrachtungen. Ausgewählte Aufsätze* (Munich, 1937), 331.
31. R. Oldenbourg, "Malerei," in *Jahrbuch der Münchner Kunst*, 1 (1917–18) (Munich, 1918), xii.
32. Oldenbourg, XVII.
33. H. Brenner, *Ende einer bürgerlichen Kunst-Institution. Die politische Formierung der preußischen Akademie der Künste ab 1933* (Stuttgart, 1972), 146.
34. *Ernst Ludwig Kirchner 1880–1938* (Berlin, 1980), 104.
35. D. Schmidt, ed., *In letzter Stunde. 1933–1945* (Dresden, 1964), 153.
36. J. Frecot, "Marginalien zur nationalsozilistischen Kunstpolitik," in *Zwischen Anpassung und Widerstand. Kunst in Deutschland 1933–1945* (n.p., 1980), 77.
37. Wulf, 390.
38. M.-A. v. Lüttichau, "'Deutsche Kunst' und 'Entartete Kunst': Die Münchner Ausstellungen 1937," in *Die "Kunststadt" München*, 99.
39. Wulf, 406.
40. A. Zweite, "Franz Hofmann und die Städtische Galerie 1937," in *Die "Kunststadt" München 1937*, 261–288.
41. K. Arndt, "Die Münchner Architekturszene 1933–34 als ästhetisch politisches Konflikfeld," in M. Broszat, ed., *Bayern in der NS-Zeit*, vol. 6 (Munich, 1981), 489.
42. Arndt, 495.
43. Arndt, 496.
44. Arndt, 505.
45. Helmut M. Hanko, "Kommunalpolitik in der 'Hauptstadt der Bewegung,'" in *Bayern in der NS-Zeit*, 6:429.
46. See also F. Euler, "Theater zwischen Anpassung und Widerstand," in *Bayern in der NS-Zeit*, 2:91–173.
47. B. Drewniak, *Das Theater im NS-Staat. Szenarium deutscher Zeitgeschichte 1933–1945* (Düsseldorf, 1983), 223.
48. J. Wulf, *Die Musik im Dritten Reich* (Berlin, 1983), 195.
49. Wulf, 198.

50. F. Prieberg, *Musik im NS-Staat* (Frankfurt, 1982), 211.
51. "Salzburger Festspiele 1937 und 1938," special edition by the Salzburg Festival (Salzburg, 1988), 71.
52. Wulf, 425.
53. Prieberg, 353ff.
54. Prieberg, 31.
55. A. Dümling and P. Girth, *Entartete Musik. Zur Düsseldorfer Ausstellung von 1938. Eine kommentierte Rekonstruktion* (Düsseldorf, 1988), 58.
56. Prieberg, 131.
58. Wulf, 334.
59. Wulf, 73.
60. Drewniak, 300.
61. Prieberg, 224.
62. K. Arnold, "Volk im Raum," *Simplicissimus*, Feb. 12, 1933, 312.
63. D. Grünewald, "Die Einfalt der 'Einfältigsten.' Der 'Simplicissimus' von 1933 bis 1944," in *Zwischen Widerstand und Anpassung*, 42.
64. Grünewald, 45.
65. N. Gidal, *Die Juden in Deutschland von der Römerzeit bis zur Weimarer Republik* (Gütersloh, 1988), 256ff.
66. Frecot, 80.
67. Fröhlich, 358.
68. Piper, 191ff.
69. Fröhlich, 374.
70. *Ein Protest deutscher Künstler*, with an introduction by Carl Vinnen (Jena, 1911), 2.
71. *Ein Protest*, 15.
72. "Protest der Richard Wagner-Stadt München," in R. Bauer and E. Piper, eds., *München. Ein Lesebuch* (Frankfurt am Main, 1987), 260.
73. "K.-H. Meißner, Karl Caspar—Maler der Hoffnung—Leben und Werk," in P.-K. Schuster, ed., *"München leuchtete." Karl Caspar und die Erneuerung christlicher Kunst in München um 1900* (München, 1984), 231–253.
74. Kiener, 334.
75. K. Vierneisel, ed., *Der Königsplatz 1812–1988* (Munich, n.y.), 41.

JÖRG WOLLENBERG, The Expropriation of the "Rapacious" Capital by "Productive" Capital

1. H. G. Adler, *Der verwaltete Mensch. Studien zur Deportation der Juden aus Deutschland* (1974), 451.
2. Raul Hilberg, *Die Vernichtung der europäischen Juden* (1982).
3. See also the excellent dissertation by Helmut Genschel, *Die Verdrängung der Juden aus der Wirtschaft im Dritten Reich*, Göttinger Bausteine zur Geschichtswissenschaft, vol. 38 (Göttingen, 1966), 124, and the recently completed thorough study by Avraham Barkai, *Vom Boykott zur "Entjudung." Der wirtschaftliche Existenzkampf der Juden im Dritten Reich 1933–1943* (Frankfurt, 1988).
4. See also Bruno Blau, *Das Ausnahmerecht für die Juden in Deutschland 1933–45* (Düsseldorf, 1965).
5. For further statistics and general context see, in addition to Barkai and Genschel, the well-documented studies by Arnd Müller, *Geschichte der Juden*

in Nürnberg 1146–1945 (Nuremberg, 1968), 210ff., and Wolf Kristian Schneider, *Der Arisierungsskandal in Nürnberg und Fürth,* an unpublished diploma thesis submitted in 1969 to the School of Economics and Social Sciences at the University of Erlangen–Nuremberg; there especially App. 2–5.

6. See also Bernt Engelman, *Deutschland ohne Juden* (1988), 338ff.; Heinrich Uhlig, *Die Warenhäuser im Dritten Reich* (Köln, 1956).

7. Hilberg, 87ff.

8. Barkai, 111ff.; Stephan Leibfried and Florian Tennstedt, *Berufsverbote und Sozialpolitik 1933* (Bremen, 1979).

9. See also Charlotte Niermann and Stephan Leibfried, *Die Verfolgung jüdischer Ärzte in Bremen in der "NS"-Zeit* (Bremen, 1988); Bennathan Esra, "Die demographische und wirschaftliche Struktur der Juden," in Werner E. Masse, ed., *Entscheidungsjahr 1932. Zur Judenfrage in der Endphase der Weimarer Republik* (Tübingen, 1965); Otto Lohr, "Die wirtschaftliche Tätigkeit der Juden von 1870–1933," in *Geschichte und Kultur der Juden in Bayern. Aufsätze* (1988), 397–409.

10. Franz Oppenheimer, *Erlebtes, Erstrebtes, Erreichtes* (1964), 64.

11. A. Müller, *Juden in Nürnberg* (1968), 219ff.

12. Müller, 236ff.

13. Genschel, 241.

14. Schneider, App. 3 and 4, and Müller, 202ff.

15. Many important documents on the "Aryanization" are located in the Federal Archives in Koblenz (Aktenbestand R 22/52). Schneider especially analyzed the materials located in the State Archives in Nuremberg, City Archives in Nuremberg and Fürth, the District Financial Office in Ansbach, and in the Restitution Chamber of the state court in Nuremberg.

16. See also Rudolf Endres, "Familie Bing, Fabrikanten in Nürnberg," in *Geschichte und Kultur der Juden in Bayern. Lebensläufe* (1988), 173–177.

17. This information is taken from Schneider, 22ff. and App. 2; Bernhard Kalb, *Die Juden in Nürnberg,* manuscript in State Archives in Nuremberg; and Müller, 202–203.

18. Schneider, 23.

19. *Deutschland-Berichte der SPD, SOPADE,* 5 (1938) A III/70–71; reprinted in 2001 (Frankfurt am Main, 1980), 203ff.

20. Reprinted in Uhlig, 177.

21. Müller, 220ff.

22. Müller, 223ff.

23. See, e.g., also "Reichsthaler jetzt arisch" (Hermann Meyer), *Nürnberger Zeitung,* March 5 and 6; "Manufakturwarengeschäft W. B. Schloss ist in arischen Besitz übergegangen" (Ley & Co.), *Fränkische Tageszeitung,* May 11, 1938; "Oettinger & Co. jetzt arisches Unternehmen" (Kneidl o.H.), *Fränkische Tageszeitung,* June 11, 1938; "Adolf Frank (Befindet sich) nunmehr in arischem Besitz," *Fränkische Tageszeitung,* June 18, 1938.

24. *Deutschlandberichte der SOPADE,* Feb. 1938, A III, 64–65; reprinted 1980, 196–199.

25. See also Schneider; Müller, 245; and H. Froschauer and R. Geyer, *Quellen des Hasses—Aus dem Archiv des "Stürmer"* (1988), 57ff.

26. As a supplement to the documents of the Göring Commission, which are located in the Nuremberg State Archives (KV, PS 1757), one can recommend looking at the fifty-two folders of the state court president of Nu-

remberg with reports by State Prosecutor Joël and the district court in Fürth (Leis), which Genschel had consulted in part, and which are now located in the Federal Archives in Koblenz.

27. Federal Archives in Koblenz, R 22/52-01/51–53.
28. Federal Archives in Koblenz, R 22/52-01/17–27.
29. Federal Archives in Koblenz, R 22/52-01/96–98.
30. Federal Archives in Koblenz, R 22/52-01/99, 99A.
31. The protocol of the conference on Nov. 12, 1938, according to Hilberg, 94.
32. State Archives in Nuremberg, KV, PS 1757, 16–75.
33. State Archives in Nuremberg, KV, PS 1757, 25–26.
34. State Archives in Nuremberg, KV, PS 1757, 192ff.
35. State Archives in Nuremberg, KV, PS 1757, 186ff.
36. Utho Grieser, *Himmlers Mann in Nürnberg* (1974), 162ff.
37. Dr. Wegner, the former police physician and collaborator of Martin, claims in his *Kurs Martin—Polizei einmal anders* that Martin fully supported Streicher.
38. For further information on the Katzenberger case, which was made into a distorted movie by the Americans after 1948 *Judgment at Nurenberg*, starring Spencer Tracy, Burt Lancaster, and Marlene Dietrich, see Jörg Friedrich, *Freispruch für die Nazi-Justiz. Die Urteile gegen NS-Richter seit 1948. Eine Dokumentation* (Reinbek, 1983), 274–301.
39. See also Wilhelm Stuckart and Hans Globke, eds., *Kommentar zur deutschen Rassengesetzgebung* (Berlin, 1937), 67ff.
40. Excerpts from the trial can be found in Jörg Friedrich, *Die Kalte Amnestie. NS-Täter in der Bundesrepublik* (1984), 78.
41. See also Friedrich, *Freispruch fur die Nazi-Justiz*, 300.
42. See also Hilberg, 87ff., and Friedrich, *Kalte Amnestie*, 108–112.
43. Friedrich, *Kalte Amnestie*, 112. See also Friederike Littman, "Vom Notstand eines Haupttäters—Zwangsarbeit im Flickkonzern," *1999*, 1 (1986): 4–43.
44. See also Omgus, *Ermittlungen gegen die Deutsche Bank, 1946/47* (Nördlingen, 1985); Omgus, *Ermittlungen gegen die Dresdner Bank, 1946* (Nördlingen, 1986); Omgus, *Ermittlungen gegen die IG Farbenindustrie AG, September 1945* (Nördlingen, 1986). All three volumes were edited by Hans Magnus Enzensberger as special editions of the Anderen Bibliothek and published by Franz Greno. See also Joseph Borkin, *Die unheilige Allianz der IG Farben. Eine Interessengemeinschaft im Dritten Reich* (Frankfurt, 1986).
45. H. W. Armbruster, *Treason's Peace* (New York, 1947), 383.
46. Friedrich, *Kalte Amnestie*, 2.
47. On the role and function of Benno Martin, see the dissertation by Utho Grieser submitted to the University of Würzburg and published as volume 13 of the Series of the City Archives of Nuremberg: *Himmlers Mann in Nürnberg. Der Fall Benno Martin. Eine Studie zur Struktur des Dritten Reiches in der Stadt der Reichsparteitage* (Nuremberg, 1974).
48. Grieser, 294–295, note 3.
49. J. Walk, ed., *Das Sonderrecht für die Juden im NS-Staat* (Karlsruhe, 1981), i/xiii.

JÖRG FRIEDRICH, "The Apartment Keys Are to Be Relinquished to the House Manager"
Selected Bibliography

Adler, H. G. *Der verwaltete Mensch*. Tübingen, 1974.

Sauer, Paul, ed. *Dokumente über die Verfolgung der jüdischen Bürger in Baden-Württemberg*, vol. 2. Stuttgart, 1966.

Rockenmaier, Dieter W. *Aus den Akten der Würzburger Gestapo. Buchführung des Todes*. Würzburg, 1981.

Sentence by the State Court in Cologne (June 9, 1954); AZ 24 Ks/3/53, reprinted in Christian F. Rüter, *Justiz und NS-Verbrechen* (Amsterdam, 1968–81), 12:574ff.

Sentence by the State Court in Würzburg (April 30, 1949); AZ KLs 63/48

Sentence by the Bavarian Supreme State Court (Nov. 15, 1950); AZ III 37/49. In Rüter, 4:468ff.

Sentence by the State Court in Nuremberg (May 10, 1949); AZ KLs 230/48

Sentence by the Bavarian Supreme State Court (Nov. 15, 1950); AZ III 12/50. In Rüter, 4:524ff.

Sentence by the State Court in Nuremberg (June 2, 1951); AZ 213 Ks 1/51. In Rüter, 8:462ff.

Sentence by the State Court in Nuremberg (July 1, 1953); AZ Ks 1/51. In Rüter, 11:184ff.

DICK DE MILDT, Collaboration and Deportation in Holland

1. L. de Jong, *De Bezetting* (Amsterdam, 1985), 103.
2. Important publications on the persecution of Jews in the Netherlands are A. J. Herzberg, *Kroniek der jodenvervolging* (Amsterdam, n.y); J. Presser, *Ondergang. De vervolging en verdelging van het Nederlandse jodendom 1940–1945*, 2 vols. (Gravenhage, 1965); and L. de Jong, *Het koninkrijk der Nederlanden in de tweede wereldoorlog*, 12 vols. (Gravenhage, 1969–88).
3. E. A. Cohen, *De negentien treinan naar Sobibor* (Amsterdam and Brussels, 1979), 20–22.
4. In comparison in Norway and Belgium approx. 40 percent; in France approx. 25 percent; in Denmark almost none. J. C. H. Blom, "De vervolging van de joden in Nederland in internationaal vergelijken perspectief," in *De Gids*, July 1987, 494.
5. B. A. Sijes, *Studies over jodenvervolging* (Assen, 1974), 133, 135–136.
6. De Jong, 5:996.
7. De Jong, 6:345–350; Presser, 2:180–182.
8. Presser, 2:129–130.
9. De Jong, 6:37–41; Presser, 2:175–180.
10. De Jong, 5:456–475.
11. De Jong, 5:475–482.
12. De Jong, 4:693.
13. De Jong, 1:295–302. E. Fraenkel-Verkade and A. J. von der Leeuw, eds., *Correspondentie van Mr. M. M. Rost van Tonningen*, 1 (1921–May 1942) (Den

Haag, 1967), 57 and reference 2; N.C.K.A. in 't Veld, *De SS en Nederland. Documenten uit SS-archieven 1935–1945*, 2 vols. (Den Haag, 1976), 536.

14. See also A. A. de Jonge, *Het nationaal-socialisme in Nederland. Voorgeschiedenis, onstaan en ontwikkeling* (Den Haag, 1979).
15. De Jong, 1:484–89; Verslag der Handelingen van de Tweede Kamer der Staten-Generaal, 1938–39, Nov. 15, 1938, 252ff.
16. About Mr. Cleveringa and his protest, see L. E. Van Holk and I. Schöffer, eds., *Gedenkschriften Prof. R. P. Cleveringa* (Leiden, 1983).
17. For additional information on the general strike of February 1941, see B. A. Sijes, *De februaru-staking 25–26 februari 1941* (Amsterdam, 1961); de Jong, 4:807–876; Presser, 1:78–96.
18. Presser, 2:239–283; De Jong, 7:665–804.
19. De Jong, 6:12–22.
20. Raul Hilberg, *The Destruction of the European Jews*, 3 vols. (New York and London, 1985), 2:597.

The Contributors

AXEL EGGEBRECHT (born in 1899): Contributor, since 1925, to the *Weltbühne* (World Stage) and many other newspapers; arrested by the Nazis after concentration camp detention and in spite of a professional ban, he survived by working for the Ufa movie company as a contributor to several entertainment films. After 1945 he became a writer and the co-founder of the Northwest German Broadcasting Company (NWDR) in Hamburg. Numerous publications, among them *Der halbe Weg. Zwischenbilanz einer Epoche* (Halfway. An Interim Account of an Epoch), 1975. [Died on July 14, 1991; Am. ed.]

JÖRG FRIEDRICH (born in 1944): Writer and radio author in Berlin; author of works on contemporary history, among them *Die kalte Amnestie: NS-Täter in der Bundesrepublik* (The Cold Amnesty: The National Socialist Perpetrators in the Federal Republic) and *Freispruch für die Nazi-Justiz* (Acquittal for Nazi Justice). He published, under commission from the City of Nuremberg, the Nuremberg follow-up trials, of which volume 1 (1989) has been published in the Piper Series.

WOLFGANG GERLACH (born in 1933): Minister in Essen; author of a 1970 dissertation, *Zwischen Kreuz und Davidstern. Bekennende Kirche in ihrer Stellung zum Judentum im Dritten Reich* (Between the Cross and the Star of David. The Confessing Church and Its Position toward Jewry in the Third Reich), which was first published in 1987 by the Institute of Church and Judaism under the title *Als die Zeugen schwiegen. Bekennende Kirche und die Juden* (When the Witnesses Were Silent. The Confessing Church and the Jews).

HERMAN GLASER (born in 1928): Scholastic and Cultural Reviewer for the City of Nuremberg; professor at the Institute for Communication Sciences, Media, and Music Sciences at the Technical University Berlin. His numerous publications include works on the National Socialist period and the cultural history of Germany.

MARIA COUNTESS VON MALTZAN (born in 1909): Veterinarian in Berlin-Kreuzberg. After 1933 she joined a resistance group in Munich around the Jesuit monk Friedrich Muckermann. In 1939 she met the Jewish writer Hans Hirschel in Berlin whom she hid along with other Jews in her small Berlin apartment. Her memoirs were published in 1986 under the title *Schlage die Trommel und fürchte dich nicht* (Beat the Drum and Don't Be Afraid).

MANFRED MESSERSCHMIDT (born in 1926): Up until 1988 he was the director of the Military History Research Office in Freiburg/Breisgau. Author of articles and books on the role of the German military in the National Socialist system; member of the Waldheim Commission.

DICK DE MILDT: Historian; research assistant at the Criminal Law Institute at the University of Amsterdam since 1987. He is preparing a study there on the motivating factors for the "Close to the Act" perpetrators of the Jewish Holocaust. This study is based on the sentences given for National Socialist killings, published in the collection *Justiz und NS-Verbrechen* (Justice and National Socialist Crimes).

ERNST PIPER (born in 1952): Historian; manager of the Piper Publishing House; author and publisher of numerous books on historical and contemporary themes, among them *Nationalsozialistische Kunstpolitik* (National Socialist Art Policy), 1987.

RADO PRIBIC (born in 1947): Professor and Chair of the International Affairs Program at Lafayette College in Easton, Pennsylvania. A native of Germany, he has published extensively in the area of Germano-Slavic cultural relations.

ERNST WALTEMATHE (born in 1935): Member of the Bundestag representing the Social Democratic party of Germany from Bremen. He was persecuted by the Nazis as a "mixed-breed of the first degree" and had to emigrate to the Netherlands.

WALTER GRAB (born in 1919): Emigrated in July of 1938 as a student from Vienna to Jerusalem. Up until 1986, when he became professor emeritus, he was a professor of contemporary history at the University of Tel Aviv and the director of the Institute for German History, which he founded. Author of books on "Pre-March" (Vormärz) and German Jacobinism.

ARNO HAMBURGER (born in 1923): President of the Jewish Cultural Community in Nuremberg; deputy chairman of the Social Democratic City Council Faction in Nuremberg.

ROBERT M. W. KEMPNER (born in 1899): Lawyer and government official in the Prussian Ministry of Interior; denied citizenship in 1935; after 1945, he was the chief prosecutor at the Nuremberg trials and a secondary prosecutor at many other trials against Nazi criminals. Numerous publications, among them *Ankläger einer Epoche. Errinerung* (Prosecutor of an Epoch. Memoirs), 1983.

ULRICH KLUG (born in 1912): Professor (emeritus) for Public Law in Cologne; retired Justice Senator of the City of Hamburg, for many years the president of the Humanistic Union.

HEINER LICHTENSTEIN (born in 1932): Writer and editor at the West German Broadcasting Company (WDR); author of books on the role of the railroad and the Red Cross in the Third Reich; reporter at important trials against the Nazi criminals after 1945.

JÖRG WOLLENBERG (born 1937): Director of the Educational Center of the City of Nuremberg and professor for continuing education at the University of Bremen. Author of numerous articles; along with Jörg Friedrich, editor of the volume *Licht in den Schatten der Vergangenheit. Zur Enttabuisierung der Nürnberger Nachkriegsverbrecherprozesse* (Light into the Shade of the Past. Toward Removing the Taboos of the Nuremberg Postwar Criminal Trials), 1987.

Index

207